For Our Parents

The four of us were dressed in the height of fashion
which in those days was a pair of black very tight tights with
the old jelly mould, as we called it, fitting on the crotch
underneath the tights, this being to protect and also a sort of
a design you could viddy clear enough in a certain light, so
that I had one in the shape of a spider, Pete had a rooker (a
hand, that is), Georgie had a very fancy one of a flower, and
poor old Dim had a very hound-and-horny one of a clown´s
litso (face, that is), Dim not ever having much of an idea of
things and being, beyond all shadow of a doubting thomas,
the dimmest of we four. Then we wore waisty jackets without
lapels but with these very big built-up shoulders ("pletchoes"
we called them) which were a kind of a mockery of having
real shoulders like that. Then, my brothers, we had these off-
white cravats which looked like whipped-up kartoffel or
spud with a sort of design made on it with a fork. We wore
our hair not too long and we had flip horrorshow boots for
kicking.

From A Clockwork Orange

by

Anthony Burgess

© Thomas Johansson and Fredrik Miegel
ISBN 91-22-01489-6
Graphic Systems AB, Malmö 1992

PREFACE

This is actually two theses published in one and the same book, which makes it necessary to say something about the division of labor between the two authors. Thomas Johansson has had the main responsibility for chapter two, three, four, five, eight, twelve and fifteen, whereas Fredrik Miegel has had the main responsibility for chapter six, nine, eleven, thirteen, sixteen and seventeen. Chapter one, seven, ten, fourteen, eighteen, nineteen, twenty and twenty-one are co-written by the authors. The work has all the time been integrated and both authors are responsible for the book as a whole.

To write this book has been a long, sometimes painful and sometimes enjoyable journey. We have now finally arrived at our goal, we have finished our manuscript. During the four years this journey has lasted, several different persons have helped us catching the right trains, going to the right stations and choosing the right tracks. We cannot mention all of them here, but just some of the most important

First and foremost, we would like to thank each other for support, friendship, intellectual stimulation and good partnership. Our advisor, professor Karl Erik Rosengren, has all the time provided us with constructive and sometimes crushing, but necessary critique, when our brains have slipped away too far. It is hard to imagine a better advisor. We would also like to thank our collegues at the department of Sociology: Per Källström for drawing the tables and figures and for deconstructing and reconstructing our computer when needed. Thanks to Jim Dalquist for his relevant as well as irrelevant comments on our work and for his extremely silly jokes, Ulla Johnsson-Smaragdi for her useful comments on chapter twelve, the staff at the Department of Media and Communication for general support. Joke Esseveld for reading and commenting certain parts of the book.

Thanks to Bo Reimer, at the Department of Journalism and Mass Communication at The University of Göteborg, for stimulating discussions and a good friendship. A special thanks to Robert Goldsmith who read the entire manuscript and corrected our English. We would also like to thank British Council and especielly Eva Sterndahl, for giving us the possibility to spend three months at the Teesside Polytechnic in Middlesbrough. Thanks also to Mike Featherstone for accepting us as guests at the poly, and for reading and commenting on the theoretical parts of the book.

The seven young people portrayed in the case studies deserve a special thanks for letting us into their lives and for becoming not merely research objects, but also friends. Without their generous cooperation we could not have written this book.

Finally we must thank our parents for their support and love, and last but not least our girlfriends, Bibbi and Ulrika, for putting up with us during these years. Thanks also to Tyson for company during the late night walks.

Lund in March 1992
Thomas Johansson and Fredrik Miegel

CONTENTS

CHAPTER 1
INTRODUCTION

This is a book about young people and their lifestyles. The reasons behind our choice of this subject are several. Both of us have been working for approximately five years within a project entitled *Lifestyle and Mass Media Culture* (LOM). This project is the latest of a number of interrelated projects conducted at the Department of Sociology of Lund University during the past two decades, focusing on different aspects of children's and adolescents' mass media use (Rosengren & Windahl 1989; Rosengren 1991a).

The LOM-project is an extension of a research program called MEDIA PANEL, which focused mainly on different types of *mass media use* and their *effects* on children and adolescents (Rosengren & Windahl 1989). On two different occasions, in the spring of 1988 and of 1990, postal questionnaires were distributed to two panels within the research program MEDIA PANEL. Although the two projects are similar or overlapping in certain respects, there are a number of important differences between them.

First, the theoretical perspectives of the projects differ. MEDIA PANEL builds mainly on a combination of two theoretical traditions - that of *uses and gratifications* and of *effect studies* - whereas the perspective taken within the LOM-project involves a combination of sociological theory and cultural study.

Secondly, the data collected within the two projects differ. Whereas MEDIA PANEL focused mainly on children's and adolescents' uses of different kinds of media, LOM focuses on young people's values, attitudes, taste, leisure time activities *and* media use.

The differences between the two projects are based partly on the fact that the individuals studied empirically in the longitudinal surveys (1988 and 1990) have now reached the age of twenty-two. They are thus no longer to be considered as children or adolescents, but as young people gradually entering adulthood. To understand this age-group, and what we call their lifestyles, one has therefore to broaden the focus to embrace not only the group's mass media use, but also other cultural, personal and social activities, processes and phenomena involved in the development of these young people's lifestyles.

Another reason for our choice of subject is the increasingly widespread interest in questions concerning different aspects of youth culture. In a sense, the culture of the young population in a society can serve as a sensitive seismograph, registrating future cultural movements early. In studying questions pertaining to youth, one is also indirectly studying changes in society at large. In recent research on youth culture, therefore, there has been a tendency to look at youth and its lifestyles in endeavoring to asses the cultural condition of society.

During the last few decades the concept of lifestyle has become dangerously diluted. Nevertheless, it does have a long history within social science, not least among such classical writers as Weber, Simmel and Veblen. During the past century, the concept of lifestyle has played an important role in the sociological analysis of changes in relations between the individual and society. To construct a theory of lifestyle today, therefore, implies that one starts with classical sociology and follows conceptual and theoretical developments which have occurred on into modern times. A major tendency in the development of theories of lifestyle is that the individual has come to be increasingly seen as a willing and active subject in the creation of her or his own lifestyle. This tendency has been accompanied by increasing discussion of what is usually called the process of modernization, and, in a similar vein, of the process of individualization. That is why we have devoted two chapters of the book to a description of the main developmental lines of the concept of lifestyle, and to theories relating to it.

Connected with theories of modernization and individualization is a growing interest in theoretical questions concerning individual identity. The earlier emphasis on social position - that is, on age, gender, class and status — as factors determining the lifestyle of the individual has decreased in relation to the present emphasis on qualities located within the individual. The concept of identity has thus gradually come to play a central role in lifestyle theories. The concept has a number of different components, however. It is actually quite complex and thus in need of theoretical analysis. Therefore, a chapter on identity seems well motivated here.

A major feature of the process of modernization is the constant change in societal values. In every culture or society there has to be some values which are commonly held and guide the behavior of its members. As society changes, so does its value structure. The existence of commonly held values within society does not exclude, however, that there be considerable variation within the population. Indeed, the value structures of different classes, status groups, age groups and gender groups show considerable variation. Consequently, the emergence of new social positions also means that positionally determined value changes will occur. Furthermore, within each position the values held by the individuals occupying that position vary.

One of the most important components of the identity of an individual is what values she or he holds. In connection with a theory of lifestyle there is thus also a need for a theoretical discussion of the values of society, of the values which are predominant in its various class, gender and status groups and among the individuals belonging to these. Therefore, a major portion of this book is devoted to a theoretical discussion of the concept of human values and their relation to identity and lifestyle.

The two central concepts in the theoretical discussion of lifestyles which we put forward in this book are thus identity and value. Our theoretical assumptions are intended to be rather *general*, but for reasons mentioned above, we concentrate in the empirical and in much of the theoretical parts of the book upon young people (in fact, on individuals born in one particular year, 1969).

The empirical study of youth culture and lifestyles is by no means an easy task. Depending on the purpose of a study, it can be conducted from quite differing theoretical and methodological points of view. In our study we combine both qualitative methods and quantitative ones (mainly questionnaires and semi-structured interviews). Quantitative methods make it possible to identify a number of general patterns concerning tastes, leisure activities, values and attitudes among the young people studied. Qualitative interviews allow us to illuminate the differences existing between individuals belonging to a given quantitatively identified pattern. The interviews also provide important information concerning, structurally and positionally determined aspects of individual lifestyles, on the one hand, and the individual's attempts to create her or his own lifestyle, on the other.

The empirical analyses presented in this book do not primarily serve the purpose of answering any specific and clear-cut research questions or to verify or falsify any particular hypotheses. The analyses we present are instead aimed at *illustrating* and *exemplifying* empirically the assumptions we present within our theoretical discussions of the relations between values, identity and lifestyle. Since the theory developed in this book is a *general* theory of lifestyle, it covers a wide range of more specific relations and phenomena within the field of lifestyle research. The empirical data we make use of allow us simply to measure and analyze certain specific relations and phenomena covered by our general theory. The empirical analyses presented are thus analyses of special cases of more general phenomena. As such they can simply serve as exemplifications and illustrations, and cannot be employed as a means of either verifying or falsifying our theory as a whole. Our intention has been to apply the general theory to a number of central areas of young people's lifestyles, specifically, their leisure time behavior and their tastes for music, film and clothes. Thus, we have tested the applicability of our theory empirically on only a few of the wide range of areas it is intended to cover.

We hope nevertheless to provide a modest contribution not only to lifestyle research but also to an understanding of young people and their culture at large. How well we have succeeded is for the reader to judge.

PART ONE:

LIFESTYLE: IDENTITY AND VALUE

Lifestyle is not a term which has much applicability to traditional cultures, because it implies choice within a plurality of possible options, and is "adopted" rather than "handed down". Lifestyles are routinised practices, the routines incorporated into habits of dress, eating, modes of acting and favoured milieux for encountering others; but the routines followed are reflexively open to change in the light of the mobile nature of self-identity. Each of the small decisions a person makes every day — what to wear, what to eat, how to conduct himself at work, whom to meet with later in the evening — contributes to such routines. All social choices (as well as larger and more consequential ones) are decisions not only about how to act but who to be. The more post-traditional the settings in which an individual moves, the more lifestyle concerns the very core of self-identity, its making and remaking (Giddens 1991a:81).

CHAPTER 2
THE CONCEPT OF LIFESTYLE: CLASS AND INDIVIDUALITY

INTRODUCTION

The concept and term *lifestyle* is used widely within various fields of social research, fields which concern radically differing aspects of human life. One common way of employing the term is to use it to denote various determinants of consumer attitudes and consumer behavior and the processes these involve. The usefulness and popularity of the lifestyle concept in market research has often been stressed (Schwartz et al. 1979; Mishra 1982; Pitts & Woodside 1984; Veltri & Schiffman 1984; Holman & Wiener 1985). In such research lifestyle is conceived in a manner directly relevant to marketing problems and advertizing campaigns. The very purpose clarifies the way in which the concept is defined there, that is, largely in terms of patterns of consumption.

Another use of the term is to be found in medical research. In such research lifestyle often refers to ways of living which can in one sense or another be harmful or pathological. Certain individual characteristics, habits and attitudes are regarded as leading to unhealthy living, which in its turn increases the risk, say, of heart disease, of cancer of the lungs or of becoming a drug addict (see, for example, Berardo et al. 1985).

In a sense the goals of the two research fields just mentioned are much the same. The aim in both fields is to change people's habits in one direction or another. The differing contents of the two fields in terms of the human attitudes and behavior they involve illustrate the terminological confusion which use of the lifestyle concept can sometimes lead to.

The term lifestyle has also been used in the study, for example, of different aspects of social life such as gender roles, of the relationship between industrialized and third world countries, of social mobility, of identity construction, or of the use of the communication media (Bourdieu 1979/1984; Steenbergen & Feller 1979; O'Connel 1980; Kothari 1980; Mishra 1982; Mitchell 1983; Roos 1983; Donohew et al. 1987; Ewen 1988; Ziehe 1989). In comparing such cases, on the other hand, one is dealing with more fundamental problems in use of the lifestyle concept, problems based on broad differences in theoretical approach, methodological considerations and choice of a micro or a macro perspective.

In this chapter, we shall present and discuss a number of important theories of lifestyle. Although it has frequently been used in an atheoretical way, we must not forget that the notion of lifestyle has strong roots in classical social science as represented, for example, by Veblen, Weber and Simmel. We will start our theoretical exposition, therefore, by considering the works of these classical social scientists, approaching the contemporary theoretical debate step-wise.

CLASSICAL THEORY

There are at least three main contributions to a theory of lifestyle in classical social theory. First, there is Weber's distinction between classes and status groups. Secondly, there is Veblen's theory of conspicuous consumption, and thirdly, there is Simmel's essay on the mechanisms operating in the dissemination of fashion.

A basic distinction in the Weberian sociology of lifestyle is the distinction between classes and status groups (Weber 1924/1968; Turner 1988). According to Weber it is appropriate to use the term class to designate a large number of persons with similar, and economically determined living conditions and life experiences. In contrast with classes, status groups are determined by assessments of social honor or esteem. Status distinctions are often linked with class distinctions, but income and property as such are not always acknowledged as qualifying for status. Social status is normally expressed in the form of a specific *style of life*. As Weber puts it in an oft-quoted passage:

> With some over-simplification, one might thus say that "classes" are stratified according to their relations to the production and acquisition of goods; whereas "status groups" are stratified according to the principles of their *consumption* of goods as represented by special "styles of life" (Weber 1922/1968:193).

According to Weber, different status groups at the time could be distinguished on the basis of their material monopolies. Such *honorific preferences* consisted, for example, of the privilege of wearing special clothes, of eating special food and of playing certain musical instruments. This meant that in public life it was not very difficult to distinguish between different status groups (and their lifestyles), since they were rather conspicuous and easily identified through such symbolic signs (cf. Sennett 1976; Heller 1970/1984).

The classical thinker most strongly associated with the description of such conspicuous differences between status groups is Thorstein Veblen. He describes how the transition from feudal society to modern industrial society influenced the use of status and power symbols (Veblen 1899/1979). In premodern society the aristocracy could express and display their power by conspicuously cultivating — in the absence of work — the art of leisure. In modern industrial society the ruling classes no longer display their superiority by the absence of work, but by means of conspicuous consumption. Possessing wealth or power is not enough. It has to be put in evidence through clothes and jewellery or other accessories, for example. Veblen can thus be said to be a predecessor to contemporary analysts of consumer culture. During the development of industrial society and mass production an increasing numbers of persons gained access to an ever greater variety of goods. According to Veblen the result was that the lower classes tried to imitate the lifestyle of the classes above them by means of mass produced, cheap copies of former aristocratic status symbols.

> In modern civilized communities the line of demarcation between social classes have grown vague and transient, and wherever this happens the norm of reputability imposed by the upper class extends its coercive influence with but slight hindrance down through the social structure to the lowest strata. The result is that the members of each stratum accept as their ideal of decency the scheme of life in vogue in the next higher stratum, and bend their energies to live up to that ideal (Veblen 1899/1979:84).

In a classical essay on fashion, Simmel analyses the same phenomenon as Veblen, albeit in a somewhat different way. Like Veblen he notes the lower classes' inclination to imitate the fashion of the upper classes. He finds the result of this process to be that, as soon as the lower classes adopt their style, the higher classes abandon it and develop a new one in order to maintain the distinction. He thus agrees with Veblen that fashion is used to make distinctions in terms of social status and access to power, but he also stresses another important function of fashion. Fashion can serve as a force uniting people who belong to the same group (Simmel 1904/1971).

Simmel sees these two different aspects as engendering a continuous process which has led to an ever continuing development in the area of fashion. When these continual changes in fashion become so frequent as was the case in the modern urban life with which he was concerned, the fashion industry becomes one of the major institutions in society. It is not fashion itself that is the key concept any more, but rather the constant need for change and the new sensations and experiences, which according to Simmel are typical for modern city life.

> The decisive fact here is that in the life of a city, struggle with nature for the means of life is transformed into a conflict with human beings and the gain which is fought for is granted, not by nature, but by man. For here we find not only the previously mentioned source of specialization but rather the deeper one in which the seller must seek to produce in the person to whom he wishes to sell ever new and unique needs. The necessity to specialize one's product in order to find a source of income which is not yet exhausted, and also to specialize a function which cannot be easily supplanted is conducive to differentiation, refinement and enrichment of the needs of the public which obviously must lead to increasing personal variations within this public (Simmel 1903/1971:336).

Simmel also maintained, however, that the urban city itself contradicts this tendency towards diversification through implanting in its inhabitants a blasé attitude of indifference toward the distinction between individuals and things.

The impact of classical sociologists on matters relating to lifestyle has continued on into modern sociological theory. During the last few decades the many concepts relating to the notion of lifestyle have become increasingly important in sociological thinking. Parallel with this, the importance given to cultural dimensions has increased considerably within sociology. a number of leading sociologists have contributed to the area, Norbert Elias's well known works on the civilizing process being an example (Elias 1939/1978, 1939/1982). Most of this work is beyond the scope of the present investigation. Rather, we will concentrate on the two sociologists most relevant to our work, namely, Herbert. J. Gans and Pierre Bourdieu.

MODERN SOCIOLOGY I: GANS AND BOURDIEU

Gans is mainly interested in the relation between popular culture and high culture. The thesis he puts forward is that the struggle for power between different groups and aggregates in society is not limited to the areas of economy and politics, but also includes the struggle for cultural dominance (Gans 1972; 1974).

Gans rejects the distinction between high culture and mass culture, so popular at the time. He considers the notion of mass culture, which suggests that most people belong to an undifferentiated collectivity which is distinguished by its lack of culture, to be false. Rather, he claims there to be a number of different popular cultures, arguing that these popular cultures — just as is the case with high culture — can be conceptualized as *different kinds of taste cultures*. In this view there are thus many similarities between high culture and different forms of popular culture. Gans defines taste cultures in the following way:

> Taste cultures, as I define them, consist of values, the cultural forms which express these values: music, art, design, literature, drama, comedy, poetry, criticism, news, and the media in which these are expressed — books, magazines, newspapers, records, films, and television programs, paintings and sculpture, architecture, and, insofar as ordinary consumer goods also express aesthetic values or functions, furnishings, clothes, appliances, and automobiles as well. In addition, taste cultures include the values, forms and media of the natural and social sciences and philosophy — including their commercial popularizations and even "folk wisdom".Finally, taste cultures have political values; although they do not often express them explicitly, they do so implicitly, and even when not, they frequently have political implications (Gans 1974:10).

According to Gans, the concept of taste culture is an analytical abstraction; it separates a culture from the people who create and use it. He therefore distinguishes between taste culture, the creators of that culture, and its users. People who share the same aesthetic values and make similar choices of taste culture content he designates as *taste publics*.

A large number of factors influence to a greater or lesser degree a person's choice among taste cultures, such factors as class, religion, age, race and personality. The major source of differentiation, however, is to be found on the socioeconomic level (income, occupation and education). According to Gans (1974) a person's educational achievement will predict his or her cultural taste better than any other isolated factor. Consequently, Gans assumes that in American society the range of taste cultures and taste publics is closely related to the range and hierarchy of classes. He thus distinguishes between five taste cultures and publics: high culture, upper-middle culture, lower-middle culture, low culture, and quasi-folk culture (for a description of these cultures, see Gans 1974).

The different taste cultures and taste publics co-exist within what Gans calls a *taste structure*. The main reason for the existence of a taste structure is the socioeconomic hierarchy in society. Taste cultures and taste publics are thus structured in a hierarchical way, with high culture at the top and low culture at the bottom. Consequently, decisions about cultural consumption often reflect status considerations. Even if most people tend to restrict their cultural consumption to "their" taste culture, everyone now and then chooses from a higher or a lower culture. If this happens too frequently the content of the higher culture becomes devalued, and analogously the content of the lower culture increases in value (cf. Veblen 1899/1979; Simmel 1904/1971). Gans expresses this in the following way:

> As I suggested earlier, when Ingmar Bergman's films became popular with upper-middle moviegoers in the 1960s, they lost much of their standing among high culture film buffs (Gans 1974:114).

Gans's theory has gained some influence in the sociology of popular culture (see, for example, Denisoff & Levine 1972; Fox & Wince 1975; Lewis 1978, 1981, 1989). However, a more elaborated theoretical view on the subject of the relation between high and popular culture, power relations and lifestyles, is represented in the works of the French sociologist Pierre Bourdieu.

In several of his books Bourdieu has tried to throw light upon the relation between cultural consumption and the power relations between and within different classes and status groups in society (Bourdieu et al. 1965/1990; Bourdieu & Passeron 1977/1990; Bourdieu 1979/1984; 1988). His major work in this respect is *Distinction* (1979/1984), in which he puts forward his theory of *the social space of lifestyles* (cf. Broady 1990; Harker et al. 1990; Fenster 1991; Rosengren 1991b).

Bourdieu considers there to be an ever ongoing struggle for power and status, not only between but also within the different classes in society. This struggle concerns not only position in relation to matters of production (income, occupation, education). Rather, Bourdieu also defines a class or a class fraction in terms of such features as sex-ratio, geograpical distribution or ethnic origin (Bourdieu 1979/1984). Struggles of this sort take place within what he calls a social space, where relations between the classes are structured in accordance with the amount of and access to different forms of capital, for instance, economic, cultural and social capital characterizing the different classes and class fractions. (Different forms of capital are more thoroughly discussed in chapter eight of this book.)

It is the dominant classes and class fractions that primarily interest

Bourdieu, since that is where he finds there to be the most accentuated struggle for power, the struggle for not only economic but also cultural dominance. According to Bourdieu, the dominant class in a society has a monopoly on legitimate culture defining the latter and determining what tastes are the best and what lifestyle is to prevail.

Other classes and class fractions constantly try to promote their cultural preferences and lifestyles so as to become legitimate and predominating. This struggle for dominance between classes and class fractions leads to continual changes in lifestyle. This symbolic battle is fought in different fields of cultural preference (Bourdieu 1979/1984). These fields consists of different cultural goods within the areas of, for example, music, art, theatre and literature. Bourdieu claims that the heart of these symbolic struggles is taste, and that the aim is to achieve acceptance of a specific taste as the legitimate one within a particular field of preference. The "right" taste and lifestyle thus stand as symbols for power and status.

This brief summary of Bourdieu's theory of lifestyle will be followed later by a more thoroughgoing discussion of his key concepts of habitus and of different forms of capital (see chapter five and eight).

In classical theory as well as in the sociology of Gans and Bourdieu the concept of class occupies a central position. Within more recent brands of sociology relating to lifestyle, however, a quite different line of thinking has developed, one in which class assumes only a minor position. In the next section, we will take up this tendency towards moving away from a class-related analysis of the lifestyle-phenomenon.

MODERN SOCIOLOGY II: FROM CLASS DIFFERENTIATION TO COLLECTIVE SELECTION

The movement away from a class-oriented analysis of lifestyle has taken a number of different forms, but in most of them the stress laid upon the individual is significant. Thus the individual has come to a greater extent to be seen as responsible in one way or another for the lifestyles she or he develops. This tendency can be noted in several contemporary articles and books on lifestyles (Blumer 1969; Zablocki & Kanter 1976; Lewis 1978; Reimer 1989; Lüdtke 1989; Lööv & Miegel 1989, 1991). This tendency can also be traced to the rich sociological literature on modernity, individualization and cultural change (Bell 1976; Habermas 1981/1984;1981/1987; Berman 1983; Beck 1986). We will not discuss the works of these latter authors in any detail, however, important as they may be. Rather, we shall concentrate on two pioneering articles of specific relevance to the area of interest.

Ierbert Blumer (1969) was probably one of the first sociologists to relate lifestyle-related phenomena to the twin processes of modernization and individualization. In his discussion of the character of modern fashion, he takes Simmel's essay on fashion as a starting point. His critique of Simmel's analysis is directed mainly at the notion of the elite class as a style-setting group in society. According to Blumer's analysis of the relation between the elite class and the fashion mechanism, the prestige of the elite affects, but does not control the creation of new fashions. The fashion mechanism is more complicated. There is much more to it than the mere exercise of prestige and status:

> The fashion mechanism appears not in response to a need of class differentiation and class emulation but in response to a wish to be in fashion, to be abreast of what has good standing, to express new tastes which are emerging in a changing world. These are the changes that seem to be called for in Simmel's formulation. They are fundamental changes. They shift fashion from the fields of *class differentiation* to the area of *collective selection* and center its mechanism in the process of such selection (Blumer 1969:282).

Rather than pointing to the importance of power relations between classes and status groups in society, Blumer's reformulation of Simmel's analysis of fashion emphasizes the individual's use of fashion in her or his attempts to adjust to an ever changing world.

In an illuminating article *The Differentiation of Lifestyles*, Zablocki and Kanter (1976) further develop the thesis presented by Blumer. Like Blumer they deny that class is the dominant factor in lifestyle. Although they agree that class and position are important, they maintain that other matters are at least as central. Their definition of lifestyle runs as follows:

> A life-style might be defined over a given collectivity to the extent that the members are similar to one another and different from others both in the distribution of their disposable incomes and the motivations that underlie such distribution (Zablocki & Kanter 1976:270).

What Zablocki and Kanter stress is that the role of the free choice of the individual must not be forgotten in discussing lifestyle. Since in contemporary society lifestyles are not as bound to class and status as they were in traditional society, Zablocki and Kanter maintain that it is now more important to study the intra-generational transition of individuals among different lifestyles than to try to place an individual in a specific lifestyle category. Consequently, they talk about *lifestyle mobility* and *lifestyle careers*.

Zablocki and Kanter, as well as Blumer, work in a sociological context which allows them to identify and speak of socially constructed groups and collectivities. During the past decade a tradition has developed in lifestyle-research which is both more individualistic and more closely related to market research. This tradition has gained rather wide influence among social scientists working in different areas. The founder of this tradition, Arnold Mitchell, has become especially influential, not least because he has developed a technique for the empirical measurement of the values and lifestyles of the individuals in a society. His theoretical ideas are the topic of next section.

THE NINE AMERICAN LIFESTYLES

Mitchell's theory is probably the best known psychologically oriented theory of lifestyle (Mitchell 1983). His typology of values and lifestyles (VALS), a typology of the American consumer, has been widely used in market and consumer research (see, for instance, Zetterberg 1977, 1983; Holman 1984; Veltri & Schiffman 1984; Holman & Wiener 1985). In this section we shall present briefly the most central portions of Mitchell's lifestyle theory.

Mitchell conceptualizes and describes *The Nine American Lifestyles* on the basis of Maslow's well known hierarchy of needs (Mitchell 1983). In brief, Maslow's theory states that certain elementary physical needs have to be fulfilled before people will become concerned about activities and interests aiming at self-realization (Maslow 1968). Accordingly Mitchell distinguishes between three different categories of lifestyles: *need-driven* lifestyles, *outer-oriented* lifestyles and *inner-oriented* lifestyles. In Mitchell's theory the outer-directed and the inner-directed groups represent two different, albeit not incompatible, ways of achieving psychological maturation (cf. David Riesman's concepts of inner and *other* directed, Riesman et al. 1950). Lifestyle changes are explained from the point of view of psychological forces driving people to develop new lifestyles.

At the lowest levels in Mitchell's typology come the need-driven groups, called *Survivors* and *Sustainers*. Although they are different, these two groups share some basic characteristics. Both are poverty-stricken. Basically people belonging to these groups struggle to achieve a minimum standard of living.

According to Mitchell, outer-directed lifestyles make up about two-thirds of the American population. Three distinct lifestyles belong to this category: *Belongers*, *Emulators* and *Achievers*. Characteristic of these lifestyles is a sensitivity to signals from others. People belonging to outer-directed lifestyles create ways of structuring everyday life that are geared to the visible, tangible, and materialistic. Belongers typify the middle-class American. They are traditional, conforming, conservative and family-oriented. Emulators strive to be like those whom they consider richer and more successful than themselves. Emulators are people with high ambitions who are not always successful in realizing their ambitions. Achievers are at the top of society. Mitchell describes them as a gifted, hard-working, self-reliant, successful, and happy group. Achievers typify the successful status-seeking American.

Inner-directed lifestyles are so named because their driving forces are internal, not external. Inner-direction adds another layer of values to the ones just mentioned, offering to individuals new ways of expressing their self, new perspectives and new ways of structuring everyday life. According to Mitchell there are three inner-directed lifestyles: *I-Am-Mes*, *Experientals*, and *Socially Conscious*. I-Am-Mes seek the new, often resenting old values and lifestyles. Experientals seek direct, vivid experience. In a psychological sense experientals are the most inner-directed group. Characteristic of this group is a feeling for the mystical, and a quest for inner exploration. Socially conscious persons, in contrast, are concerned with societal issues, trends and events. Their greatest interest in life is political matters.

Finally, Mitchell discerns a category of lifestyles that he calls *Integrateds*: people who have succeeded in combining outer-directed and inner-directed personality characteristics. Maturity and a sense of "fitting" are prime characteristics of this particular group.

A major part of Mitchell's book is dedicated to a discussion of the question of how people change their lifestyles.

It should be recognized from the start that lifestyles are, happily, not fixed and immutable. People change levels as children, as adolescents, and as adults. Many people — possibly most — move one or two levels upward from their "entry point" into our typology at about age eighteenth. Some very few may move from the bottom to the top in a lifetime. "Slipping back" is also a common phenomenon, as discussed later. To make the situation even more complex, some people seem to exhibit different lifestyles in various areas in their lives (Mitchell 1983:28).

Mitchell argues that personal growth and change are widespread phenomena in all social classes of American society. Although he admits that societal forces can obstruct individual growth, he is mainly concerned with psychological explanations for the blockage of personal growth and for changes in lifestyle. According to his view, certain people tend more often than others to get "stuck" at a particular lifestyle level.

In the next section we will present a critical discussion of the different traditions in lifestyle research referred to above, and will also draw various conclusions regarding our own position in this field of research.

CONCLUSIONS

The chronologically and in substance widely divergent group of writers discussed in the previous section have all contributed to developing the very complex and important concept of lifestyle. The term *lifestyle* does not denote today the same as it did earlier. What was valid and true about the concept earlier is not necessarily true to an equal degree today. In each of the theories referred to above there are some aspects which are more or less taken for granted today in discussions on lifestyle. Nevertheless, it is easy to criticize most of these theories— in some cases regarding quite central points. This is not to deny their importance but simply to stress the fact that all concern a concept, which has changed in accordance with social and historical developments.

Against the background of the historical development of the concept, the aim of this chapter is to provide a critical discussion of the applicability of different theories in contemporary Western capitalistic societies. Our aim in so doing is to gradually arrive at a theory relevant to lifestyle in general, and to the lifestyle of youth in particular.

Classical sociologists were almost exclusively occupied with class and status relations. That is where their insufficiency for a modern analysis of lifestyle lies. In the early industrial societies which confronted Weber, Simmel and Veblen, this was the obvious starting point, although Simmel in a way foreshadows the impact of the individual. In the society of the classical sociologists, lifestyles and class or status were intimately interconnected (cf. Sennett 1976; Braunstein 1985/1988). However, the theoretical contributions of classical sociologists do provide valuable insights into the different ways in which lifestyles were created and maintained in the societies of the time. The concept of lifestyle was defined by the classics as basically being rooted in the access to power, in cultural and material goods, and the like. If different persons belonged to a particular class, they were regarded as having approximately the same lifestyle. In contemporary society, where individual variations in terms of lifestyle are supposedly much greater, this obviously provides an insufficient notion of lifestyle. Class and status are still important but are not as crucial as the classics once suggested (cf. Clark & Lipset 1991).

Within a modern sociology of lifestyle and lifestyle-related matters, two opposing tendencies can be distinguished. The one is to still basically be concerned with class and power relations, whereas the other is to put greater emphasis on the role of the individual in lifestyle development.

Both Bourdieu and Gans, for example, represent the tendency towards class and power orientation. In analyzing the origins and development of lifestyles they emphasize class, status, and power relations in much the same way as did the classics. They differ from the classics, however, in that they have expanded the class concept and achieved a more sophisticated theoretical understanding of the relation between the complexity of cultural consumption and its role in the struggle for power and status between and within the classes or fractions of society. They also have a multidimensional conception of the very notion of culture. Thus they distinguish between different forms of culture, such as, say, high culture, popular culture and mass culture.

What can be held against them is that, despite their achievements regarding cultural analysis, they still overemphasize the impact of class, status and the struggle for power, and accordingly underestimate the role of the individual (cf. Fenster 1991). It is to such tendencies that representatives of the other directions within modern lifestyle analysis object.

Authors such as Blumer, Zablocki and Kanter have come to the view that class, status and power relations need not be the major explanatory factors for the way in which lifestyles develop in contemporary society. Instead, they look for alternative forces in the process of lifestyle development, and the impact of the individual is considered to be the most significant force in this respect. This is an important achievement. However, these authors have difficulty in explaining how the individual impacts upon the creation and change in modern lifestyles. They thus lack a theory of individual lifestyle.

One of the most influential representatives of the tradition placing emphasis upon the individual is Arnold Mitchell in his study *The Nine American Lifestyles*. Mitchell's theory has at least two advantages. First, Mitchell has actually developed a theory of how the single individual develops her or his lifestyle. Secondly, he identifies different types of human values as crucial components in this development. These two advantages also represent, however, his areas of weakness. In the first place, he makes crucial errors in defining and identifying what he calls human values. This criticism will be developed in detail in chapter six. Secondly, like so many others, he overstates the role of the individual, almost completely neglecting any discussion of social and cultural structures and positions, thus making the individual almost the sole locus of lifestyle.

In Figure 1 we offer a simple scheme for the different theoretical traditions which have thus far been discussed.

The aim of the criticism we have directed against various theoretical positions is to provide a background to the theory of lifestyles which we shall develop in this book. We will maintain that in order to comprehend present-day lifestyles, one has to account not only for structural and positional factors (as did the classics), but also for the important role of the individual (which certain modern sociologists do). This requires an understanding of how individuals relate, not only to the social and cultural structures and positions in which they conduct their lives, but also to themselves, their personality, their identity and their struggle for self-development. Furthermore, there is a need for a specific theory of the relation between human values and lifestyles, since the values of the individual, though influenced by the values of society and the individual's position within society, constitute a substantial part of the individual's identity.

Figure 1. Theoretical Traditions in Lifestyle Research.

	CLASSICAL THEORY	MODERN SOCIOLOGY I	MODERN SOCIOLOGY II	ARNOLD MITCHELL	THE LIFESTYLE THEORY OF THIS BOOK
NUMBER OF LIFESTYLES IN A SOCIETY	As many as class and status groups	As many as class and status groups	As many as collectives	Nine	Not fixed
DYNAMICS OF CHANGE	Status and power relations	Status and power relations	Social and cultural development (modernization)	Needs	Social and cultural development Status and power relations Identity development
TYPES OF VALUE	Material	Material Aesthetic	Material Aesthetic	Material Aesthetic Ethical Metaphysical	Material Aesthetic Ethical Metaphysical
LEVEL OF DETERMINATION	Structure Position	Structure Position	Structure Position Individual	Individual	Structure Position Individual
SOCIAL MOBILITY	None	Some	Yes	Yes	Yes
CULTURAL MOBILITY	None	Some	Yes	Yes	Yes

The aim of the following chapters is thus to develop a general theory of lifestyle which takes account not only of the structurally and positionally determined features of lifestyle, but also of the important individually determined component, and of the crucial role of the individual's identity and values, which we will argue constitute the locus of the process of individual lifestyle development.

CHAPTER 3
LIFESTYLE AND THE QUEST FOR INDIVIDUALITY

INTRODUCTION

The aims of this study are twofold. We aim on the one hand to suggest a solution to the sometimes confusing terminological ambiguity inherent in most theories confronting the multitude of phenomena conceptualized as lifestyles, and on the other to operationalize the concept in order to study various aspects of youth culture empirically. In parts one and two of the book, we discuss the concept of lifestyle on a theoretical level. In parts three, four and five we discuss both methodological questions and the empirical results of our study.

The first theoretical question to be dealt with is how to use the term lifestyle as distinguished from other similar terms and concepts: subcultures, counter cultures, ways of living, forms of life, style, taste culture, style of life, and the like. We believe that it is possible to use the concept in different ways depending on the object of investigation, and that one way of using the term does not necessarily exclude other ways of using it. *However, it is always necessary to define the context in which one uses the term.* As the British philosopher R M Hare puts it:

> The crucial point is that, although we can ask what questions we wish, *whatever* questions we ask will be posed in terms of certain concepts; and that means that *whatever* questions we ask, we shall have, if we are going to think rationally about the answers to them, to understand the concepts (Hare 1981:19).

FORMS OF LIFE, WAYS OF LIVING AND LIFESTYLES

In this section we shall distinguish between three different but interrelated levels on which it is possible to study aspects of living relevant to a discussion of lifestyle: *a structural level, a positional level,* and *an individual level*. The purpose of this distinction is to clarify how a multitude of phenomena on each of these three levels affect and lead to the development of lifestyles (Lööv & Miegel 1989; cf. Heller 1970/1984; Thunberg et al. 1982).

Each society and each culture within it has a structure which distinguishes it from other societies and cultures. This structure involves various institutions, legislative acts, modes of production, norms, values, ideals, convictions, customs and mores. On this level — the structural level — one can examine differences and similarities between various countries, societies and cultures, as well as differences evolving over time within one and the same society. At this level of analysis, the fundamental differences between, for example, Islamic and Christian or, agrarian and industrial societies, religious and secular cultures, and the like, are to be found. This is the level of conceptualization we use, for example, in comparing the American way of life with the Swedish or the Russian. The configurations involved, reflecting primarily differences in social structure, will be referred to as *Forms of Life*. They basically represent different forms of society or culture.

The second level of analysis concerns differences and similarities existing in a given society or culture between large categories, classes, strata or groups. the latter are characterized and distinguished on the basis of their differing positions within the social structure. Their relations with various institutions differ; as do their role in production, their access to power, the cultural and economic resources they possess, and so on. At this level — the positional level — one can study differences and similarities between, say, different status groups, social classes, or age categories, between men and women or whatever. Configurations of this kind, primarily determined by the position held in a given social structure, will be termed *Ways of living* (cf. Höjrup 1983; Rahbek 1987).

The third and last level of analysis deals with the individual. On this level — the individual level — one endeavors to understand differences and similarities between the varying ways in which individuals face reality and lead their lives, how they develop and express their personality and identity, their relations toward other individuals or groups of individuals, and so on. To the extent that such differences are primarily determined by individual characteristics other than positional ones, we shall refer to these as differences in *Lifestyles*. In this sense, lifestyles are expressions of individuals' ambitions to create their own specific, personal, cultural and social identities within the historically determined structural and positional framework of their society.

The reason for distinguishing between these three levels of analysis or determination is that the application of the concept of lifestyle in the social sciences, as mentioned earlier, has changed in accordance with societal changes.

In classical sociology the concept of lifestyle was used to distinguish between social classes and status groups on the basis of their cultural characteristics, as related to access to the means of production, and to power, social status and other resources (Weber 1922/1968; Veblen 1899/1979; Simmel 1904/1971). This was quite a natural starting point in examining a society in which different groupings represented differences in most aspects of life, not only in access to economic capital, education, material goods, standards of living and the like, but also in values, tastes and styles.

In contemporary society, however, lifestyles have become less tied to the social position of the individual. Instead, individually determined conditions have become increasingly important (Toffler 1970; Zablocki & Kanter 1976; Schudson 1986; Turner 1988). Theories of the lifestyles in contemporary society, therefore, must pay regard to the individual and his or her identity. Particular attention must be given to the distinctive features of the *individualization process*, that is, to the historical process through which individuals acquire a consciousness of their own position within different cultural and societal systems (Elias 1939/1982; Abercrombie et al. 1986).

It is important to distinguish between the process of individualization and the *process of individuation* (cf. Blos 1962, 1967, 1979). Whereas the former is a historical process, the latter is an individual one (cf. the roughly parallel concepts of phylogenesis and ontogenesis). These processes are of course related in various ways.

The historical process of individualization takes place within a structurally and positionally determined framework. In order to arrive at a reasonable understanding of lifestyles, it is thus not sufficient to account for only one or two of the levels of determination. All three must be taken into consideration. To maintain that lifestyle is an individually determined phenomenon is thus not to deny the impact of societal constraints. In the final analysis, however, there is no denying that judgements by the individual form an important basis for his or her lifestyle.

The relationship between human beings, culture and society is indeed complex. As Berger and Luckmann (1966/1987:79) put it so well more than 25 years ago: "*Society is a human product. Society is an objective reality.*

Man is a social product." To grasp this complex relationship Berger and Luckmann use three concepts: *Externalization, Objectivation* and *Internalization.*

Berger (1967:4) defines externalization as the "ongoing outpouring of human beings into the world, both in the physical and the mental activity of men". The human need for interaction and communication leads to the ever continuing creation of new cultural and social patterns. In that sense society is a human product. Externalization is thus an active and creative process in which individuals express and create their own unique selves.

In later chapters we shall argue that lifestyles are externalizations of the values and attitudes of individuals. To comprehend the complexity inherent in lifestyle one must therefore understand the values and attitudes underlying such externalizations.

What Berger (1967:4) terms objectivation is the "attainment by the products of this activity (again both physical and mental) of a reality that confronts its original producers as a facticity external to and other than themselves". Through objectivation society becomes a reality in itself.

Internalization, finally, is, according to Berger (1967) the process by which the objectivized social world is retrojected into subjective consciousness during the course of socialization. It is through internalization that man becomes a social product.

In order to understand lifestyle development it is important to study the interplay between the interconnected processes of externalization, objectivation and internalization. Lifestyles are created by human beings, but they are also transformed into an objective reality which, to be sure, can be deconstructed as well. In the line with Berger and Luckmann one could thus say: *Lifestyles are human products. Lifestyles are objective reality. Individual's lifestyles are social products.*

According to our theory, then, lifestyles are structurally, positionally and individually determined phenomena. In order to comprehend lifestyles in modern society it is necessary to understand the different processes taking place within and between these three levels.

On the structural level one focuses upon relatively stable cultural and social formations and changes in them. According to Berger and Luckmann the institutionalized world is to be regarded as objectivized human activity. Social and cultural institutions are relatively impervious to changes generated by individuals. Constant changes do take place however, but only slowly (cf. Inglehart 1977, 1990). In a short-time perspective they are almost invisible to the ordinary individual.

Through the process of socialization individuals internalize and are made to internalize, social and cultural structure. That is, they are taught or learn the rules, norms, values, morals and modes of behavior, of their society and culture. All this forms an *internalized structure*, which in turn constitutes an important part of the social and cultural identity. Through different internalized structures individuals become members of different collectivities such as tribes, religious communities, and cultures, for example. The concept of *collectivities* can be used to designate large numbers of people, among by far the greater part of whom there is no social interaction (Merton 1963). People who belong to such social formations share a common body of social norms and values, and a sense of moral obligation to fulfill certain role expectations. Collectivities can be recognized on the basis of differences in mode of living which characterize them.

Although in every society there are commonly held norms and values, individuals and groups of individuals also differ with respect to norms, values, opinions and attitudes, depending upon which position they occupy in the given structure. On the positional level we focus on relationships between different structurally determined positions in society and changes in these. Individuals internalize various role-expectations depending among other things upon their access to power, to cultural and social competence, to economic capital, and to education.

Whereas it is difficult or almost impossible for the individual to change his or her structurally determined characteristics, it is somewhat easier for the individual to move between different positions, through what is usually called *social mobility*. The term social mobility was often used in classical sociology to portray individual trajectories in the economically defined class or status hierarchy of a society. Analogously we can use the term *cultural mobility* to conceptualize individual trajectories in the cultural sphere. Such changes do not always have any correspondence within the area of the appropriation of real power by members of lower classes or of status groups. Ewen (1988) uses the term *symbolic democratization* to describe how symbols of the dominant classes and status groups have been made available on a mass scale through the mass production of services and goods. Such symbolic democratization sometimes creates an illusory transcendence of class (cf. Veblen 1899/1979).

Although class is an important factor in the formation of lifestyles, one must also explain how abstract culture is internalized by individuals and used by them. We maintain that the core of lifestyle is to be found in the identity of the individual. Identity, however, is a highly complex concept consisting of many different components.

We have divided the concept of identity into three different but interrelated types: personal identity, social identity and cultural identity (Lööv & Miegel 1991). The reason for introducing this distinction is that each of the three types of identity has a different part to play in producing the lifestyle of an individual. We will argue that it is cultural identity which is most important for the lifestyle of an individual. Personal and social identities are important insofar as they influence and are influenced by cultural identity. In chapter five and six we will discuss and further motivate the distinction between the three types of identity, their mutual relations, and their connections with the concepts of value and lifestyle.

As already mentioned, in order to understand how individual identity — as well as cultural identity, in particular — are constituted, we must understand how abstract culture is internalized and is used by the individual. In this context, Bourdieu's concept of habitus seems appropriate (cf. Bourdieu 1977, 1979/1984). Habitus may be regarded as mediating between societal structures and subjective interpretations of and attitudes towards these structures. A habitus consists both of the cultural style of a class, gender, age group, etc., and a personal manner of comprehending and relating to these structurally and positionally determined features. A habitus is a structure internalized by the individual during the course of his or her life. The externalization of habitus will be conceptualized here as the basis for individual lifestyles. In the course of a lifetime, habitus and individual lifestyle alter, sometimes drastically so.

Habitus is the internalized structure in which structurally, positionally and individually determined influences converge and become the unity which constitutes cultural identity. One of the most fundamental elements of habitus and thus of cultural identity is that of the values held by the individual. On the one hand, the individual holds a set of basic values shared by the vast majority of the members of his society. On the other hand the variations in values between different status groups and social classes express and define these groups' positions in the value structure of society.

The unique value structure of the individual, finally, is influenced — but not totally determined — by structurally and positionally determined values.

By definition, values are rather abstract. They are made more concrete by the individual in his or her attitudes. Attitudes, in their turn, are visualized and expressed in different kinds of actions. Since human values are of different kinds, there are also different kinds of attitudes and actions corresponding to these which are to be considered in discussing lifestyles. We believe that the concept of value should be the key concept in any analysis of lifestyles. In chapters six and seven, we will therefore outline a theory of the relationship between different kinds of human values and lifestyles.

Although value has no doubt been a key concept in most theories of lifestyle, the relationship between the two concepts has tended to not be made explicit. Instead, theories of lifestyle have often concentrated upon the visible and expressive elements of lifestyles, that is the style (fashion), activitities and consumption of the individuals involved (Simmel 1904/1971; Veblen 1899/1979; Bourdieu 1979/1984). As we will argue later, such aspects of lifestyle are primarily related to certain kinds of what we term outer-directed values. There are also other kinds of values, however, what we term inner-directed values. These are not as visibly expressed, but it is nevertheless important to include them in an analysis of lifestyles (cf. Kamler 1984).

In the following chapters we shall discuss in some detail the three problematic areas touched upon in this section: the development of an identity, the human values and the importance of these two concepts as related to the main concept at issue, the concept of lifestyle.

We have argued that lifestyle is a phenomenon which throughout recent history has gradually become determined less and less by structural and positional conditions, being determined to an increasing extent by the individual and his or her identity. Before going further we will attempt to account for the historical process of individualization which has led to this increasing relevance of the individual in contemporary society. Here we will turn to four classical sociologists.

CHAPTER 4
THE PROCESS OF INDIVIDUALIZATION

THE DISCOVERY OF THE INDIVIDUAL

> There is no reason that all human existence should beconstructed on some one or some small number of patterns. If a person possesses any tolerable amount of commonsense and experience, his own mode of laying out his existence is the best, not because it is the best in itself, but because it is his own mode (Mill 1859/1984:132).

> Men make their own history, but they do not make it just as they please; they do not make it under circumstances chosen by themselves, but under circumstances directly encountered, given and transmitted from the past (Marx 1852/1969:15).

The notion of the individual as being separate from society is by no means a modern one. As far back as the ancient Greeks we can find discussions of the relationship between the individual and society (Arendt 1978; d'Epinay 1991). During the Enlightenment the link between man and God was seriously questioned. This led to a reformulation of the relationship between the individual and his society, and to what could be called the *theoretical revolution of individualism* (d'Epinay 1991). Whereas previously the individual was in many ways defined in relation to a cosmic order, the individual was now regarded more and more as a rational and free subject (Lukes 1973a; Taylor 1975; Rundell 1987; Connolly 1989).

The discussion of the relationship between the individual and society gained new significance during the nineteenth century in the classical sociological works of Marx, Weber, Durkheim and Simmel. However, it was primarily the social and personal consequences of the rupture between the individual and society which occupied these new social scientists, the sociologists. Marx's (1844/1975; 1852/1969) most important contributions to this discussion are the theory of free labor and the concept of alienation (cf. Lichtheim 1968; Israel 1979). Marx maintained that in capitalistic society individuals in one sense gained a certain degree of freedom which they had not experienced in the previous feudal societal system. The kind of freedom Marx had in mind was basically the freedom of the worker to sell his or her labor as a commodity on the market. This was rather a freedom *from* than a freedom *to* something (cf. Fromm 1962). It was a freedom *from* the bonds of serfdom in a feudal society, but it was not, according to Marx, a "real freedom", that is, not a freedom *to* something.

Workers had the choice of selling their labor to capitalists, but in the end they were required to expose themselves to the exploitation of capitalists. Marx also analyzed the consequences for the worker of the division and specialization of labor. He felt that the division and specialization of labor created a distance between the worker and the products the latter produced. The worker never saw the completed results of his or her efforts but only fragments of the finished product. This together with the fact of becoming an interchangeable link in the chain of production, created in the worker a feeling of dissatisfaction, which Marx referred to as *alienation*. This was a feeling of being robbed of any possibility of affecting the creation and design of the product, the disappearance of any direct relation between the worker and the work the latter carried out, as well as a loss in value of the individual worker.

What Marx did was to analyze the paradox of the process of individualization. On the one hand, individuals had gained a certain amount of freedom; on the other hand, they had lost the value which the skilled craftsmen or the peasants possessed on the basis of their work. Industrial workers thus had the possibility of choosing, but the range of choices was, indeed limited.

> What constitutes the alienation of labour? First, that the work is external to the worker, that it is not part of his nature; and that consequently, he does not fulfill himself in his work but denies himself, has a feeling of misery rather than well-being, does not develop freely his mental and physical energies that is physically exhausted and mentally debased. The worker, therefore, feels himself at home only during his leisure time, whereas at work he feels homeless. His work is not voluntary but imposed, forced labour. It is not the satisfaction of a need, but only a means for satisfying other means. Its alien character is clearly shown by the fact that as soon as there is no physical or other compulsion it is avoided like the plague. External labour, labour in which man alienates himself, is a labour of self-sacrifice, of mortification (Marx 1844/1975:326).

Like Marx, Durkheim was occupied with the question of the relationship between the individual and society. Like Marx he also considered the division of labor to be a fundamental power in a developing industrial society — but in quite a different way. Whereas Marx was mainly interested in conflicts between different classes and the disintegration of capitalistic society, Durkheim was instead primarily concerned with the integration of society. The dichotomy between the society and the individual is thus the keystone of Durkheim's entire system of thought (cf. Parsons 1968b; Lukes 1973b; Alexander 1988, 1989).

Durkheim claimed that in pre-modern societies with little division of labor and no individualism, social integration was achieved through the construction and maintenance of what he called a *collective consciousness*, i.e., a common stock of values, beliefs and attitudes held by the members of a particular society (Durkheim 1893/1988). The term which he used to describe the integrative principle in this type of society was mechanical solidarity. In brief, this means that solidarity within society is based upon — and maintained through — the sameness of individuals. In societies characterized by *mechanical solidarity* individuals are in a way interchangeable since everyone performs the same tasks and possesses similar functions, similar knowledge, and the like.

In modern society, through the development of specialization and the division of labor, collective consciousness has become weaker and less important. Social integration basically rests instead on the mutual dependency between individuals which results from the division of labor. Modern societies are thus based on and maintained through what Durkheim calls *organic solidarity*. By this he means that social integration depends upon differences between individuals. Since division of labor has advanced to such an extent in modern societies, and since the individuals thus have different roles to play and different tasks to fulfil, each individual has become dependent upon a number of other individuals and on various institutions. In Durkheim's view, it is these widespread mutual dependencies which lie at the basis of the organic solidarity characterizing modern Occident.

> Yet if the division of labour produces solidarity, it is not only because it makes each individual an agent of exchange, to use the language of the economists. It is because it creates between men a whole system of rights and duties joining them in a lasting way to one another. Just as social similarities give rise to a law and a morality that protect them, so the division of labour gives rise to rules ensuring peaceful and regular co-operation between the functions that have been divided up (Durkheim 1893/1988:337f).

According to Durkheim, it is hardly possible to talk about individuality in pre-modern societies with their mechanical solidarity, and only possible to a limited extent there to speak of separate individuals, since collective consciousness is so dominant and in sole control. Through certain processes (which we will not take up here) collective consciousness had according to Durkheim been gradually weakened so that room for individual development and creativity had successively increased. In Durkheim's view, it had reached its peak in the modern society of his time.

> Indeed to be a person means to be an autonomous source of action. Thus man only attains this state to the degree that there is something within him that is his and his alone, that makes him an individual, whereby he is more than the mere embodiment of the generic type of his race and group (Durkheim 1893/1988:335).

Beside stressing that this gradual process of individualization was necessary and inevitable, Durkheim pointed out certain consequences of the process. He also claimed that in order to restrain individual desires and passions, an authority is needed, capable of imposing collective order on individuals. Such regulations must come from a power which dominates individuals and is obeyed on the basis of respect. According to Durkheim, the power which exercises this controlling function is society. When a drastic change strikes, society becomes momentarily incapable of maintaining collective order. During such periods society is characterized by what Durkheim calls *anomie*. Anomie is, in brief, a disproportion between the expectations, desires and needs of individuals, on the one hand, and the actual possibilities of fulfilling or realizing these, on the other.

The third classical sociologist we shall briefly discuss is Georg Simmel. In many of his essays Simmel described the relationship between the individual and society. He was mainly interested in the social psychological aspects of this relationship. Concepts such as *social structure, system* or *class* played a minor role in Simmel's sociology. Simmel was more interested in social interaction and phenomenological aspects of social reality (cf. Mayntz 1968). In his essays on the metropolitan personality type, fashion and the develement of individuality, he analyzed the social psychological consequences for the individual of the processes of industrialization and modernization. Simmel's social theory may thus be regarded primarily as an attempt to analyze different modes of experiencing modern life. Simmel's theory of modernity, however fragmentary and incomplete it may be, takes up many important themes in analyzing modern life (cf. Frisby 1985). From our point of view one of the most important of these themes is the one concerning the meaning of individuality and the process of individualization (cf. Nedelmann 1991).

For Simmel individuality and sociability were in no way incompatible. On the contrary, he held that individuality was gained and maintained through individuals' adherence to different social groups (Simmel 1908/1971). Thus, in his view, individuals develop their individuality both through their membership in a specific social group and through differentiation within this group. Simmel expressed this relationship in the following way:

> The differentiation drive receives satisfaction from the contrast of one's particular personality with one's fellow members, but this plus corresponds to a minus in the satisfaction that the same person, as a purely social being, derives from oneness with his fellows. That is to say: intensified individualization within the group is accompanied by decreased individualization of the group itself, and vice versa, whenever a certain portion of the drive is satiated (Simmel 1908/1971:259).

Simmel's analysis of the meaning of individuality seems still more explicitly formulated in his essay on fashion. Through the development of a distinct taste and style in fashion, for example, an individual is able to express his or her individuality, or separateness from other individuals, and at the same time to express his or her adherence to other individuals who possess a more or less almost identical taste and style in fashion (Simmel 1904/1971) Therefore, according to Simmel, individuality can only be developed and maintained within social groups.

Max Weber, the last of the four influential thinkers we deal with here briefly, was perhaps the most individually oriented of the four. In several of his writings he developed and refined the thesis of the relationship between the processes of secularization and individualization. Probably the most important of these writings is *The Protestant Ethic and the Spirit of Capitalism* (Weber 1904/1930), but one should not forget his presentation of these thoughts in the collection of his papers *Economy and Society* (Weber 1924/1968), as well (cf. also Parsons 1968a; Bendix 1968).

In these classical works Weber outlined his influential theory of the dialectical process by which a particular religious doctrine can provide extremely favorable conditions for a specific economic order, and vice versa. He attempted to explain in his way how different societal processes could contribute to the growth of capitalist society. Weber perceived how various branches of Protestantism — particularly Calvinism — provided religious and spiritual support for the development of economic ways of thinking and behaving which were characteristic of the Occident.

Calvin's teachings contained an element of predestination. Man was seen as predestined from birth to either salvation or condemnation, without any possibility of changing his or her faith through earthly actions. One can say that Calvinism separated "heaven and earth" by removing the channels — for instance, the sacraments — through which individuals had earlier "communicated" with God. The belief in godly predestination led to a need among Calvinists for signs of whether one belonged to the chosen or to the condemned. Earthly success became such a sign of divine selection.

> But this was precisely the case with the pious Puritan. He could demonstrate his religious merits through his economic activity because he did nothing ethically reprehensible, he did not resort to any lax interpretations of religious codes, or to systems of double moralities, and he did not act in a manner that could be indifferent or even reprehensible in the general realm of ethical validity. On the contrary, the Puritan could demonstrate his religious merit precisely in his economic activity. He acted in business with the best possible conscience, since through his rationalistic and legal behaviour in his business activity he was factual objectifying the rational methodology of his total life pattern. He legitimated his ethical pattern in his own eyes, and indeed within the circle of his community, by the extent to which the absolute — not relativized — unassailability of economic conduct remained beyond question (Weber 1924/1968:616).

The different historical processes Weber described, among which religion was one powerful driving force, led to what has often been described as the Puritan ethic, that is, an ethic based upon principles such as asceticism, duty, and the value of hard work. According to Weber this interplay between religious and economic practice led to certain paradoxical consequences. The process of secularization actually accelerated once religious motives for the accumulation of capital had gradually diminished. As God became viewed less and less as an important agent in everyday life, people increasingly developed their individuality.

The heritage of Weber has been continued in the works of several modern social scientists. Weber's theses concerning the relationship between religion and economy, the process of individualization and the disenchantment with the nature of reality are themes that have been taken up, for example, in *The Lonely Crowd* by David Riesman and his co-authors (1950), *The Achieving Society* by David McClelland (1967), *The Sacred Canopy* by Peter Berger (1967), *The Theory of Communicative Action* by Jürgen Habermas (1981/1984, 1981/1987), and recently in Colin Campbell's Weberian analysis *The Romantic Ethic and The Spirit of Modern Consumerism* (1987).

As we have seen, the notion of an ongoing process of individualization has been a central theme in the writings of the classical sociologists. The theme has continued to attract the attention of later or contemporary social theorists (see, for example, Fromm 1962; Berger et al. 1973; Bell 1976; Abercrombie et al. 1986; Beck 1986; Connolly 1989). It has also been discussed in terms of agency and structure (cf. Giddens 1984; Archer 1988).

The idea that the individual gradually becomes separated from society, however, has not remained unquestioned. On the contrary, the opposite perspective has been put forward now and then by philosophers and social scientists concerned with analyzing the relation between the individual and modern society and culture.

Some (post)modern philosophers and social scientists have gone so far as to say that in reality the individual has no existence separate from society, and that individualism is instead an ideology (Baudrillard 1988; Jameson 1989).

> Yet today, from any number of distinct perspectives, the social theorists, the psychoanalysts, even the linguists, not to speak of those of us who work in the area of culture and cultures and formal change, are all exploring the notion that that kind of individualism and personal identity is a thing of the past; that the old individual or individualist subject is "dead"; and that one might even describe the concept of the unique individual and the theoretical basis of individualism as ideological (Jameson 1989:17).

In these so-called postmodernist analyses of modern culture and the relationship between the individual and society, the classic distinction between the individual and society is put aside, so to speak. The individual is regarded instead as being almost absorbed by culture, and in a sense is almost totally objectified and made theoretically redundant.

The problematic questions of the relation between the individual and society, and of the process of individualization, are by no means theoretical questions alone. They have various implications for the way in which people live their everyday lives. Although a continuing interest in the process of individualization has been an important feature of social science in the 19th and 20th centuries', there are, of course, many other issues which have been important during this period. Obviously theories of different social and cultural structures, and of positions within these structures has been just as important or possibly even more important in the social theory of this period. The reason why the process of individualization is given such a prominent position in this book is that it is one of the basic elements in our theory of lifestyle. However, we do not deny that class and gender, for example, are also strongly related to the lifestyle concept. We do maintain nevertheless that, in addition to structural and positional determinants, lifestyle also contains individually determined components. Therefore, it is crucial for our outline of a theory of lifestyle to examine the connections between these three levels of determination. David Riesman emphasizes as follows the importance of not exaggerating the importance of either structure or individuality:

> Sometimes the point is pushed to the virtual denial of individuality. Since we arise in a society, it is assumed with a ferocious determinism that we can never transcend it. All such concepts are useful correctives of an earlier solipsism. But if they are extended to hold that conformity with society is not only a necessity but also a duty, they destroy the margin of freedom which gives life its savour and its endless possibility for advance (Riesman 1954:38).

THE PROCESS OF INDIVIDUALIZATION AND LATE MODERN IDENTITY

As already discussed in chapter three, the process of individualization is a central theme in numereous theoretical and empirical studies of the lifestyles found in modern Western societies. There has been a tendency in lifestyle research to overrate the impact of structurally and positionally determined conditions on the formation of lifestyles. During recent decades there has been an analogous tendency to attach an exaggerated importance to individual influence on the formation of lifestyles. We are convinced that in order to gain a realistic picture of the lifestyle phenomenon, one must realize that structural, positional *and* individual influences are all involved in the differentiation of lifestyles in modern Western societies. The degree to which each level is the dominant determinant probably varies between different cultures and societies and also from one period of time to another within one and the same culture or society.

We are concerned with young people's lifestyles. The fact that the period of youth is characterized by important changes in personal identity makes individuality particularly important during this period. Therefore, we must look closer into the relationship between identity and lifestyle.

In classical sociology, and also in some contemporary sociology — for instance in Bourdieu's theory of the social space of lifestyles — identity and lifestyle tend to be looked upon as intimately related to the individual's position in the social structure. In recent lifestyle theory the discussion has taken a different, more *individualistic turn*. This has sometimes led to exaggerated notions about the individual's freedom to form her or his life and lifestyle. In some theories applied within research on youth, young people are described as being almost totally capable of forming and changing their own lives, lifestyles and identities, and of doing this in whatever direction is best suited to them (see, for instance, Ziehe 1989; Willis 1990). The discussion, has not always gone to the extremes. In *The Homeless Mind* (1973) Berger and his co-authors distinguish four different features of modern identity (cf. also Berger & Luckmann 1966/1987; Berger 1967).

First, they say that modern identity is *peculiarly open*, by which they mean that the individual is peculiarly "unfinished" as he enters adult life. This open-ended quality of modern identity makes the individual more vulnerable to the shifting definitions of her- or himself by others.

Second, they state that modern identity is *peculiarly differentiated*. Since in modern society a manifoldness of social worlds exists, the individual experience of each of them is unstable and relative. Consequently the individual becomes more aware of herself/himself as the bearer of many different and often even incompatible social roles.

Third, they describe modern identity as being *peculiarly reflective*, by which they mean that ever-changing social experiences force modern man to reflect upon her or his own existence. Berger and his co-authors (1973:79) state: "Not only the world but the self becomes an object of deliberate attention and sometimes anguished scrutiny."

Fourth, they consider modern identity to be *peculiarly individuated*, and, in brief, individual freedom, autonomy and rights to have become the superior values for the modern individual.

Berger and his co-authors do not deny that, as a result of different conditions inherent in the process of socialization, important features of the individual are relatively stable. They thus do not entirely neglect questions of structure and position. Indeed, they have pointed out some important features of modern identity which make identity of utmost relevance to a theoretical understanding of the concept of lifestyle.

It is probably true that in modern society the individual has gained greater freedom to choose and create her or his own specific lifestyle. This is not to say, however, that structure and position no longer play a significant role in the making of lifestyle. Perhaps the very freedom of choosing one's lifestyle is at least partly, determined by class. In several articles, and in his book *Consumer Culture and Postmodernism*, Mike Featherstone has discussed this issue (Featherstone 1987; 1990b; 1991b). He maintains that the urge to create and renew one's lifestyle is a matter primarily for the new middle class and for intellectuals. According to Featherstone (1987:59) these "new heroes of consumer culture make lifestyle into a life project". Featherstone maintains that the new middle-class, promotes a particular style, but rather a general interest in style itself. This process can also be described in terms of the aestheticization and stylization of everyday life. In these terms, life is turned into a work of art (Featherstone 1992).

From this discussion we may conclude that in modern society neither structure, position, nor the individual, is the sole determinant of lifestyles. Modern lifestyles are the result of a complex interplay between phenomena at all three of these levels. As Raymond Williams states:

> We have at our command, now, a number of ways of defining our existence, in terms of nationality, class, occupation and such, in which we in fact offer a personal description in terms of membership of a group. Yet for most of us, when all these terms have been used, an area of conscious and valued existence remains, which in this mode of description could not be expressed at all. It is in relation to this area of existence that the problem of "the individual and society" takes shape (Williams 1961/1978:93).

Individuality is thus a necessary but not a sufficient condition for the creation of lifestyle. In the next chapter we will concentrate upon the individual and how she or he develops the different characteristics referred to as identity.

CHAPTER 5
IDENTITY AND LIFESTYLE

> Corresponding to the ideal communication community is an ego-identity that
> makes possible self-realization on the basis of autonomous action. This identity
> proves itself in the ability to lend continuity to one's life history (Habermas
> 1981/1987:98).

The aim of this chapter is to define and distinguish between a number of
different but interrelated concepts important to an understanding of the
concept of identity. To this end, we distinguish between three different
components of identity — personal, cultural and social identity — each
playing a central role in the making of an individual's lifestyle. Later in the
book the definitions of these three aspects of identity will be employed in an
attempt to develop a theoretical understanding of the specific cultural, social
and individual circumstances characterizing the period of youth.

THE CONCEPT OF IDENTITY

The term identity has been used and defined in differing ways by social and
behavioral theorists within various fields of research. Just as is the case with
many other terms used within different disciplines and theoretical schools
(for instance, value and lifestyle), the definition of the term identity is
dependent on the user's scholarly identity and purpose. It is necessary,
therefore, to clarify how one intends to apply the concept. In this chapter we
distinguish between three different components inherent in individual
identity. Each of these can be traced back to an influential theoretical
tradition:

The concept of *personal identity* has perhaps been most thoroughly
developed within a psychoanalytical tradition. We will exemplify this
tradition by *Blos*'s theory of adolescence viewed as a second individuation
and *Winnicott's* discussion of the relation between dependence and
independence. The concept of *social identity* constitute a central element in
role-theory. The concept of *cultural identity*, in the sense in which we use it,
is not employed very widely, but is often incorporated into, or confused
with, that of social identity. The former concept has also been frequently
employed to designate aspects of culture basically related to ethnicity.

Although he does not use the term cultural identity as such, Bourdieu's theory of the meaning of cultural taste is probably the most thoroughly elaborated theory of what we will call cultural identity.

It is important to distinguish between these three different components of identity. However, it is also important to examine relations between them. Attempts to do this, primarily as regards the relation between personal and social identity, can be found in the works of G.H. Mead and of E.H. Erikson.

Personal Identity

Peter Blos (1962, 1967, 1979) elaborated much of Freud's theories regarding adolescence and the development of personal identity. He regards adolescence as a maturation period during which the individual has to work through his or her earlier life experiences, in order to develop a stable personal identity (Blos 1962). Blos (1967) distinguishes between primary and secondary individuation (cf. Mahler 1963; Mahler et al. 1975).

Primary individuation is the process by which the child gains a first sense of own personal identity through gradually being able to differentiate the self from one's primary caretaker, so as to finally become an autonomous person.

The second individuation process involves the relinquishing of the intrapsychic structures formed during childhood. During the period of adolescence individuals thus have to re-evaluate and restructure internalizations formed during early childhood. Blos (1962) distinguishes four different stages of adolescence:

Early adolescence, according to Blos, is characterized primarily by biological maturation. Young people become less dependent upon their parents, and same-sex friendships become increasingly important.

Adolescence proper is characterized by an increased interest in the opposite sex. Life is in turmoil generally, and young people re-evaluate their earlier relationships with parents, relatives and friends.

During *late adolescence*, a positive, more self-evident awareness of personal identity emerges. According to Blos (1962:58) "It is only during late adolescence that the capability to form one's own view of the past, present, and future emerges". Late adolescence is primarily a time of consolidation. Individuals establish firm representations of the self and of others, and develop a greater sense of individuality.

The transition from adolescence to adulthood is marked by an intervening phase, *post-adolescence*. During this period the psychic structure of personality acquires a certain stability.

Late adolescence and post-adolescence are both integrative periods. During late adolescence different lifeplans and goals for the future are developed. During postadolescence some of these lifeplans and goals are transformed into clearly defined social roles and permanent relationships.

Blos's theory of the process of second individuation is primarily a theory of the psychological relationship between adolescents and their parents, and of the development of personal identity. Personal identity is thus a subjective sense of continuous existence and a coherent representation of one's own needs, abilities, knowledges, hopes, wishes and dreads (cf. Kroeger 1989). Contrary to social and cultural identity, personal identity concerns features that are to be considered as unique expressions of the individual. Even though personal identity is formed in a social and cultural context, it represents above all the active component of one's total identity.

However, personal identity concerns, not simply the process of individuation, but also such aspects of life such as intimacy and dependence on others. The British psychologist Donald Winnicott describes the development of personal identity in terms of a journey from dependence to independence (Winnicott 1963/1987). Furthermore, he distinguishes between three phases in this development: *absolute dependence*, *relative dependence* and *towards independence*.

In the beginning, according to Winnicott, the infant is entirely dependent on the environment and on the parents, that is on these caretakers' sensitive adoption of the needs, wishes and desires which the infant has. If the caretakers can provide a facilitating environment, this makes a steady maturational process possible.

The next stage — relative dependence — is characterized by growth in the intellectual and emotional capacity of the child. At this stage of development the infant begins to become aware of its dependence, beginning to differentiate between "Not Me" and "Me". This development and growth take the form of a continuous interplay between inner and outer reality. The child now becomes a potential creator of the world, enriching reality with samples of his or her own inner life.

During the last of Winnicott's developmental phases — towards independence — the child gradually becomes able to balance between personal existence and outer social reality. In his book *Playing and Reality* (1971), Winnicott also speaks of a *potential space*, which exists between inner psychic reality and the outer social world. Through playing and through use of cultural symbols, the child tries to bridge over the incongruity between inner and outer reality. Culture is thus created in this continuous interplay between personal experiences and the outer social reality.

According to Winnicott the journey towards independence is an endless one. Adolescents are all the time widening the circle, embracing new and more strange phenomena. In this process parents play an important role, providing guidance and support to their children. However, this process must also be expected to continue in adulthood, since in adolescence full maturity is seldom reached. It is also necessary to point out that the journey towards independence contains not only progressive elements but also regressive ones. That is, it is not necessarily a linear and continually progressing journey towards independence, but can also involve a frequent or constant pull towards, or urge for, dependence.

Personal identity is thus created in this constant interplay between the striving for independence and autonomy, and the need of and dependence upon others. In order to become a full person it is necessary to internalize aspects of significant others, as well as to develop a capacity for distinguishing between the self and others. The process of psychological differentiation, described by both Blos and Winnicott, thus leads as well to a reflexive attitude towards others and towards society at large, in the form of a heightened sensitivity for other people's needs, wishes and desires. The process of individuation must thus be interpreted in terms of the delicate balance and interplay between dependence and independence. This balance differs, not only between different individuals generally, but also between individuals occupying different positions in society (cf, Chodorow 1974, 1978).

In his book *I — The Philosophy and Psychology of Personal Identity* Jonathan Glover stress the importance of self-creation and thus of the individual's personal identity in the development of total identity.

> I shall make several claims here. The main one is that our individuality is not something just given to us, but is, in part, something we ourselves create. The way we think of ourselves, and of our past, has a special role in this self-creation. Other things in the world, and other people, are not changed directly by the way we think of them. But our conception of ourselves does directly

influence what we are like. I shall argue that, contrary to a common belief, a scientific view of people is compatible with our shaping our own characteristics. And I shall suggest that shaping ourselves is a more important aspect of us than is usually supposed. It should be given a central place in our thinking about social and political issues (Glover 1985:110).

Whereas social and cultural identity must be defined primarily in relation to different collectivities and groups, personal identity is defined primarily through a multitude of unique experiences of the individual and in terms of the conceptions the individual has elaborated of the self and of life generally. Personal identity determines, therefore, how the other two types of identity are shaped, maintained and expressed. That is why personal identity is of importance for the development of lifestyle as well. Although the identity in one sense becomes stable during youth, the individual is still developing ever new desires and wishes (see, for instance, Ewen & Ewen 1982; Campbell 1987). These wishes and desires are based on more or less stable personal identity.

Social Identity

As early as in the 1920s the dramaturgical metaphor and concept of *role* was developed and systematically exploited by George H. Mead (Mead 1934/1962). The term role is commonly used to represent the behavior expected of the holder of a given position in the societal structure (Mead 1934/1962; Goffman 1969, 1982; Turner 1990). An individual actor assigned to the position of policeman, for instance, is expected to enact the role of a policeman as characterized by certain typical actions and qualities.

According to Turner (1968:552) the following elements are included in the definition of role:

> It provides a comprehensive *pattern* for behavior and attitudes; it constitutes a *strategy* for coping with a recurrent type of situation; it is *socially identified*, more or less clearly, as an entity; it is subject to being played recognizably by *different individuals*; and it supplies a major basis for *identifying* and *placing* persons in society.

According to Burke and Franzoi (1988) identities are internalized through a process of *role-enactment*. A student identity, for instance, is based on the behavioral expectations and meanings that the individual internalizes through her or his enactment of the role of student. We shall call this type of identity *social* identity.

Each person has several different roles in her or his repertoire. Social

44

identity thus consists of a wide array of different roles, such as psychologist, teacher, father, son or friend (cf. Merton's (1963) concept of *multiple roles*).

There are of course great differences between different individuals' ways of playing their roles. It is therefore important to distinguish between the role as *expected* behavior, and role as *enactment*. Goffman uses the term *role distance* to describe the effectively expressed separateness between the individual and his role.

> A set of visible qualifications and known certifications, along with a social setting well designed as a showplace, provides the individual with something more than an opportunity to play his role self to the hilt, for this scene is just what he needs to create a clear impression of what he chooses not to lay claim to. The more extensive the trappings of a role, the more opportunity to display role distance. Personal front and social setting provide precisely the field an individual needs to cut a figure in a figure that romps, sulks, glides, or is indifferent (Goffman 1969:68).

Individuals' social identities are more or less coercive. Role distance, for instance, may be attributed to the lack of personal involvement that a person feels when playing various roles. Such lack of personal involvement in a particular role often leads to *role transition*, that is, the individual's movement out of one role and into another (Turner 1990).

To be able to participate in a specific social context it is necessary to have learned the rules, norms, mores and modes of behavior guiding interaction in that context. That is what social identity is primarily about: to enable the individual to decode and respond correctly to the signals, symbols, and actions of a specific social situation. Social identity is thus the identity through which the individual becomes a social being.

Intimately connected with the development of personal and social identity is the development of cultural identity. In the next section we will define the concept of cultural identity. Later we shall return to a discussion of the relations between the three different components of identity.

Cultural Identity

The term cultural identity is not employed very frequently, but the idea of such an identity is often implicit in theories of lifestyle. Pierre Bourdieu developed a theory regarding processes by means of which cultural distinctions between and within different status groups in society are generated by a struggle for cultural dominance or power. Although he was primarily interested in the struggle for power between different fractions of the dominant societal class, Bourdieu also does discuss how the individual learns to understand and use the cultural symbols and artefacts available in society. In this sense, Bourdieu's theory may be regarded as an attempt to deal with the relation between the structurally determined regularities of social action, on the one hand, and individually determined actions, on the other.

Bourdieu's concept of habitus may be regarded as a mediating concept accounting for the relation between social and cultural structures, and the subjective interpretation of and attitude towards such structures (Bourdieu 1977; Bourdieu 1979/1984; Garnham & Williams 1986). Bourdieu describes habitus in the following way:

> The structures constitutive of a particular type of environment (e.g., the material conditions of existence characteristic of a class condition) produce *habitus*, systems of durable, transposable *dispositions*, structured structures predisposed to function as structuring structures; that is, as principles of the generation and structuring of practices and representations which can be objectively "regulated" and "regular" without in any way being the product of obedience to rules, objectively adapted to their goals without presupposing a conscious aiming at ends or an express mastery of the operations necessary to attain them and, being all this, collectively orchestrated without being the product of the orchestrating action of a conductor (Bourdieu 1977:72).

A habitus works primarily as an individual structure in the cultural field. A habitus is not, however, an exclusively individual phenomenon (Bourdieu 1977). Rather, it is an internalized structure derived from a common set of material conditions of existence. This structure is primarily shaped and internalized in early childhood. The habitus acquired in the family underlies, for example, the structuring of school experiences; the habitus transformed by schooling in turn underlies the structuring of later experiences. The habitus is constantly being restructured in the course of life, but experiences of early childhood and the material conditions of it are of decisive importance for the formation of the individual habitus.

Bourdieu's theory accounts primarily for the process of cultivation, i.e., the societal transmission, and internalization of values, attitudes and manners. However, it is also possible to use the concept of habitus to account for the development of individuality, i.e., an individual's awareness of one's own specific position within different societal and cultural systems, and one's unique way of expressing a specific cultural identity.

Through one's cultural identity the individual develops her or his individual values, style and cultural taste. Therefore, it is the cultural identity which forms the core of individual lifestyle. As we shall see, however, cultural identity cannot be understood without reference to personal and social identity.

IDENTITY AND LIFESTYLE — TOWARDS A SYNTHESIS

Various attempts have been made to develop a theory of the relation between personal and social identity. We shall present two of the most influential of these, namely, Mead's theory of the self and Erikson's theory of psychosocial identity.

In Mead's terminology, the concept of *self* is used to describe an internal structure which organizes social experiences into a relatively coherent unit. The self arises during the lifelong process of social experience and activity. It is therefore a dynamic and constantly changing structure (Mead 1934/1962:144).

> The unity and structure of the complete self reflects the unity and structure of the social process as a whole, and each of the elementary selves of which it is composed reflects the unity and structure of one of the various aspects of that process in which the individual is implicated (Mead 1934/1962:144).

Furthermore, Mead (1934/1962) differentiates between what in our terminology, are personal and social identity. Mead distinguishes between "I" (cf. personal identity), and "Me" (cf. social identity), through giving them different contexts in which to operate.

In analyzing an individual's membership in different groups, as well as the individual's status position or role-specific behavior, emphasis is on the Me. In analyzing individuals' capacities to distinguish themselves from other people, and to express their individuality, emphasis is on the I.

In a way somewhat similar to Mead, Erikson (1959, 1968a,b) distinguishes between personal identity and the psychosocial identity. Personal or inner identity involves a subjective sense of continuous existence and the capacity to live and think in isolation from others. Psychosocial identity is on the one hand subjectively defined (cf. personal identity), and on the other hand, defined objectively in terms of the individual's adherence to different collectivities, categories and groups. Psychosocial identity forms a bridge between early childhood stages in which personal identity is given its specific meaning and the later stages in which a multitude of social roles become available and increasingly important.

> The gradual development of a mature psychosocial identity, then, presupposes a community of people whose traditional values become significant to the growing person even as his growth assumes relevance for them. Mere "roles" that can be "played" interchangeably are obviously not sufficient for the social aspect of the equation. Only a hierarchical integration of roles that foster the vitality of individual growth as they represent a vital trend in the existing or developing social order can support identities. Psychosocial identity thus depends on a complementarity of an inner (ego) synthesis in the individual and of role integration in his group (Erikson 1968a:61).

According to both Mead and Erikson, therefore, social development is a life process built upon a paradox. We are connected with others in a multitude of ways, and at the same time are ultimately alone in the world. In the course of life most individuals become better able both to establish connections with others and to achieve a separateness from others (Berger & Luckman 1966/1987; Zigler & Seitz 1978). In short, we become more social while at the same time becoming more individual, reflexive and unique (cf. Damon 1988).

Within modern sociological theory, theories of the reflexive character of identity have been put forward, for example, by Peter Berger, Jurgen Habermas and Anthony Giddens. According to Giddens each of us not only *has*, but also lives, a biography reflexively organized in terms of "flows of social and psychologiocal information about possible ways of life" (Giddens 1991:14). Each day we have to answer questions about how to behave, what to eat, what to wear, etc. In this reflexive process of identity creation mass media and experts in different areas play a central role. They provide a kind of raw material of images and knowledge about the human being which can be used in the process of development of both identity and lifestyle. According to Giddens, the social world should not be viewed simply as a multiplicity of situations in which "ego" faces "alter", or in Mead's terms "I" faces "Me", but as one in which each person is equally involved in the active process of organizing predictable social interactions.

The distinction between personal and social identity has been applied in social scientific theories (Mead 1934/1962; Breakwell 1986; Ewen 1988; Willis 1990). This distinction is important also in a theory of lifestyle as well, since individual lifestyle is an expression both of personal identity and of an individual's membership in more or less *socially* defined groups.

However, it is not sufficient to distinguish between personal and social identity. One must also take into consideration the form of identity which we call cultural identity.

The three different types of identity are to be considered, of course, as aspects of one and the same phenomenon — that is, of the individual's total identity. The reason for separating them are purely analytical. By keeping them as separate concepts we can attain a better understanding of the complex system which constitutes the identity of the individual. As we shall see, this also makes it easier to analyze the relation between identity and lifestyle. It is especially in this context that cultural identity comes in handy.

Through personal identity, the individual develops the capacity to live and think in isolation from others as an autonomous being.

Through social identity the individual becomes a member in different types of groups and learns the roles she or he is expected to play. In a sense, social identity serves the function of integrating the individual in different social contexts.

Through cultural identity, finally, the individual becomes able not only to express one's unique characteristics within the groups to which one belongs, but also to express towards other groups one's own group membership or belongingness. For such expressions of cultural identity we often use the terms *style* and *taste*.

The three types of identities are formed in different ways. We shall distinguish, therefore, between the *individual*, *social* and *cultural* spheres in the formation and development of an individual's identity (cf. Parsons 1966; Habermas 1981/1987).

Personal identity is primarily developed through the relationship between the individual and *significant others*, the latter often being parents, siblings, relatives or friends. Personal identity is thus formed in the individual sphere.

Social identity is developed through the internalization of those specific obligations, privileges, rights and duties which are the defining characteristics of each position that an individual holds in the social system. Social identity is thus formed in the social sphere.

Cultural identity is developed through an individual's membership in more or less well-defined cultural and social groups, and through the internalization of values, attitudes, tastes, and styles. Cultural identity is thus formed in the cultural sphere.

To summarize: we have made an analytical distinction between personal, social and cultural identity. Personal identity is formed and developed in the individual sphere. This process we refer to as *individuation*; it results in the *personality* of the individual.

Social identity is formed and developed in the social sphere through the process of socialization. It manifests itself in the processes of *role-enactment*, *role-distance* and *role-transition*. The outcome of these processes is the ability of the individual to play certain roles in social life.

Cultural identity, finally, is formed and developed in the cultural sphere through a process we term *lifestyle development*. The result of this process is the *habitus*.

The different distinctions and relations that have been employed in chapter five are summarized in Figure 2.

Figure 2. The Three Levels of Structuration and Interrelated Levels of Individual Structures and Individual Processes

SPHERE OF IDENTITY-FORMATION AND DEVELOPMENT	INDIVIDUAL STRUCTURE	INDIVIDUAL PROCESSES	TYPE OF IDENTITY
Cultural	Habitus	Lifestyle-Development	Cultural
Social	Role	Role-Enactment/ Role-Distance/ Role-Transition	Social
Individual	Personality	Individuation Dependence/ Independence	Personal

---

The reason for distinguishing between different components of identity in a theory of lifestyle is that this makes it easier to grasp the complexity inherent in the individual's shaping and maintenance of lifestyle. Since most contemporary researchers on youth have failed to note and take account of the different components of identity, some of them — for example Willis (1990) and Ziehe (1989) — have come to clearly overestimate the lack of stable identity in youth, maintaining instead that young people constantly change and experiment with different identities. In reality, personal identity is relatively stable. Its being mainly social and, above all, cultural identity which is undergo change during youth.

There are many different ways of defining and characterizing an individual. It can be done on the basis of the individual's class, gender, religion, nationality and age, for example, that is, on the basis of his social identity. It can also be done in terms of such unique characteristics as the individual's personal thoughts, desires, longings, dreams, memories and experiences, that is, his or her personal identity. It can be done as well on the basis of the individual's values, cultural tastes, preferences, interests and style, that is, his or her cultural identity.

In youth culture research cultural identity is classified basically in terms of how the young individual has been identified — for instance, as a punk, a skinhead, a rocker, a biker, a teeny-bopper, a hippie, a mods, a hip-hopper or a rapper. Each of these branches of youth culture is linked with certain tastes in clothing, hairstyle, film, music, cars, motorcycles, etc. In earlier analyses of youth culture — for instance, the class, ethnicity and gender studies of the Birmingham school — the connection has often been made between cultural identities and social identities. Generally, however, the most fundamental and relatively stable component of identity, personal identity, has been neglected. In earlier studies of youth culture there has also been a tendency to look upon what we term cultural identity as being almost completely determined by social identity, that is, by such factors as class, gender and race. In the most recent youth culture theories, on the other hand, one can note a tendency to regard cultural identity as either the central component of identity, or as being primarily determined by the unique characteristics of the individual (Ziehe 1989; Willis 1990).

We believe that it is not sufficient to consider identity as being determined by social position or as being equivalent with cultural consumption. Neither is it correct, we believe, to consider only the unique characteristics of the individual. We maintain that the cultural consumption of the individual is influenced by his or her social positions as well as by his or her unique personal identity.

There are also important forces, however, located outside the individual influencing the cultural tastes and styles of modern youth. These are, for instance, the fashion industry, the music industry, and the mass media. This is obvious from the fact that most young people do not belong to specific and conspicuous subcultures but use much of the central youth cultural goods such as music, film and clothes quite homogeneously. In other words, they like very much the same music, watch the same movies, dress in a similar way and spend their leisure time in similar activities.

To say this, however, is not to claim that differences do not exist. Rather, it is to state that only in exceptional cases are such differences as obvious and conspicuous as they are in subcultures. More often the differences are located in the realm not of cultural but of personal identity. In most cases, therefore, differences are more subtle and must be studied on a purely individual level. The absence of this theoretical insight is, we believe, one of the main reasons why most previous and contemporary youth culture research has dealt with basically deviant or conspicuous youth groups and has not been much concerned about what could be called "mainstream" youth. This is a pity, since in order to understand youth as a whole, it is obviously not sufficient to study simply extreme representatives. Above all, it is necessary to understand the more anonymous majority. We shall argue that it is extremely important, as well, to understand the differences which exists between various individuals who belong to mainstream youth. To achieve such an understanding it is necessary to concentrate not only on the social or the cultural identity, but also to consider to a greater extent the personal component of identity.

The three different components of identity are of course not isolated from each other. Indeed, they depend upon each other and are moulded together, so to say, within the individual, constituting a more or less coherent unity. In order to further clarify our view, we will close this chapter by turning to some concrete exemples of how the relations between the different components of identity can function in reality.

During youth, the individual is often uncertain about what the future contains and what he or she wants from it. Therefore, it is quite natural that young people try out different roles and possibilities in many different areas of life. Another way of putting this is to say that during youth the individual shapes his or her social identity through continually changing roles. This insecurity and the changes it brings about, do not necessarily mean that the individual continually changes his or her identity. The personal and cultural components involved need not change accordingly and may, in fact, remain relatively unchanged, even though change in these respects may occur too.

Analogously, changes in cultural identity do not automatically imply that the other components of identity change. Often, to be sure, changes in one component of identity influence the other components, but the degree to which this occurs can differ greatly. For example, when an individual chooses to use cultural goods typical to a certain youth group — say, punks — cultural identity obviously changes as well. It does not follow from this, however, that social identity changes to the same extent. Much the same goes for personal identity. It is probable that change in this will influence the other components, but this need not be dramatic. This has to do with the fact that the most unstable component of identity is the cultural, which is thus the easiest for the individual to change at will. It is not as easy to change social identity, and to change personal identity dramatically is difficult indeed.

The dramatic lifestyle-changes noted by some contemporary lifestyle researchers may thus well be illusory. By this we mean that such changes may only seem dramatic, since they involve the most visible component of identity. A deeper analysis of such changes would probably in most cases show that social and personal identity have not changed radically.

In modern Western society, individuals often become consumers of identities offered on the market. Some of these identities have a reasonable durability, others are more ruled by fashion. However, this does not mean that identity has to be regarded as something fluid and unstable; in order to exist, individuals must somehow integrate the different parts of their identity and develop a certain sense of their own identity involving a relatively stable system of thoughts, knowledge, tastes, styles, etc., even if these structurations may in some be regarded as preliminary. Modern identity is thus at the same time stable and unstable, unique and general. The process of identity creation is a life process aimed at the achievement of a sense of one's own place in reality and a continuity in one's own life history.

In the next chapter we shall discuss the most central of the many concepts related to identity and lifestyle: the concept of human values. After that we will be in a position to fit the pieces of the lifestyle-puzzle together by analyzing the relations between all these concepts.

CHAPTER 6
VALUES

INTRODUCTION

> Of all widely invoked concepts, few are as difficult to specify as the concept of
> value (Wilson 1988:1).

As we have already indicated, the concept of value can be considered indispensable to any adequate theory of lifestyle. Thus we direct attention now at this key concept, complex and at the same time so important to our work.

As with the concept of lifestyle, the concept of value is based by many difficulties, including ambiguities and theoretical as well as methodological disagreements and disputes. The question of the nature of human values has been a major issue throughout the history of philosophy. Over the centuries, a large number of differing and often conflicting theories of value have been advanced. The matter is complicated further by the fact that various areas of knowledge — alongside philosophy, such fields as those of psychology, economics, sociology, theology and law — have been concerned with problems regarding the value concept. Thus, no single concept of value is agreed upon. Even within each of the disciplines named, the term value is used in differing ways.

> In many behavioral science inquiries into alleged value phenomena, the term
> "value" is used in conflicting and incoherent ways, and a wide variety of
> methodological and substantive problems emerge (Handy 1969:vii).

In view of the vastness of the problem, it would be presumptuous of us to try to settle the longstanding dispute over the nature of human values. In order to be able to make adequate use of the concept in a theory such as the one we propound, it is nevertheless important to pinpoint and discuss certain controversies concerning value which are of relevance here.

Over the years several attempts to operationalize human values and measure them empirically have been made by scholars within various scientific disciplines, some of them sociologists. The methodological problems this has entailed are obviously as important and necessary to consider as are the theorethical ones. We will leave aside the empirical and methodological questions in this chapter, however, returning to them instead in a later chapter devoted to methodology (chapter 11).

When in the present chapter various general theoretical questions regarding value have been dealt with, we will focus on the application of the concept of value to questions of lifestyle. This will involve relating the concept of value to a number of other concepts in such a way that these various concepts and the relations between them form a consistent theory of lifestyle.

Earlier in this book we have argued that in analyzing lifestyle it is useful to distinguish between three different but interrelated levels of detemination — structure, position and individual. In this chapter we will argue that this distinction can be applied analogously to the concept of value.

We will furthermore argue that the value aspect of lifestyle can be analyzed on three different conceptual levels, which we refer to as the *value-level*, *attitude-level* and *action-level*. This latter distinction, as we will see, is quite useful for understanding the relation between the concepts of value and lifestyle.

Yet another type of distinction it is necessary to make is between different types of human values. In the literature both on lifestyle and value, a number of such distinctions have been suggested. The distinction between different types of values can thus be made in various ways, depending on the purpose the distinction is intended to serve. We will suggest here that a distinction be made between four types of values, namely, *metaphysical*, *ethical*, *aesthetic* and *material values*.

In a previous chapter we argued that the values of individuals constitute one of the most important components of their identities. It is also necessary, therefore, as will be undertaken here to discuss the relation between value and identity.

Finally, we will try to fit all the pieces together and present our suggestions regarding how to conceptualize and understand the relations between value, identity and lifestyle. Once this has been done, we have reached our goal of presenting here our theory of the complex notion of lifestyle.

THE CONCEPT OF VALUE

Value Theory

What does the term value mean? This is far from an easy question to answer. Although many have tried, no one has yet managed to come up with a definition sufficiently convincing to gain universal acceptance. Rather, ever since the question of the nature of human values first became an object of theoretical discussion and analysis at some early period in the history of philosophy, it has been a matter of continual disagreement. Discussions regarding it have resulted in at least four differing assumptions concerning the nature of human values. Each of these assumptions has been used as a platform for a number of more specific value theories. Combinations of two or more of these basic assumptions have also appeared in various theories.

We believe it to be relevant, as a theoretical background for an understanding of the theoretical and empirical disagreements concerning the value concept, to provide a brief account of these four differing and partly conflicting assumptions about the nature of human values which have appeared within value theory.

Value theory, or axiology, is a branch of analytical philosophy concerned with interpreting the meaning of value propositions, i.e. of propositions in which the predicate is a value expression such as good, bad, evil, right, wrong, beautiful, or ugly.

The first of the four basic assumptions is that of what is usually called *objectivism*. This is characteristic of *deontological theories*. Such theories start with the assumption that objects and actions either have or do not have certain qualities, for example goodness and beauty. Deontological theories assume, therefore, that value expressions designate value qualities of objects or actions.

Subjectivism, second, is characteristic of *teleological* theories of value. these consider the value of an object or an action to depend upon the attitude of a subject towards it. The subject in question may be anything from I, to the majority of mankind, and even to God. The probably best known among the subjectivistic value theories is utilitarianism which in Peter Singer's rendering of it states that an action is good or right if "... it produces as much or more of an increase in the happiness of all affected by it than any alternative action, and wrong if it does not" (Singer 1983:3).

Characteristic of *naturalistic* theories, thirdly, is the assumption that value terms

> ... designate natural characteristics, processes etc., and that ethical *statements* are descriptive, cognitive, and in principle either true or false (Handy 1969:19).

Naturalistic theories define value terms, for instance ethical or aesthetic, in non-ethical or non-aesthetic terms. "Need" is an example of such a non-value term used to define value terms.

> In general, much self-defeating, antisocial or otherwise damaging behavior develops from the inability to satisfy needs in a more adequate way. Making needs central is useful for incorporating psychological findings into value inquiry (Handy 1969:157).

Naturalistic theories, however, have been subjected to much criticism by a number of different value theorethicans. R. M. Hare puts his criticism in the following way:

> It is a common mistake, whose name is "naturalism", to think that a fact cannot be a reason for a moral judgement unless the moral judgement is deducible from the fact with or without some other factual premises (Hare 1981:217).

Also Rokeach is critical towards the naturalistic use of the value concept, and he states his critique in a rather concrete fashion, aimed primarily at Maslow's theory that values are equivalent to needs.

> If values are indeed equivalent to needs, as Maslow and many others have suggested, then the lowly rat, to the extent that it can be said to possess needs, should to the same extent also be said to possess values. If such a view were adopted, it would be difficult to account for the fact that values are so much at the center at attention among those concerned with the understanding of human behavior and so little at the center of attention among those concerned with the understanding of animal behavior. That values are regarded to be so much more central in the one case than in the other suggests that values cannot altogether be identical to needs and perhaps that values possess some attributes that needs do not.
>
> Man is the only animal that can be meaningfully described as having values. Indeed, it is the presence of values and systems of values that is the major characteristic distinguishing humans from infrahumans. Values are the cognitive representations and transformations of needs, and man is the only animal capable of such representations and transformations (Rokeach 1973: 20).

Naturalistic value theories are particularily interesting since they have been widely adopted by sociologists and psychologists concerned with the value concept. One of the most clear-cut examples is Arnold Mitchell's influential values and lifestyle theory based on Maslow's hierarchy of needs, which we will discuss in some detail later.

Emotivism and *value nihilism*, finally state that values are not judgements at all, but represent, for example, recommendations, commandments or expressions of emotion.

> Emotivists held that ethical statements are noncognitive and nondescriptive and thus neither true nor false, and they denied that ethical terms designate unique nonnatural characteristics (Handy 1969:19).

These four differing assumptions regarding the nature of human values as well as the value theories corresponding to them can be criticized on various grounds. It is beyond the scope of the present study, however, to take up such criticisms. Our purpose here is rather to provide the background necessary for a basic understanding of the varying uses of the concept of value among not only different philosophers, but also different theoreticians in the area of value and lifestyle research.

We shall see somewhat later that two of the most influential value theories within the field of research considered here make naturalistic assumptions regarding the nature of human values: the theories of Arnold Mitchell (1983) and of Ronald Inglehart (1977). The highly influential value theory of Milton Rokeach (1973), on the other hand, rests on subjectivistic assumptions. In the sections of this chapter which follow we will brief account of these three theories and of their assumptions regarding the value concept.

Each of the three authors named has also undertaken empirical studies of value. Although such studies contain a number of methodological problems, these will not be taken up in this chapter, but we will return to them later on.

Value as Need

In chapter 2 we provided a brief account of Mitchell's theory of lifestyle. In this theory, the concept of value occupies a central position. It is a psychological theory of individual mobility within what might be called a hierarchy of lifestyles. According to Mitchell, each of the positions in this hierarchy is characterized by different values and needs. Mitchell holds that when the needs of an individual are satisfied on a particular level in the hierarchy, he or she will develop new values and needs, and consequently change his position in the hierarchy of lifestyles. According to Mitchell, the causes behind such changes of position in the hierarchy can have various origins: particular events or circumstances, age, history, experiences from childhood, paradigm changes, natural development, evolution, etc. In order for change to take place, the individual must in one way or another be dissatisfied with his or her present situation.

What does the term value mean, according to Mitchell? Actually, the definition he offers is not very clear-cut:

> By the term value we mean the entire constellation of a person's attitudes, beliefs, opinions, hopes, fears, prejudices, needs, desires and aspirations that, taken together, govern how one behaves (Mitchell 1983:vii).

It is not too exaggerate to say that this is a very broad and unprecise definition of value, since it contains a number of concepts that are usually distinguished from the value concept.

If one examines Mitchell's value theory further, one will find that the central and basic concept in it is *need*. This is made clear not least by the fact that his theory basically rests on Maslow's well-known hierarchy of needs. The consequence of Mitchell's use of Maslow's theory as a theoretical framework is that of his basically defining values in terms of needs. Thus, he defines value in non-value terms, just as do the naturalistic value theories.

The Silent Revolution

The fundamental difference between Mitchell's and Ronald Inglehart's value theories is that, whereas the former is basically concerned with how the values and lifestyles of individuals develop, the latter is mainly interested in how the value structure in modern Western societies change over time. One could say that Mitchell is operating basically on the individual level, and Inglehart first and foremost on the structural level.

Although he does not state it as clearly as does Mitchell, Inglehart is as much influenced by Maslow's hierarchy of needs as Mitchell is. Just as that of Mitchell's, Inglehart's theory of values, therefore, builds on basically naturalistic assumptions about the nature of human values.

Inglehart (1977, 1990) aims at understanding, first, how the structural changes that take place in Western societies contribute to changes in human values and competences, and, secondly, which consequenses these changes in turn have on social structure. He starts out from the rather reasonable assumption that people who have grown up in the Western post-war welfare states have enjoyed considerable benefits of material and economic security. To the extent that their material and economic needs have been satisfied, he assumes that new needs have emerged. In accordance with this assumption, Inglehart maintains that the values of the Western public have undergone a change from having emphasized material welfare and physical security, to an increased emphasis on quality of life values. The former type of values he calls *material*; the latter, *post-material*. His main thesis is thus that post-war Western societies have witnessed a gradual shift in their value structure, a shift from materialist to postmaterialist values.

Inglehart's theory is dynamic. He tries to illustrate a process of change, or, in his own words, a silent revolution in modern Western societies. He believes that what he calls *System-Level Changes* — for instance, economic and technological development, distinct cohort experiences, rising levels of education and the expansion of mass communications — have led to considerable *Individual-Level Changes*, i.e., to changes in values and skills among the public. The value changes result in an increasing emphasis on needs for belonging, self-esteem and self-realization, whereas changes in skills have led to more people having the skills needed to cope with politics on a national scale. According to Inglehart, these *Individual-Level Changes* have in turn brought about strong *System-Level Consequences*, that is, changes in prevailing political issues, in lifestyles, in the social bases of political conflict, in support for various institutions, in political participation and so on (Inglehart 1977, 1990).

Value As the Preferable

The originator of the last of the three important and influential value theories we shall account for here is Milton Rokeach. His theory of human values is much more complex and thoroughly elaborated than are those of Mitchell's and Inglehart's. Like Mitchell, Rokeach is primarily interested in the values of the individual, but unlike Mitchell and Inglehart he does not make any naturalistic assumptions about the value concept. That is, Rokeach does not define a value in non-value terms. Of the three theories of value discussed here, Rokeach's theory, we shall argue, has several advantages compared to the other two. It is probably the most useful one for an analysis of the relation between individual values, identity and lifestyles. That has partly to do with the fact that Rokeach does not make naturalistic assumptions about the value concept. He distinguishes clearly between human values and other concepts — such as for instance lifestyle, attitudes and needs — which, as we have seen, Mitchell and Inglehart do not.

First, Rokeach makes a distinction between values and attitudes. He maintains that value refers to a single belief which guides actions, attitudes and judgements, whereas an attitude refers to an organization of several beliefs towards a specific object or situation. Thus, whereas values transcend objects and situations, attitudes are focused on specific objects or situations; values are standards, whereas attitudes are not. A person has only as many values as he has learned beliefs concerning desirable modes of conduct and end-states of existence, but as many attitudes as he has encountered specific objects and situations. Finally, according to Rokeach, values are more immediately linked to motivation than are attitudes.

Secondly, Rokeach distinguishes between values and social norms, stating that values may refer to a mode of behavior as well as to an end-state of existence, whereas a social norm refers only to the former. According to Rokeach, a social norm is a prescription or proscription to behave in a specific way in a specific situation. Furthermore, he holds that value is personal and internal, whereas a norm is consensual and external to the person.

Thirdly, Rokeach makes a distinction between values and needs, claiming that values are cognitive representations of not only individual needs, but also of societal and institutional demands; values are also results of sociological as well as psychological forces.

Fourth, Rokeach distinguishes between values and traits, stating that through regarding a person as a system of values it is possible to conceptualize his or her undergoing change as a result of changes in social conditions, whereas the trait concept has an inbuilt characterological bias which precludes such possibilities for change.

Fifth, Rokeach distinguishes between values and interests, stating that interests are not standards; rather they represent attitudes directed towards certain objects or activities.

According to Rokeach, a value is an enduring belief, either prescriptive or condemning, about a preferable or desirable mode of conduct or an end-state of existence. Values referring to end-states of existence he calls *terminal values*; they can be either personal or social. Values referring to modes of conduct he terms *instrumental*, and they are either moral values or values of competence. Furthermore, Rokeach maintains that a value is a preference as well as a concept of the socially or personally preferable. He also considers that the values held by an individual are relatively few — about twenty terminal, and seventy instrumental values — they are universal and their origins can be traced to culture, society and its institutions, and to personality. According to Rokeach, the values of an individual are organized into value systems. The difference between a value and a value system is that a value is an:

> ... enduring belief that a specific mode of conduct or end-state of existence is personally or socially preferable to an opposite or converse mode of conduct or end-state of existence (Rokeach 1973:5),

while a value system is described as

> ... an enduring organization of beliefs concerning preferable modes of conduct or end-state of existence along a continuum of relative importance (Rokeach 1973:5).

Rokeach believes that values are taught to human beings, and once taught they are integrated into an organized value system in which each value is arranged in relation to other values. According to Rokeach, the values serve different functions for the individual. They constitute standards guiding our behavior, helping us to make decisions, for example, in our presentation of ourselves to others, on our comparisons of different actions or objects, in our attempts to influence others, in our formulations of our attitudes; in our evaluations and our condemning of others, and so forth.

Rokeach's theory of value is accompanied by a number of assumptions about human nature. He maintains that there is a group of conceptions more central to an individual than are his values. These are the conceptions individuals have about themselves. Rokeach argues that the total belief system of an individual is functionally and hierarchically structured, and that if some part of the system is changed, other parts of it will be affected too, and consequently their behavior as well. The more central the changing part of the belief system is, the more extensive the effects will be. A change in the conception of one's self would thus affect and lead to changes in the terminal values, instrumental values, attitudes, etc. Rokeach's main thesis is that

> ... the ultimate purpose of one's total belief system, which includes one's values, is to maintain and enhance ... the master of all sentiments, the sentiment of self-regard (Rokeach 1973:216).

As already indicated, Rokeach is not a value naturalist. We are inclined to interpret him as a subjectivistic value theoretician. This statement, however, requires explanation.

Subjectivistic theories of value maintain that ascribing a value to an action or an object means that some kind of person has a certain attitude towards the object or action in question. The proposition "X is good" would thus be the same as to say "the subject (S) has the attitude (A) towards X." In Rokeach's terms it is the attitude "to be morally, personally or socially preferable", which ascribes an object or an action its value.

Subjectivistic value theories state that the basic criteria for what is morally good, for example, is the non-moral value it produces. The instrumental and terminal values distinguished are such products that can be identified with what is preferable or desirable.

One major advantage with the value theory suggested by Rokeach is that it clearly distinguishes between values, attitudes and actions. Rokeach believes that a limited number of human values constitute the cognitive components underlying all the attitudes an individual has. An attitude is thus a manifestation of a group of either terminal or instrumental values. According to Rokeach, if one knows how the value system of an individual is structured, one can predict how he will act in a given situation.

VALUES, IDENTITY AND LIFESTYLE

Introduction

We can study human values on the three distinct but interrelated levels of determination which we have previously discussed in relation to the concept of lifestyle. Since the line of argument in this respect is very similar for the two concepts of value and lifestyle, we need not say very much about the distinction between structure, position and individual here. It should be sufficient to briefly summarize the line of argumentation.

Every society or culture has a social and cultural structure, and people living in that structure necessarily share some basic values. Thus, in all societies, there must exist some general code of behavior for its members to act upon. Some basic values, convictions and beliefs — often formulated as imperatives or norms — must be shared and held in common by the vast majority of societal members. Such values, convictions, and beliefs are essential and characteristic features of all cultures. They represent social and human ideals of various kinds: moral, material, aesthetic, metaphysical, religious and political. These structural values serve as the basis for human interplay and coexistence.

Since they constitute society's belief system, and since they also establish the framework for the variations in the positionally and individually determined values, convictions, and beliefs of its members, these fundamental values are important parts of the structure of any society, and they distinguish one culture from another. Different means are used by society to maintain, strengthen, distribute and reproduce these fundamental values. Several social institutions, such as law, school, church and the mass media, serve this purpose.

All social structures contain a number of positions, defined along several basic dimensions such as social status, class, gender, age, education and ethnicity. Depending on which positions individuals occupy along such dimensions, the degree to which they embrace certain values is likely to vary. Another way of expressing this is to say that the values of the individual contain an element of positional determination. Individuals belonging to a certain status group, social class, gender or age group may therefore inculcate and develop certain values to a higher or lesser degree than do individuals belonging to another class, gender or age group.

Finally, apart from the values which an individual shares with most of the members of the society to which he or she belongs, or with people occupying the same position within that structure, there is still room for value differences between single individuals. To the degree that such variations are basically due to individuals' differing identities and personalities, they are individually determined, of course.

We have already argued that a certain amount of individual determination is a necessary but not sufficient condition for a phenomenon to be designated as a lifestyle. Consequently, we will concentrate here upon individually determined values, although aware of the fact that individually held values are also to various degrees structurally and positionally influenced.

Different Types Of Values

According to most theories of lifestyle, one of the basic features of lifestyles is that in one way or another they are expressions of individually held human values. This basic idea, however, is more or less explicitly formulated and expressed within the various lifestyle theories, each drawing on one or more differing types of values to a varying degree.

One can distinguish between different types of values. This is by no means a very original idea. Inglehart, Mitchell and Rokeach all make distinctions between different kinds of human values. Inglehart (1977, 1990) distinguishes between material and post-material values, Mitchell (1983) between inner- and outer-directed values, and Rokeach (1973) between terminal and instrumental values. Such distinctions between different types of values can be made from different starting-points, depending, for example, on the value theory the researcher employs, and the aims of his or her research.

One interesting way to distinguish between different types of values within a lifestyle context is provided by the American philosopher Howard Kamler (1984). As we shall see, Kamler's distinction partly resembles both Inglehart's and Mitchell's distinctions. On the basis of the psychological functions which each of the value categories serves for the individual, Kamler distinguishes between what he calls *Life Philosophy Values* and *Life Style Values*. One important psychological function of values, according to him, is to help the individual to develop and form his sense of identity. Kamler distinguishes between social and personal identity. He maintains that the lifestyle values help the individual to shape and strengthen his or her social identity. The life philosophy values, he argues, help the individual to shape and strengthen his or her personal identity. He maintains that life philosophy values are held by the individual irrespectively of what others think, whereas life style values are held by the individual precisely because of what others think.

> Life philosophy values secure a person's sense of personal identity; they are held regardless of what anyone else thinks of his value choice. Life style values secure a person's sense of social identity; they are held precisely because of what others think of his value choice (Kamler 1984:69).

Very probably, however, life philosophy values are also influenced by the individual's social background and type of personality. Perhaps it is more accurate to say, therefore, that life philosophy values — to the degree that they are influenced by what others think — first and foremost are influenced by the individual's immediate environment, for example his family and close friends. Life style values, on the other hand, are influenced not only by the immediate environment but also by a more distant and broader surrounding — for instance by the environment provided by the mass media.

Thus reformulated, the distinction suggested by Kamler is quite relevant for our lifestyle discussion. The idea implied by Kamler — that an individual's lifestyle is basically founded on a need to mark or express social affiliation or status — is a fundamental assumption often stated in theories of lifestyle. In such theories the concept of lifestyle is often defined in social psychological terms, since it is used primarily to designate aspects of the individual's strivings and aspirations to gain a position in the society to which he or she belongs and be incorporated into it.

A more traditional sociological approach is to look upon lifestyles as closely tied to different social classes or strata. In such theories, it is not the individual, but his social position that is central to the lifestyle concept. Several of these theories claim that what generates lifestyles is a striving for status and power. The perhaps best known example of such an approach is the theory which Pierre Bourdieu puts forward in his *Distinction*. In Bourdieu's theory, the development of lifestyle is intimately connected with a symbolic struggle for power between different class fractions or status groups in society. Obviously, then, Bourdieu is concerned primarily with positionally determined features of cultural differences. In our terminology, he does not discuss lifestyles but forms of life and ways of living. The struggle for power or status, we will argue, may well be highly relevant to different forms or to all forms of life, but it is not a necessary element in a person's lifestyle.

The assumption that lifestyle expresses an individual's social status has of course affected the way the relation between values and lifestyles has been understood. According to theories making this assumption, lifestyles are regarded as a way for the individual to express his position in relation to other individuals or groups. Consequently, it is primarily values which the individual holds because of what other people think that have been put in focus when the relation between value and lifestyle has been discussed. This becomes even more obvious when we note that within most lifestyle theories lifestyle are distinguished on the basis of consumption, taste and preferences in different areas. The notion of taste, which has become a key concept in this context, is frequently used when discussing how people's values are concretely expressed. The type of values which Kamler calls life philosophy values, on the other hand, have been almost completely left outside the discussion of values and lifestyles.

Kamler's distinction, therefore, illustrates a fundamental mistake often made in discussions of value and lifestyle, since it so clearly puts the life philosophy values outside the lifestyle discussion. All the same, the distinction between life style values and life philosophy values is relevant since it distinguishes between values referring to different components of identity. We will argue that both life style values and life philosophy values are important to a person's lifestyle. We suggest, however, that two other terms be used to express the distinction. We will use the term *outer-directed values* to refer to values held by the individual in order to express his or her social identity, and the term *inner-directed values* to refer to those values relevant to personal identity.

Finally, yet another component of identity should be mentioned, namely, the cultural one. This part of the identity, we argue, is located between social and personal identity. It relates, so to speak, to both these identity components, and in so doing helps the individual to relate his social and personal identities to one other. That is, it helps one to unite and make compatible one's need for a sense of individuality and uniqueness, and one's need for expressing one's social position and aspirations. Of the three types of identity, therefore, cultural identity is the one closest and most relevant to an individual's lifestyle.

Some Further Distinctions

Before proceeding to a more detailed discussion of the connection between human values and lifestyles, we will suggest and take up a distinction between four different types of values — *material, aesthetic, ethical and metaphysical* (Miegel 1990).

The distinction between different types of values suggested here is by no means the only one. It is possible to also distinguish a number of other types of values such as political, ecological, economic, etc., but the four categories presented above, we believe, are general enough to satisfactorily cover these more specific types of values as well. Political values, for instance, may be basically located among the ethical and metaphysical, economic values among the material, and so on.

Any distinction between different values depends basically on what purpose the distinction is meant to serve. The distinction put forward in this book can be conceptualized as representing a dimension reaching from matter to mind. Therefore, it serves well for studying the beliefs underlying lifestyles, since the lifestyle of an individual also reaches from a very obvious and visible consumption of goods and services to less obvious concerns and thoughts about life and what life is all about.

Since lifestyles are often distinguished on the basis of consumption, taste and preferences in different areas, they are often distinguished and identified on the basis of what we will call *aesthetic* and *material* values.

By the term *material values* we mean an individual's fundamental conceptions when considering material utility and preferability. Material values constitute the basis for an individual's preferences in relation to consumption of time as well as capital.

By the term *aesthetic values* we will mean an individual's fundamental conceptions of the beautiful and the ugly. These values constitute the basis for the individual's judgements concerning, for example, art, music, literature, film and the aesthetic qualities of various types of consumer goods.

The idea that taste, and consequently lifestyle, is ultimately based on aesthetic and material values is shared by several theoreticians in the field.

> Taste cultures, as I define them, consist of values and the cultural forms which express these values: music, art, design, literature, drama, comedy, poetry, criticism, news, and the media in which these are expressed — books, magazines, newspapers, records, films and television programs, painting and sculpture, architecture, and insofar as ordinary consumer goods also express aesthetic values or functions, furnishings, clothes, appliances, automobiles as well (Gans 1974:10f).

> The idea that style is a way that the human values, structures, and assumptions in a given time are aesthetically expressed and received is a powerful insight (Ewen 1988:3).

In most lifestyle theories it is also commonly held that taste is a manifestation of the status of the individual, of his or her position in the social hierarchy. Taste is thus often studied as status or class, i.e., in terms of positionally determined patterns. Much more seldom such patterns are studied as individually determined phenomena.

Even though the values of the individuals depend on the individual's position in the social hierarchy, they are not positionally determined entirely, but are also determined subjectively — by the individual. In addition, one and the same value may be expressed by means of any number of different actions and artefacts, and in different patterns of actions and artefacts. In discussing matters of lifestyle, therefore, it is the individual level of determination that interests us most.

It is no doubt possible to distinguish certain positionally determined patterns of taste dominating different class, status or age groups in a society, but we should keep in mind that such taste patterns are abstract theoretical constructions and generalizations, in short: ideal types. In the final analysis, a person's tastes involves subjective aesthetic judgements. However influenced these may be one's background, upbringing, age and gender, in the end the judgement is subjective and individual. That is why taste is interesting from the point of view of lifestyle.

The thesis that all individual value judgements in the end are subjective embraces all value types: aesthetic, material, moral and metaphysical. In the end all are all subjectively determined by the individual. This is not to say, however, that they are completely arbitrary. In all societies there are commonly held moral norms and principles, metaphysical and/or religious convictions, and aesthetic and material value standards. For all four types of values and value judgements distinguished here, there are thus structurally and positionally determined frameworks within which individual variations occur. However, it is individually determined variations which are of particular interest in connection with lifestyle.

Aesthetic and material values are important components of lifestyle. How about the other two kinds of values, ethical and metaphysical values, however? In most lifestyle theories they are simply neglected. One reason for this may be that ethical and metaphysical values are not as easily distinguished, since they are not as visibly expressed as are aesthetic and material ones. Nevertheless, we maintain that they are at least equally important determinants of individual lifestyles. They are the values which lie behind the individual's subjectively determined strivings and aspirations. They form the basis of the individual's judgements of what he or she considers important and worthwhile in life, what is right or wrong, and what is good or bad in various areas. These values are often expressed in terms of aesthetic and material values. Individual lifestyle, therefore, expresses not only the individual's position in the social structure, but also

— and more important as far as lifestyles are concerned — his or her personal and subjective strivings, aspirations, wishes and desires — in short: a number of very subtle phenomena which are important components of a lifestyle.

In endeavoring to understand lifestyle it is thus not sufficient to take into consideration only outer-oriented values, such as the aesthetic and material values, in considering to the social identity of the individual. Neither is it sufficient to only consider inner-oriented values connected with the individual's personal identity. What we are basically interested in is instead the individual's cultural identity, which embraces all the different value types, as well as the relations between them, making them meaningful in relation to each other. Thus, we must take into account the two inner-directed types of values as well, namely the ethical and metaphysical.

With the term *ethical values* we refer to the individual's fundamental conceptions of what is right or wrong, good or bad. Such values help the individual to act and reason in connection with different kinds of moral dilemmas and conflicts — inner conflicts as well as interpersonal ones.

With the term *metaphysical values*, finally, we refer to the individual's fundamental conceptions of the true, the eternal, and the real. Metaphysical values shape the individual's outlook toward, and philosophy of, life and reality. These are the kind of values that guide us through various types of existential questions, concerning for example, what is important in life, or the meaning of life and religion. Such values also help us define our position within reality.

Yet another important distinction with respect to the functions of values is between *security and developmental values*. This distinction resembles Rokeach's distinction between the *ego-defensive function* of values and the *knowledge or self-actualization function* of values (Rokeach 1973). The security values (cf. ego-defensive) serve the function of helping one to fit in and adapt in an unproblematic way to society, avoiding conflicts and ensuring that one's actions and attitudes are justified. Such values represent in Rokeach's terms "ready made concepts provided by our culture that such justifications can proceed smoothly" (Rokeach 1973:15f). The developmental values (cf. knowledge or self-actualization) serve the function of fulfilling the individual's needs and desires to search for meaning, understanding, knowledge and self-realization.

Any kind of values can serve both functions, but some values are nevertheless more likely either to function ego-defensively or to relate to knowledge and self-actualization. According to Rokeach, those values primarily serving security functions are, family security, national security and salvation, whereas values such as wisdom and a sense of accomplishment function primarily in a developmental sense.

The distinction between security and development is also important in both identity and lifestyle theories. In both Blos's and Erikson's psychological theories of identity, for example, identity development is described as a continuous process in which, as identity development progresses, the individual gradually becomes more independent and self-reliant and at the same time better able to establish connections with others. Thus, the need and desire for security develops hand-in-hand with the need and desire for development. However, there are significant differences between individuals concerning the relative priority given to security and development, respectively. For some individuals, security is the more important function of values, and vice versa. Obviously, which function an individual emphasizes most has a considerable impact on how his or her lifestyle is constructed (cf. Zablocki & Kanter 1976; Mitchell 1983).

The Complex Lifestyle

We will argue that values constitute the most fundamental component of lifestyle. From this perspective the lifestyle of an individual is basically an expression of his or her values. As we shall see, the values of an individual can be manifested in a variety of ways.

The values of the individual constitute a set of abstract and general conceptions of physical objects and of conditions within reality. These conceptions are, of course, not generated in a vacuum. On the contrary, the values of the individual depend to a high degree on the values commonly held within his or her culture or society. In any given culture there exist a number of fundamental conceptions about metaphysical and ethical conditions, but also about aesthetic and material objects and qualities. Such general and culturally defined conceptions are located at the level of determination which we call the structural level. Within a given structure individuals occupy different positions in terms of gender, social class and age, for example. One's position within the structure to a large extent determines which values one will hold. This means that a person is not *tabula rasa* in developing one's lifestyle. Lifestyles are generated within certain structurally and positionally determined frames. Therefore, it is not correct to say that a lifestyle is an individually determined phenomenon. Rather, a lifestyle is structurally, positionally *and* individually determined. What makes a lifestyle a lifestyle, however, are the individually determined features lacking in ways of life as well as in forms of life.

The lifestyle phenomenon can be studied on three conceptually different levels. Let us call these levels the *value level, the attitude level* and the *action level*. The value level consists of the individual's *general* and abstract conceptions about material, aesthetic, ethical and metaphysical conditions and qualities. These conceptions are made concrete by the individual on the attitude level. The attitudes of an individual involves his or her outlook on *specific* objects, phenomena and conditions of reality. Finally, on the action level the individual manifests her or his attitudes in the form of different actions. The values and attitudes of the individual become visible and observable when they manifest themselves in action. To summarize: the individual embraces a number of values which he or she makes concrete in the form of attitudes. Such attitudes are expressed in the form of certain actions and behaviors.

The four different types of values distinguished above result in four different types of attitudes. Attitudes primarily anchored in material values will be called *interests*. By the term *interest* we mean an individual's attitudes towards different ways of consuming and using his or her time, and material or immaterial resources. (Note in this context that the term is used here in a distinctly different way from more specific uses of it, for instance when used as in the terms *economic interest* and *vocational interest*).

Attitudes based primarily on the aesthetic values of an individual will be termed *taste*. Taste thus involves attitudes towards the aesthetic qualities of different objects, for instance toward a piece of music, a play, a film or a painting.

Attitudes based primarily on ethical values will be termed *principles*. A principle may refer to an individual's attitudes towards abortion, promiscuity, suicide, capital punishment or euthanasia, for example.

Attitudes based primarily on the individual's metaphysical values will be termed *convictions*. Convictions, for example, may concern the individual's attitudes towards religion, the meaning of life, as well as fate and death.

Just as the four types of values stand in various relations with each other, different types of attitudes are mutually related in various ways. Two persons may, for example, have similar material values but differing aesthetic values. Both may thus have a very strong interest in music, spending for that reason a great deal of money and time on music. All the same, they may have different aesthetic values, and consequently different tastes. One of them may prefer, say, experimental and progressive jazz music, while the other may be a dedicated listener to Finnish folk music. The material values in this case are probably subordinated to aesthetic values. However, in purchasing material objects such as records, stereo equipment and other types of goods needed to satisfy an interest in music, the individual may also make use of his material values. A new record player may, for example, be regarded as much more urgent and necessary than, say, a new suit or a vacuum cleaner.

Similarly, two individuals may hold an ethical value in common but have different metaphysical values. An exemple of such a case would be two individuals believing that killing is always morally wrong, and therefore refusing to do military service. However, whereas one of them motivates his attitude with his religious beliefs, the other is an atheist basing his refusal on a profane life philosophy. Both of them have the same ethical principle, and yet they have different metaphysical convictions.

Each of the four types of attitudes just distinguished correspond to a certain type of action. In the case of material attitudes, interests tend to be expressed in terms of what we will call *actions of interests*. Generally such actions are expressed in different types of consumption. An individual interested in music buys records, attends concerts and watches music programs on TV. An individual interested in sport buys sport magazines, attends soccer games and plays tennis.

Aesthethic attitudes (tastes) are expressed in actions which we shall call *style*. By style we refer to the individual's ways of dressing, gestures, choice of music, films, literature, etc.

Ethical attitudes, i.e. the principles behind them, become manifest in the individual's *actual moral behavior* in particular situations, especially where conflicting moral alternatives are at hand. To boycott South African products, to not eat meat, or to support Greenpeace are examples of actions that may be ethically based.

Actions based on metaphysical values will be called *actions of conviction*. Such actions can concern contemplation or praying, and also actions based, for example, on political, social or religious doctrines.

We maintain that the lifestyle of an individual involves a meaningful pattern of hir or her values, attitudes and actions. The arguments presented in this section are summarized in the model shown in Figure 3.

Figure 3. Values, Attitudes and Actions.

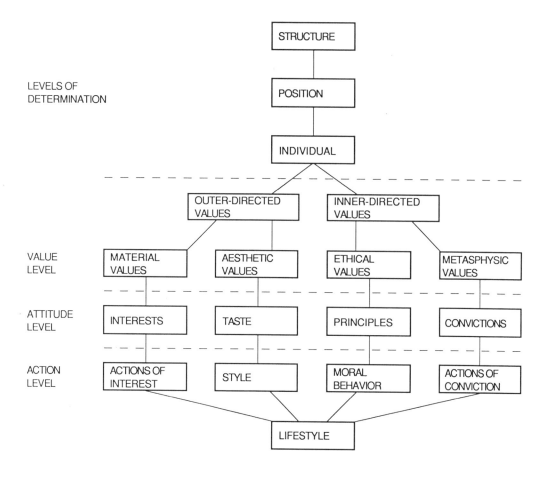

It should be noted that the purpose of the model is to organize a number of phenomena relevant to the discussion of lifestyle into a meaningful structure. The different concepts employed should be regarded as ideal types. The model should be considered as a general framework, roughly illustrating the complexity of the lifestyle concept. In reality, of course, the borderlines between different value, attitude and action types are often floating and overlapping. Furthermore, the lines presented in the figure give a very simplified representation of the relations between the different kinds of values, attitudes and actions. In reality all types of values may have at least some impact on all types of attitudes and actions, and all types of attitudes may have impact on all types of actions. The model may serve, however, as a useful analytical tool in comparing and discussing various ways of theoretically or empirically constructing lifestyles.

Values and Cultural Identity

In studying identity it is necessary to always keep in mind that the identity is a complex system of relations consisting of a multitude of conceptions about who one is, and how one is related to other individuals and to one's society and culture. Put in other words, identity has a number of different psychological functions for the individual.

First, it has the function of cultivating the personal self, that is, the qualities and characteristics we believe are tied to our own unique person. In this sense, identity functions as a means to help us to maintain and enhance the conceptions we have about ourselves, to identify ourself, define ourselves for ourselves, so to speak, as well as to express this unique self to others, to show others who we are.

Secondly, identity has a number of social functions for the individual. Apart from the desire to have a unique personal identity, people have a desire to be part of their society or culture, and of a variety of different groups existing within it. People often define themselves in relation to groups they feel they belong to. People play different social roles; consequently, they sometimes need to subordinate their personal identity in favor of various role expectations.

Thirdly, and probably most importantly, identity serves the function of integrating and making compatible with one another the desire to be unique with the desire to belong.

In a society where conditions of anonymity fertilize the desire "to be somebody," the *dream of identity, the dream of wholeness*, is intimately woven together with the desire to be known; to be visible; to be documented, for all to see Ewen 1988:94).

The integration of the two desires just mentioned is not always unproblematical. We are constantly occupied with the struggle to integrate these two poles of identity, and we do not always succeed. Conflicts often occur (cf. Turner 1978).

First, the different expectations related to the roles one plays are not always entirely compatible with one's desire to develop and express one's personality. Thus, the expectation of a certain role may be experienced as obstructing one's possibilities to achieve one's desire to maintain and develop the qualities and characteristics inherent in what one sees as one's own unique personality.

Secondly, the qualities and characteristics one identifies as one's own unique personality can lead to difficulties in adopting a certain role. Thus, although one would like to play a particular role, or to occupy a certain position in society, one is prevented from doing this by low self-esteem, or political opinion, for example.

Thirdly, one's social identity consists of a multiple of roles, and it can be difficult to combine these different into a coherent picture of one's social self. One must constantly balance between these different roles, and at the same time take into consideration all the different role expectations directed towards one. To find a satisfying balance between, on the one hand, the different roles one has to play, and on the other, these roles and one's own personal strivings and aspirations, is something which is difficult but which the individual must endeavor to achieve throughout all her life.

In order to understand how individuals construct their identity, it is important to comprehend how people reason and act in order to solve the never-ending conflicts between their different roles and between their roles and their self-images. A society's culture provides a large number of images and ideals for the way particular roles may be successfully acted out, and an equally great number of ideals and images concerning individuality and personal identity. Finally, culture provides one with a number of ideals and images concerning solutions to the problem of bringing the two poles of identity together.

With the exception of traditional agents of socialization — the family, the peer-group, and the school — the mass media of modern societies have probably become the most powerful mediator of cultural and social values, ideals and styles. Through the images provided by television, film, music, radio, popular literature, magazines and commercials, one can reflect upon one's self and one's identity, and also relate oneself to the positions and roles one occupies and has to play.

> As a panorama of apparently random images, the implicit language of style offers a way of seeing, and of not seeing, the world we inhabit, and our places within it. It affects our understanding of *value*, of *social power* and of *social change* (Ewen 1988:156).

Culture covers, so to speak, both the desire to have a personal and unique identity and the desire to be part of a group, a society and a culture. In this sense, culture serves as a mediator between society and the individual. Analogously, the cultural component of identity functions as a mediator between the personal and the social components of identity.

In the development of the lifestyle of an individual all the components of identity distinguished here are at work. Lifestyle consists not only of actions and attitudes based on material and aesthetic values, but also on metaphysical and ethical values, attitudes and actions. We have argued that lifestyle involves a meaningful pattern of relations between values, attitudes and actions of all possible kinds. It is thus impossible to keep the different types of values apart, in discussing identity and lifestyle. The same goes for the relation between the individual and society. In contemporary Western society the different types of values — material, aesthetic, ethical, and metaphysical — are mingled together in consumer goods and the mass media.

> ...in the perpetual play of images that shaped the mass-produced suburbs, and in the ever-changing styles that kept the market in consumer goods moving, "material values" and values of "mind and spirit" were becoming increasingly interchangeable and confused (Ewen 1988:232).

CHAPTER 7
LIFESTYLE: IDENTITY AND VALUE

A central feature of discussion on contemporary lifestyle is that it touches upon one of the most important themes in classical and modern sociology, namely, the complex relation between the individual and society. The historical process of individualization has gradually transformed the role of the individual in society so that the individual is given more and more freedom to act and think in his or her own right. However, this does not mean that the bonds of social structure and position are no longer important, but only that the individual has gradually increased her individual freedom within the social and cultural structure and the positions occupied within it.

The process of individualization has not gone equally far in every cultures and societies in the contemporary world. Neither is such freedom necessarily equally distributed within a specific society. It may well vary according to class, gender, race, for example. According to Elias (1939/1982), during the seventeenth and eighteenth centuries the aristocracy was the only class devoted to matters of style and manners. However, during the eighteenth century style more and more became a matter for a restricted part of the bourgeoisie, and in the nineteenth century style eventually became a matter for the whole bourgeoisie. In a similar way, Featherstone (1991b) argues that a fraction of the new middle class — which together with Bourdieu he calls *the new cultural intermediaries* — actively promotes and creates new lifestyles.

Elias's and Featherstone's views suggest that the upper classes or the higher social status-groups enjoy a greater degree of freedom than do the lower classes; therefore, they also have developed more and more varied lifestyles. We will argue that in modern Western society, especially during the latter half of the 20th century, the degree of individual freedom has increased for most people, so that also the lower classes and lower status groups have gained a greater measure of individual freedom, and this achieved the conditions necessary to develop lifestyles of their own.

As individual freedom increases, it becomes more important to consider the individual's identity and personality in discussing his or her lifestyle. Traditionally, the sociological discussion of identity has focused upon such aspects of the identity as are connected with class, gender, ethnicity and nationality. We believe that it is necessary, however, to distinguish between different types of identity in order to account for certain aspects of the individual identity that are not necessarily connected to such structurally and positionally determined features.

Identity, we maintain, is the central driving force in the making of individual lifestyles. That is because the values, attitudes, opinions, prejudices, beliefs, fears, hopes, dreams, wishes and desires of the individual are enshrined in different types of identity.

Despite the importance of the individual as a lifestyle-creator, we by no means argue that lifestyles can be reduced to being a purely individual matter. Our distinction between the three types of identity — personal, cultural and social — is made in order to encompass within the concept of identity a set of quite differing aspects of it, ranging from purely individual aspects to purely cultural and social ones.

During adult life, individual identity, of course, undergoes changes of varying degrees. Certain periods, however, are characterized by more fundamental transformations of identity. One such period is that of youth, in particular the period which we like to call culturally and socially defined youth. There are also other periods which for one reason or another involve important identity-related changes: for example the period of old age, when retirement makes it necessary for people to adapt to new lives as senior citizens. Other periods which may entail changes in the cultural and social identity are not age-related; they occur when the individual's life-situation for some reason dramatically changes. This can be the case, for example, in connection with marriage, death of a family member, divorce, parenthood, emigration and so forth.

In analyzing lifestyle in modern society one has to consider the increasing importance of the cultural component in an individual's identity development. This is because lifestyle is no longer exclusively determined by class, status, gender, ethnicity or position in a society, however important these positional determinants may be. Neither are lifestyles equivalent to total freedom for the individual in the choice of values, attitudes and actions, even though this freedom may have increased. The core of lifestyle, therefore, is located in cultural identity. Whereas the personal identity is individual and social identity is non-individual, cultural identity can be both individual or non-individual.

Personal identity consists of experiences, thoughts, dreams, desires, and so on, as interpreted and comprehended by the individual in relation to other experiences and thoughts. Personal identity thus relates to the individual. It may be described as a unique system of relations between such experiences, thoughts, dreams, hopes and desires.

Social identity, on the other hand, is non-individual. Its function is to define the individual's position within the society, relations towards other individuals sharing the same position, and the relations towards individuals occupying other social positions.

Cultural identity can be said to have a double function. On the one hand, it is related to personal identity, and on the other, to social identity. The individual uses his or her values, attitudes and actions to maintain and develop individual personal identity, but also to distinguish or relate to other individuals. Thus, one and the same value, attitude or action may, on the one hand, serve the purpose of strengthening the self, and, on the other, function as a means of expressing a sense of belonging to or holding distance toward other individuals.

One problem with much contemporary lifestyle research is the concentration upon either the non-individual or the individual aspects of lifestyle. A common tendency in classic as well as in some contemporary lifestyle studies is the attempt to divide a population into a limited number of different lifestyles on the basis of some common characteristics, whether these are class, social status, gender or a common set of needs (cf. Bourdieu 1979/1984; Mitchell 1983; Zetterberg 1983). The other tendency is represented by such contemporary scholars as Thomas Ziehe (1989) and Paul Willis (1990), who ascribe to the individual almost total freedom in developing lifestyle and identity.

Irrespective of which of these two perspectives one adopts, one misses the central set of problems within the lifestyle area, which is the relation between the individual and society. We will argue that in order to comprehend lifestyle in contemporary Western societies, one must understand the dynamic relation between the individual and society. This means also that no lifestyle theory is complete without a theory of individual identity.

What has been missing in earlier lifestyle research, we feel, are three things: first, a consistent theory of identity as related to lifestyle; second, a theory of the relations between values, attitudes and actions within a lifestyle context; third, an adequate treatment of the relations between the concepts of lifestyle, value and identity.

Although in the text thus far have called it a theory, the theoretical and conceptual distinctions and statements presented and elaborated in the book should not be regarded as a complete theory of lifestyle. Rather they should be seen as an attempt to bring some order in the terminological and conceptual diversity and confusion inherent in what might be called the sociology of lifestyle. Our intention has been to synthesize some important theoretical contributions to a theory of lifestyle and to elaborate certain of the concepts used by other authors working within this field. In the process it has been necessary to reformulate certain important concepts, such as those of values and identity. As a result, some of the terms used in different theories of lifestyle have been given either a more extended or restricted or even a new meaning.

In order to construct a more elaborated theory of lifestyle, such terminological and conceptual clarifications must be accompanied by a more thorough discussion of certain fundamental sociological and ontological questions. Such a task, however, exceeds beyond the intentions of this study. Before continuing our work in developing a theory of lifestyle, we consider it important to insofar as possible theoretically and empirically test the applicability of the assumptions we have made so far. This will be done in two separate steps. On the one hand, we will try to apply the concepts to a specific research field, namely that of youth culture. On the other hand, we will test the applicability of the concepts on the basis of both quantitative and qualitative data.

PART TWO:

CONTEMPORARY YOUTH CULTURE AND LIFESTYLE

My argument is that for youth, as for everyone else, leisure consumption and style involve a relationship between choice and constraint. The problem is that the young, since the 1920s, have come to symbolize leisure, to embody good times. Youth seem to be freer than everyone else in society, partly for the standard sociological reason — they are in a marginal position; they are not bound, like their elders, by the routines and relationships of family and career. But it is because they are *not* really free that this matters. The truth of youth culture is that the young displace to their free time the problems of work and family and future. It is because they lack power that the young account for their lives in terms of play, focus their politics on leisure. Youth culture matters for the old too: it is young people's use of leisure that raises the problems of capitalist freedom and constraint most sharply and most resonantly. Youth is still the model for consumption (Frith 1983:200f).

Today, after more than a decade of punk style, when a purple and green Mohawk on the head of a suburban American teenager only begs the question of how early he or she has to get up to fix his or her hair in time for school, it's hard to remember just how ugly the first punks were (Marcus 1990:73).

CHAPTER 8
YOUTH: SOCIAL AND CULTURAL IDENTITY

INTRODUCTION

Questions concerning young people and their culture have attracted social scientists during the entire post-war period. In Sweden, this interest has accelerated considerably during the last decade (see, for instance, Statens Ungdomsråd 1972; Dahlgren 1979; Dahlgren 1985; Fornäs et al. 1987, 1989; Fornäs 1990). The recent development of a state-financed nationwide network of youth culture researchers from a wide range of academic disciplines is probably the most obvious sign of such a development. This increased interest in youth and youth culture has led to a critical discussion of previous youth culture theories. It has increased the demand for a more differentiated concept of youth and youth culture.

In this book we endeavor to contribute to this discussion by placing our theory of lifestyle within the sphere of youth culture research. To do this, however, we must consider how the concepts of youth and youth culture have been understood earlier. We also have to locate our theoretical perspective within a social, scholarly and historical context.

Through their tastes and preferences in different areas, people express their values and their identity. By changing and adding new areas to their tastes, they also develop their values, and consequently their identity. These changes of tastes, preferences and identity might be described as a dialectic process during which changes in identity lead to changes in tastes and preferences. These in turn make further changes of identity likely, and so on. Although rather dramatic changes occasionally do occur, in most cases such changes are not very revolutionary but are slow and successive.

Such identity changes also mean that the individual — successively and in different areas — alters his or her position in relation to other individuals, groups or classes. Such positional changes can be described in terms of different kinds of mobility. Changes in social identity can thus be described in terms of social mobility, changes in cultural identity in terms of cultural mobility, and changes in both in terms of socio-cultural mobility. Therefore, the concept of mobility is of utmost importance in dealing with changes in lifestyle, and it is especially important in relation to the period of youth. During the later part of the period of youth, the individual develops a relatively stable social and cultural identity through choice of educational goals, an occupation, a partner, etc. This is not to say that social and cultural mobility does not occur during adulthood, but merely that it is during the later period of youth that the individual usually must make choices of decisive significance for his or her future adult life. Such decision-making is often very difficult, and much experimenting and tests of different alternatives take place during this period of life.

Changes in identity during the period of youth, concern the acquisition of social and cultural capital. The latter can be used to express the cultural and social competence of the individual. There are other and related competences, however, which need to be accounted for. These include personal capital, which has to do with how the individual is able to express and use what is unique to him or her as a person, and economic capital, which simply is his access to money and other material resources.

The discussion in this chapter concerning the concepts of youth, mobility and capital forms a background to an understanding young people's lifestyles, their development and change. The concepts are also important to discussing relations between the main provider of cultural and social capital for young people, namely different kinds of popular culture, on the one hand, and their lifestyles, on the other. This relation will be discussed in chapter 9.

YOUTH

Young people have been described in a multitude of ways, both in fiction and in the social sciences. In the literature on youth culture there is often a tendency to characterize youth as a homogeneous category of persons. Gillis (1981), for one, is critical towards the lack of distinction between different types of young people in youth research. He is particularly concerned about differences between middle-class youth and working class youth. According to our view, however, it is necessary to distinguish between individuals not only along the lines of class, status, gender, ethnicity and the like, but also in terms of age group. In this chapter we shall deal with that problem, that is, how to distinguish within the category of youth between different age groups.

Aristotle is usually cited as the first comprehensive source regarding a biological and psychological characterization of adolescence (Eichorn 1968). He describes a number of traits which in modern Western societies have been attributed to the adolescent. However, even if there are points of close similarity between Aristotle's way of describing adolescents and the modern way, there are also many differences. Aristotle distinguished between three different age groups: *childhood*, *youth* and *old age*. In Aristotle's philosophical writings, the term youth could thus have included any age from about seven to, say, forty years.

The lack of distinctions between different age groups in ancient and medieval Western societies can be explained in different ways. According to Eichorn (1968) the average life span was so short that it was not necessary to make fine distinctions between different age groups. Furthermore, fine distinctions between physical or mental abilities could not be achieved until the advent of a relatively high standard of living for a major part of the population. The labor of all was needed. Irrespective of age, individuals had to work.

According to Ariès (1962), the age groups of childhood and adolescence were not distinguished and treated as separate until the eighteenth century. In school Latin, for instance, the word *puer* (boy) and the word adolescent were for a long time used indiscriminately. Even at the beginning of the nineteenth century no one felt the need to distinguish childhood, this period beyond the age of twelve or thirteenth, and adolescence (Ariès 1962). Through the spread of formal education to the middle classes, the distinction between childhood and adolescence became more salient. According to Gillis (1981) the discovery or invention of adolescence as a specific developmental phase thus belonged to the middle classes. However, through the process of democratization and the expansion of the school system, the notion of adolescence, and the modern distinction between childhood and adolescence, were gradually extended to large parts of the laboring population.

Biologically, Psychologically and Socially/Culturally Defined Youth

In modern Western societies we are witnessing the emergence of a previously unrecognized stage in life, a stage that intervenes between adolescence and adulthood, namely, the stage of *postadolescence* or *youth*

(Keniston 1975; Sebald 1977; Gillis 1981). This transitional period is characterized by a prolonged experimentation with life's possibilities. As Keniston (1975:7) puts it:

> What characterizes a growing minority of postadolescents today is that they have not settled the questions whose answers once defined adulthood: questions of relationship to the existing society; questions of vocation; questions of social role and lifestyle.

The general concept of youth, however, is too imprecise to be used in a serious analysis of young peoples' lives. It is necessary, therefore, to distinguish between three different but partly overlapping ways of defining youth: as biological, as psychological and as cultural/social youth.

The *biologically* defined period of youth, or puberty, is primarily characterized by physical changes. The biological changes in puberty are dramatic and relatively rapid. One of the most important of these biological changes is the process of sexual maturation. For girls the onset of menstruation seems to have a critical significance (Magnusson 1988), whereas in boys the process of puberty proceeds, it seems, at a slower rate. Puberty, generally, speaking is two years later for boys than for girls (Petersen & Taylor 1980; Rosengren & Windahl 1989). According to Petersen and Taylor (1980) most of the differences between males and females are due to the fact that the pubertal growth spurt begins earlier in females (eleven years) than males (thirteen years).

The *psychologically* defined period of youth, or adolescence, is characterized primarily by psychological maturation. As Blos (1962:128) put it: "pubescence is an act of nature; adolescence is an act of man". Adolescents are primarily concerned with the problem of self-definition. During the period of adolescence, individuals gradually develop their capacity to differentiate themselves from other people, and to recognize their parents and other people as agents in their own right. It is during adolescence that individuals develop the capacity to frame a view of their own regarding their past, present and future life.

The *culturally* and *socially* defined period of youth is characterized primarily by experimentation with different roles and lifestyles. During this period, the young adult tries through role and lifestyle experimentation to find a unique niche in some section of society. This period can be viewed as a psycho-social moratorium, that is, a period characterized by a delay of adult commitments (Erikson 1968b).

Each society and each culture institutionalizes a certain moratorium for the majority of its young people. For the most part, these moratoria coincide with apprenticeships and adventures that are in line with the society's values. The moratorium may be a time for horse stealing and vision-quests, a time for *Wanderschaft* of work "out West" or "down under", a time for "lost youth" or academic life... (Erikson 1968b:157).

There of course are large variations between different individuals during this specific period of youth. Some individuals fairly soon develop a stable cultural and social identity, while others for a considerable period of time continue their quest for a unique niche in society.

The different periods of youth, and their relation to age, are visualized in Figure 4.

Figure 4. Biologically, Psychologically and Culturally/Socially Defined Youth.

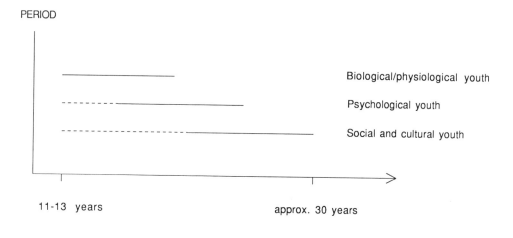

In the following section we shall deal primarily with the period of culturally and socially defined youth. The reason for this is that during late adolescence a relatively solid personal identity is in principle already formed, while cultural and social identities are characterized by constant alterations (Blos 1962; Kroeger 1989; Lüdtke 1989).

DIFFERENT TYPES OF MOBILITY

During the culturally and socially defined period of youth, young people experiment with different roles and lifestyles. However, during this period the individual also gradually forms a more stable cultural and social identity (cf. Lüdtke 1989).

During this period individuals produce different life plans, different reflections and thoughts about their future occupation, about married life, the number of children to have, etc. Some of these life plans will be realized, while others will not. To some extent, at least, it thus is possible to choose between different life plans. However, individuals always "choose" life plans within a structurally and positionally determined frame. Such things as class of origin, gender and nationality influence the individual's possibilities to realize his or her different life plans (cf. Merton 1963; Berger et al. 1973; Schutz & Luckmann 1974).

In order to understand identity formation during the period of culturally and socially defined youth, it is necessary to distinguish between the individual's present identity, and his or her optional cultural and social identities. During this period of youth, individuals find themselves in a process of anticipatory socialization, a process during which they try out the behavior and attitudes of the different groups of which they are expecting to become future members (Merton 1963; Berger et al. 1973; Rosengren & Windahl 1989).

The concept of anticipatory socialization is often used to distinguish between *class of origin*, the class from which one comes, and *class of destination*, the class which one believes one will end up in. For some young people their class of origin will be the same as their class of destination, but for many their class of origin and their class of destination will not coincide. In cases in which individuals' class of origin and their class of destination do not coincide speak of social mobility. In accordance with a well established practice, the term social mobility is used to describe individuals' trajectories, upwards and downwards, in the societal class and status hierarchy (cf., for instance, Goldhammer 1968; Erikson 1971).

In this book we will use the term social mobility in a somewhat different way, referring both to horizontal and to vertical mobility. By *horizontal social mobility* we mean changes in the individual's social identity which are not related to any changes in his or her social status. By *vertical social mobility* we mean changes in the individual's social identity which also alter his or her social status. Thus, vertical social mobility corresponds with the traditional use of the term social mobility. The concept of social mobility refers to role-changes. Horizontal social mobility does not necessarily refer to changes in occupational roles, but may also concern other types of role-changes, vertical social mobility is basically related to alterations in occupational roles.

We are not interested in changes in the social identity and status only. In a theory of lifestyle, it is of utmost importance to account for changes in the cultural identity and status as well. We shall therefore distinguish between an individual's actual cultural identity and status and his or her potential cultural identity and status. In order to understand identity formation during the culturally and socially defined period of youth, it is necessary to account for both social and cultural mobility.

We shall use the term cultural mobility to describe *horizontal* and *vertical* transformations of cultural identity and status, that is, changes of those values which constitute the core of the individual's cultural identity. Such transformations are primarily expressed and visualized through, for example, taste in different areas and the organization of leisure time. By the term *horizontal cultural mobility* we shall refer to changes in the individual's cultural identity which are not related to any changes in his cultural status. By *vertical cultural mobility* we mean changes in the individual's cultural identity which also alter his or her cultural status.

Even though social and cultural mobility are two distinct phenomena, they are related to each other in various ways. One type of mobility often coincides with the other. In Figure 5 we present an overview of the different possible combinations of horizontal and vertical social and cultural mobility. The typology gives a schematic picture of the different directions which identity and lifestyle development may take in terms of social and cultural mobility. Changes in social and cultural identity are often intimately related to each other, but sometimes changes in one type of identity do not have any particular impact on another. It is thus possible for an individual to alter social identity without altering the values and taste constituting cultural identity. Moreover, it is possible for an individual to alter both cultural or social identity without changing cultural or social status. It is not possible, however, to alter social or cultural status without also changing one's identity in one way or another.

Figure 5. Different Types of Mobility.

CULTURAL MOBILITY

	NONE	HORIZONTAL	VERTICAL
NONE	Status quo	Altered cultural identity	Altered cultural identity Altered cultural status
SOCIAL MOBILITY **HORIZONTAL**	Altered social identity	Altered social identity Altered cultural identity	Altered social identity Altered cultural identity Altered cultural status
VERTICAL	Altered social identity Altered social status	Altered social identity Altered cultural identity Altered social status	Altered social identity Altered cultural identity Altered social status Altered cultural status

The different types of mobility are related in various ways to the individual's varying access to different types of *capital*. The term capital is used here in a rather specific context, and it should not be confused, therefore, with the everyday application of the term. In order to understand the different types of mobility, it is also necessary to understand the concept of capital.

The most extensive theoretical contribution in this respect is undoubtedly found in Bourdieu's *Distinction* (1979/1984). In the next section we shall account briefly for the three types of capital Bourdieu distinguishes, namely economic, cultural and social capital. Furthermore, we shall discuss Coleman's conceptualization of human and social capital. The reason for such a discussion is that Bourdieu's and Coleman's use of the concepts each contains a number of limitations in relation to the theory which we outline here. As we shall see, these limitations are mainly due to the fact that whereas Bourdieu is primarily occupied with questions of power relations between and within different classes and status groups in society, and Coleman mainly with social integration, we consider the power relations and the issue of social integration to be equally important.

DIFFERENT TYPES OF CAPITAL

Bourdieu (1979/1984; 1988) distinguishes between three different types of capital: economic, social and cultural.

The concept of *economic capital* is not very complicated. It has to do with money, and thus refers to qualities such as income, private means and property, and other economic resources.

The concepts of *Social and Cultural capital* are more complex and in need of a thorough discussion in this context. We shall undertake such a discussion after first having in brief accounted for Bourdieu's use of the terms.

The concept of *Social capital* refers to such features as social connections, honorability and respectability. This type of capital is essential in winning and keeping the confidence of high society.

Cultural capital is equivalent to cultural competence, i.e., duration of schooling and the ability to appreciate and to understand legitimate culture, which is the culture of the dominant classes in a specific society. Bourdieu

(1984) distinguishes between acquired and achieved cultural capital (cf. Parsons's notion of *ascribed* and *achieved* status). On the one hand, cultural capital is inherited from the family, on the other, cultural capital is an effect of schooling (educational capital).

> While variations in educational capital are always very closely related to variations in competence, even in areas like cinema or jazz, which are never taught nor directly assessed by the educational system, the fact remains that at equivalent levels of educational capital, differences in social origin (whose "effects" are already expressed in differences in educational capital) are associated with important differences in competence (Bourdieu 1979/1984:63).

The notions of cultural, social and economic capital, are used as analogues to describe different ways of obtaining power in a specific society. The most important distinction, according to Bourdieu, is the one between economic and cultural capital. The distribution of different classes and status groups in a society runs from those who are well provided with both economic and cultural capital to those who lack both.

Certain strata in society combine very high economic capital with very high cultural capital, but the composition of different types of capital is often assymetrical, with cultural capital dominant in some cases, economic in other. Those fractions within the dominant class whose reproduction depends mainly on economic capital are thus opposed to those fractions which are least endowed with economic capital, and whose reproduction as a group depends mainly on cultural capital. The process of exchange between economic and cultural capital is one of the fundamental stakes in the struggle between different classes and status groups whose power and privileges are linked to either these types of capital.

One type of critique that has been directed against Bourdieu's use of the concept of cultural capital is that it is difficult to make an analogy between economic capital and cultural competence. John Fiske (1987), for instance, argues that cultural capital does not circulate in the same way as economic capital, and that there can be different types of cultural capital — for instance *popular cultural capital* and *legitimate cultural capital* — while such differing types of economic capital do not exist in the same way.

> There is a popular cultural capital in a way that there is no popular economic capital, and thus Bourdieu's validated cultural capital of the bourgeoisie is constantly being opposed, interrogated, marginalized, scandalized, and evaded, in a way that economic capital never is (Fiske 1987:314).

Although Fiske has a point in his critique, it is, however, by no means conclusive, however. Capital may be used here more as a metaphor than as a direct analogy. The term is used to denote access to the means necessary to attain certain goals, whether this be in the purchasing of a commodity or in the understanding and appreciation of a piece of art.

Another important contribution to the discussion of different forms of capital is the one provided by the American sociologist James Coleman (Coleman 1988, 1990). He distinguishes between physical, human and social capital.

> Just as physical capital is created by changes in materials to form tools that facilitate production, human capital is created by changes in persons that bring about skills and capabilities that make them able to act in new ways. Social capital, however, comes about through changes in the relations among persons that facilitate action. If physical capital is wholly tangible, being embodied in observable material form, and human capital is less tangible, being embodied in the skills and knowledge acquired by an individual, social capital is less tangible yet, for it exists in the relations among persons Coleman 1988:100f).

To provide a reasonable theoretical framework for the study of lifestyles in modern society it is necessary, we repeat, to account for the impact of economic and social inequalities in terms of class-determined conditions. However, if one uses the concept of lifestyle as we do, that is, to describe and analyze a phenomenon that by necessity and per definition always contains an element of individual and subjectively anchored components, one must also pay attention to the function of the individual's unique identity and personality in the shaping of lifestyle.

The main difference between Bourdieu's and Coleman's views concerns this very point. Whereas Bourdieu applies the concepts of cultural and social capital in order to describe and analyze *the power relations* between different classes and status groups, as well as similar variations in the access to cultural and social status within primarily the bourgeoisie, Coleman uses the concepts of human and social capital to describe and analyze various human resources as well as the possibility of realizing them in terms of social action. That is, unlike Bourdieu, Coleman is not only interested in power relations between different classes and status groups, but in moral and social integration.

Both Bourdieu's and Coleman's concepts of capital are useful tools in a theory of lifestyle. In our theory, we seek to understand the incentives for the individual to adopt the various cultural and social abilities, symbols and artefacts needed to create lifestyle. Therefore, Bourdieu's concepts of cultural and social capital are not incompatible with our efforts. Nevertheless they are not sufficient on the individual level. There — as Coleman has observed — there are other relations than those of power that are equally or even more important. We will return in more detail to these relations later. Among them are social integration in terms of, for example, family relations, kinship, friendship, brotherhood and love.

Building on both Coleman's and Bourdieu's concepts of capital, we will use the terms cultural and social capital in order to consider both functions of the different forms of capital. We will argue that both the status and the non-status dimensions of the concepts are relevant in the creation and development of lifestyles in a society.

By the term *cultural capital* we will refer to the ability and competence to understand and make use of various types of cultural goods, be it clothing, music, paintings, soccer or film. It does not matter whether the ability and competence concern the legitimate culture or popular culture, youth culture or adult culture, male culture or female culture. The individual may use his or her cultural capital both in order to achieve higher cultural status and to develop cultural identity without changing his or her cultural status.

By *social capital* we will refer to individuals' ability and competence to take part in social interaction, that is, to communicate, to socialize, to establish, maintain and develop various types of interpersonal relations, and to participate in different social contexts. Just as with cultural capital, social capital can be employed as a means for achieving a higher social status, but also for developing social identity quite apart from the status function.

These rather broad definitions of cultural and social capital serve the purpose of avoiding the limits inherent in Bourdieu's and Coleman's more narrow definitions of the concept of capital. Our intention is to broaden the scope of the lifestyle discussion so as to embrace the perspectives both of social conflicts and power relations and of social integration and identity development.

Since we are basically concerned with the lifestyles of young people, and since our main interest is lifestyle change and development, we concentrate upon social and cultural identities and mobility. We must therefore deal with a cultural area where the components of youth culture are particularly likely to be found. Such an area, we shall argue, is the area of popular culture. The following chapter offers a discussion of the relation between youth culture and popular culture.

CHAPTER 9
YOUTH CULTURE AND POPULAR CULTURE

The purpose of this chapter is, on the one hand, to give a brief summary of the most influential theories of youth culture, and on the other, to discuss these theories, together with their advantages and limitations in relation to the aims of this study, those of describing and understanding how young people in contemporary Sweden develop their lifestyles. The main thesis put forward in this chapter is that the concept of youth culture, as it has previously been employed, has certain limitations due either to its emphasis on not very representative groups of youth or its exaggerated concentration on either class or the individual. These tendencies and the limitations we distinguish within them will be discussed throughout the chapter.

YOUTH AS PROBLEM — YOUTH AS FUN

In *Hiding In the Light* (1988), Dick Hebdige distinguishes between three different historical views of how youth has been looked upon by the adult society as represented by scholars, journalists and teachers. We will use his distinction in order to present a brief summary of how youth culture research has developed and changed during the twentieth century. Some especially influential traditions will then be more thoroughly presented in the two following sections.

Hebdige uses the term *Youth as Problem* to describe the view held by the early American sociologists concerned with young people and their culture. This category of researchers developed in the USA during the late 1920s. The founding fathers of this tradition were to be found within the so called Chicago School of Social Ecology, represented by, among others, Park, Thrasher, Whyte and later Albert Cohen. Their main involvement in this respect was with criminal subcultures and gangs among youth in large American cities. They saw these delinquent youth groups as being a result of what they identified as a social and cultural breakdown of society, as the material, cultural, psychological and moral decline of the social milieu of the rapidly growing urban American areas.

One of the most important successors of the Chicago School was Albert

Cohen. In his highly influential study *Delinquent Boys* (1955) he elaborated the concept of *subculture*. Cohen used the concept to understand how young delinquent boys formed gangs in order to cope with circumstances in their social milieu constituting common problems or difficulties for them. He maintained that such circumstances constitute problems specific for the members of the given subculture; they thus do not concern the majority of the population in the same way (Schwendter 1990). Cohen regards the common needs of a group of persons to solve problems occurring during such circumstances as are found when a subculture originates. He writes:

> In this fashion culture is continually being created, re-created and modified wherever individuals sense in one another like needs, generated by circumstances, not shared generally in the larger social system (Cohen 1955:65).

As we shall see in chapter 9, Cohen's significance for contemporary youth culture theory is probably most evident in the works of representatives of the Birmingham School.

Hebdige calls his second historical category of how youth culture has been conceptualised *Youth as Fun*. With the growing affluence of the 1950s and the increasing influence of American culture on the Western European countries, a specific way of looking at youth and their culture emerged. The effect of this development on youth culture research was that the focus moved away from more or less criminal subcultures to youth as a homogeneous category separated from the adult culture. The most influential representative of this view was Talcott Parsons who shaped and influenced many of the theoretical perspectives on youth culture during the 1950s and 60s (Parsons 1942; 1964; Eisenstadt 1956; Abrams 1959; Coleman 1961). In brief, Parsons held that during this period youth became less tied to institutions such as class, family and local community. He saw youth as a transitional period between childhood and adulthood, devoted to leisure, consumption and a romantic quest for meaning in and with life. In a rapidly changing society young people are left without guidance from the adult generation, a situation which leads to conflicts between generations. These conflicts, however, are not as serious as to prevent young persons from eventually becoming integrated into adult society and its value system. Coleman describes this view as follows:

> In sum, then, the general point is this: our adolescents today are cut off, probably more than ever before, from the adult society. They are still oriented toward fulfilling their parent's desires, but they look very much to their peers for approval as well. Consequently, our society has within its midst a set of small teen-age societies, which focus teen-age interests and attitudes on things far removed from adult responsibilities, and which may develop standards that lead away from the goals established by the larger society (Coleman 1961:9).

Hebdige calls his third historical category *Youth as Image*. This category emerged in the mid 60s. During this period, he maintains, youth became extremely occupied with their own body as a sign-system. Another way of putting it is to say that style became a predominant feature of youth culture. It is also during this period that many of the conspicuous youth groups made their first appearance on the British scene. At this time, or somewhat later, groups such as mods, rockers, punks and skinheads, captured the interest of the group of humanists and social scientists known as the Birmingham School, whose theories are the subject of the next section.

YOUTH AND CLASS

During the 1970s and 1980s British youth researchers developed an interest in specific and often deviant or conspicuous youth subcultures (Willmott 1966; Patrick 1973). Another interest that developed among American and British researchers during this period was the so-called counter cultures among youth (Roszak 1969; Wilson 1970). Probably the most influential theoretical tradition concerning youth subcultures and counter cultures during the period was that of the Birmingham school, with names such as Stuart Hall, Paul Willis, Dick Hebdige, Angela McRobbie and Paul Gilroy. The work these researchers carried out has been presented in a wide range of articles and books (see, for instance, Hall & Jefferson 1976; Hall et al. 1980; Brake 1980; Turner 1990).

The Birmingham school was influenced by a wide range of theoretical tradition and was represented by such names as Gramsci, Althusser, the previously mentioned Chicago school, Lévi-Strauss, Barthes, Hoggart — who founded the school — and Williams. These influences were used to form a theory of youth and its culture in post-war Britain. We will first describe briefly the general theoretical framework of the Birmingham school, and then discuss further some of the most important single works of the school.

The general theory of the Birmingham school is probably best found in the volume *Resistance Through Rituals* edited by Hall and Jefferson (1976). In this overview of the research conducted at the Center for Contemporary Cultural Studies in Birmingham, the most prominent representatives of the school put forward the fundamental aspects of their general cultural theories. In brief one can say that a common feature of these theories was that they expressed in particular a reaction towards Parson's ideas concerning a classless youth culture. Contrary to such a perspective, the Birmingham school claimed that such features as class, race and gender constitute important forces in the formation of the various movements among young people and the different groups, subcultures and counter cultures connected with these. In their analyses of youth culture they found different mechanisms behind working-class-based subcultures as well as middle-class-founded counter-cultures.

The Birmingham school regarded youth subculture in terms of reactions towards contradictions within the culture of their parents. Perhaps more important, the formation of different subcultures was regarded as a reaction towards inequalities suffered by older generations in relation to the dominant classes in British society. Subcultures can be seen as responses to these circumstances. On the one hand, they represent the need of youth to express and create a distance and autonomy vis-à-vis their parents' generation, and on the other, to express identification and support for their parents in relation to the opressions suffered from the dominant classes in society. Youth subcultures can thus be seen as a kind of almost magical solution of the problems involved with being both young and working class.

> There is no "subcultural solution" to working-class youth unemployment, educational disadvantage, compulsory mis-education, dead-end jobs, the routinisation and specialisation of labour, low pay and the loss of skills. Sub-cultural strategies cannot match, meet or answer the structuring dimensions emerging in this period for the class as a whole. So, when the post-war sub-cultures address the problematics of their class experience, they often do so in ways which reproduce the gaps and dicrepancies between real negotiations and symbolically displaced "resolutions". They "solve", but in an imaginary way, problems which at the concrete material level remain unresolved. Thus the "Teddy Boy" expropriation of an upper class style of dress "covers" the gap between largely manual, unskilled, near-lumpen real careers and life-chances, and the "all-dressed-up- and-nowhere-to-go" experience of Saturday evening (Clarke et al. 1976:47f).

The Birmingham school's analysis of counter-cultures differs in several ways from its views on subcultures. They look upon counter-cultures among youth as responses towards the contradictions and value conflicts within the culture of the dominant class. The economic and cultural developments in post-war British society led to significant changes in the values of the dominant classes. Clarke and his co-authors express these changes as follows:

> This was an altogether different — puzzling, contradictory — world for the traditional middle classes, formed in and by an older, more "protestant" ethic. Advanced capitalism now required, not thrift but consumption; not sobriety but style; not postponed gratifications, but immediate satification of needs; not goods that last but things that are expendable; the "swinging" rather than the sober life-style (Clarke et al. 1976:64).

The representatives of the Birmingham school thus maintained that counter-cultures expressed in a manner similar to that of subcultures the search for magical solutions to the problems of being young and middle class in the 1960s and 70s.

The means used by youth to express their belonging to a certain subculture or counter culture were their taste, style and language. Symbolic elements from established contexts were often employed and were transformed into either having no at all or meaning something completely different from they traditionally had meant. In accounting for Hebdige's work on subculture later on, we will return to the expressive and stylistic components of youth subcultures and counter cultures in greater detail.

Paul Willis has perhaps written most lucidly about the two functions of subculture among working class youth. In his *Learning to Labour* (1977) he describes thoroughly both the way in which young working class lads, through their language, taste and style distance themselves from their parents and from the middle class culture represented by their teachers and schoolmates, and at the same time they become integrated into the working class culture of their parents and learn to become a part of it. Willis's somewhat paradoxical conclusions are that working class lads through their opposition to the dominant middle class culture and its values, gradually become integrated into the subordinated working class culture. He maintains that, even though the single individual may succeed in improving his or her social status by adopting and accepting the values of the middle class, the working class itself, and consequently the class system, remain intact.

Dick Hebdige represents a later tendency within the Birmingham school, in that he moves at least partly away from the class perspective, concentrating instead on the subcultures as such, and the styles, tastes and symbols, of the youth belonging to the subcultures he studies. In his best known book, *Subculture* (1979), he develops a subtle analysis of the functions and meanings of style. Although in this study he also accounts for a number of different subcultures, his main concern is the punk culture. He holds that style is used by the representatives of this subculture in order to question and destroy all forms of established cultural stereotypes, and especially the stereotypes of class and gender. Style is seen as a constant quest for new experiences and meanings, an attempt to create meanings in a constantly changing world (cf. Simmel 1903/1971; Blumer 1969). In his illuminating book *Lipstick Traces. A Secret History of the Twentieth Century* (1990), Greil Marcus studies the connections between Sex Pistols, dada and the Situationist International. In all of these music or art movements there was a reversal of perspectives and value, a quest for new and more radical ways of perceiving reality in a world were "all that is solid melts into air".

Finally we must mention the works of Angela McRobbie, for her criticism of the lack of any work being done within the Birmingham school on the culture of young women. In several articles and books she has questioned the traditionally male-oriented analyses of youth culture, and she has also developed a theorethical framework for studying female youth culture (McRobbie & Garber 1976; McRobbie 1984, 1991).

Some of the theoretical developments within the Birmingham school have been further accentuated during the latter part of the 1980s, both by former representatives of the school and other researchers. It is to these developments and their results we shall now turn.

YOUTH AND INDIVIDUALITY

During the 1980s and the first years of the 1990s, a new tendency in youth culture theory can be discerned. To the former emphasis on class, gender and race, the impact of the individual and of individual identity has been added. In some cases, the emphasis on class has even been almost completely replaced by that on individuality and identity. As we shall see, however, there are reasons for criticizing this new emphasis in youth culture research. We shall return to this matter later. Here we will simply present a few of the most distinguished representatives of this direction.

Among contemporary youth culture researchers, the German pedagogue Thomas Ziehe has drawn considerable attention in Sweden (see, for instance, Fornäs et al. 1987; 1989). Ziehe (1975/1984, 1989) argues that modern society is characterized by a continual cultural modernization. The norms and values of contemporary society are changing at such a pace that individuals lack the normative guidelines of the past. This in turn has as a consequence the fact that to an increasing extent the individuals reflect upon their own situation, their goals in life and other existential questions. The lack of generally acceptable norms and values in society leads, on the one hand, to an increased freedom of choice regarding how to lead one's life, and on the other, to an increased insecurity and vulnerability. To cope with the difficulties involved in this dual situation, individuals experience constant changes in their identities. According to Ziehe, young people especially are sensitive to these changes of identity. He uses the term *cultural emancipation* (analogously to Marx concept of *economic emancipation*) to describe the conditions of the modern society.

> Today we are experiencing something similar, an emancipation in the cultural sphere. It makes possible new, partly more subtle, mechanisms of expropriation, it often enhances the pressure upon the single individual to choose and to risk to fail — but it is nevertheless a fundamental condition of cultural freedom. Now the single individual has to sketch, try out and redraft his identity, and to do so in the light of an enormously increased social knowledge and enormously increased individual demands (Ziehe 1989:38; Translated by the authors).

In much the same way as Ziehe, in his book *Common Culture* (1990), Paul Willis argued that youth are not passive users of popular culture but active creators of it. Contrary to those researchers who argue that mass media are making its audience passive and uncritical, Willis holds that young people use mass media and clothes in their own manner, creating new meanings out of them.

> Commerce and consumerism have helped to release a profane explosion of everyday symbolic life and activity. The genie of common culture is out of the bottle — let out by commercial carelessness. Not stuffing it back in, but seeing what wishes may be granted, should be the stuff of our imagination (Willis 1990:27).

Willis's main thesis is that young people's use of different kinds of popular cultural goods no longer automatically reflect subcultural affiliations or collective social identities, but that it also involves an active process of conscious, purposeful image-making.

What is probably most significant in the area of youth culture research generally has been the view that popular cultural elements play the most central role in the making and maintenance of different youth cultures. Although we agree that such elements do play an important role, we also maintain that these elements must be related to a wider spectrum of individually held values, attitudes and actions. However, to be able to broaden the perspective we present on youth culture in contemporary society, we must first discuss relations between youth and popular culture. This is the topic of the next section of this chapter.

YOUTH AND POPULAR CULTURE

Youth culture has been conceptualized in many ways, but certain crucial elements have always been included in the concept. At least since the 1950s, young people's culture has been intimately connected with what is usually called mass culture and popular culture. Such elements as rock and pop music, certain clothes and films are often included in the concept of youth culture. In studies of young people's lifestyles, these elements are often used to distinguish between different youth lifestyles. Since these are among the most important cultural elements in young people's lives, we are in no way critical of this.

However, as we have seen in chapter six, one cannot reduce the lifestyles of young people to their merely being expressions of material and aesthetic attitudes and values. Unless the analysis is to remain rather shallow, one has to also consider young people's ethical and metaphysical attitudes and values. In this chapter, however, we shall mainly deal with attitudes and actions which are based on the material and aesthetic values of the individual. The reason for this is that most of the literature on young people's lifestyles which has been concentrates on what is generally called popular culture. This is not to say that and values have been totally missing in this kind of literature, but that when the distinction is made between different youth cultures and youth groups, this is often done in terms of taste in popular music, films, clothes, and other artefacts. It is often said that these tastes and artefacts are consciously and systematically used by youth in order to actively express their identity, attitudes and values, and it is also frequently stated that popular culture is a mass culture influencing the individual in such a way that he or she becomes a conformist and a passive slave of fashion.

There is a tendency to exaggerate each of these views. One side tends to attach too great importance to the individual's conscious and creative use of popular cultural elements as signs and symbols, whereas the other tends to view the individual more or less as a product of market forces and the mass media. The aim of this section is to present a more balanced picture of the multidimensional phenomenon of popular culture and how it is employed in youth culture.

Is There A Mass Culture?

Popular culture has often been designated as mass culture. This term has obtained several negative connotations, due mainly to the fact that it has been frequently used to describe large numbers of persons as being passive and unreflective consumers of popular cultural elements.

An influential grouping in the early debate on mass culture was the Frankfurt School. With the exception of Walter Benjamin, this theoretical school was extremely critical towards mass culture (cf. Benjamin 1968; Jay 1973). In modern books on mass culture the leading representative of the school, Theodore W. Adorno, is often used as an example of how far this negative view on mass culture could go (see, for example, Collins 1989). The following quotation serves well to illustrate Adorno's view:

> The more stereotypes become reified and rigid in the present setup of cultural industry, the less people are likely to change their preconceived ideas with the progress of their experience. The more opaque and complicated modern life becomes, the more people are tempted to cling desperately to clichés which seem to bring some order into the otherwise ununderstandable. Thus, people may not only lose true insight into reality, but ultimately their very capacity for life experience may be dulled by the constant wearing of blue and pink spectacles (Adorno 1957/1964:484).

The basic positions in the debate on mass culture can be found in Rosenberg and White's now classical anthology on *Mass Culture* (Rosenberg & White 1957/1964). In terms of their view, mass culture threatens the autonomy of man and makes the individual a passive and uncritical consumer of mass produced products, almost entirely shaped by the mass media. As Rosenberg (1957/1964:5) puts it:

> There can be no doubt that the mass media present a major threat to man's autonomy. To know that they might also contain some small seeds of freedom only makes a bad situation nearly desperate. No art form, no body of knowledge, no system of ethics is strong enough to withstand vulgarization. A kind of cultural alchemy transforms them all into the same soft currency. Never before have the sacred and the profane, the genuine and the specious, the exalted and the debased, been so thoroughly mixed that they are all but indistinguishable. Who can sort one from the other when they are built into a single slushy compost?

The critique of mass culture is also present in contemporary cultural debate — however, not as unchallenged as it was earlier. In works by theorists as different as, for example, Neil Postman and Jean Baudrillard, we find an explicit critique of the modern mass media and of information technology (Postman 1982; 1985; Baudrillard 1987, 1988). Postman's most influential book on this subject *Amusing Ourselves to Death*, reveals its author's view already in its very title (Postman 1985). Postman's main thesis is that TV's concentration on entertainment impoverishes its audience's possibilities of acquiring an adequate knowledge of the world. He claims that TV is converting the whole world to a scene of skin-deep entertainment.

Baudrillard's view on mass media is perhaps most overtly expressed in his book *The Ecstacy of Communication*, in which he maintains that human beings no longer exist as "playwrights or actors but as terminals of multiple networks" (Baudrillard 1987:16). He often exaggerates the relation between man and modern media techniques in such a way that it becomes pure science fiction (which is also his intention). However, he obviously dislikes the ecstatic obscenity which, according to him, the mass media produce (see, for instance, Kellner 1989).

> Ecstacy is all functions abolished into one dimension, the dimension of communication. All events, all spaces, all memories are abolished in the sole dimension of information: this is obscene (Baudrillard 1987:23f).

At the other extreme we have those who see the individual as an almost totally autonomous and consciously creative user of mass produced cultural elements. This view has become more and more influential in modern theories of mass media, popular culture and youth. In *Mass Culture Revisited* White strongly emphasizes the importance of avoiding the notion of an uncritically consuming mass of people (Rosenberg & White 1971).

> Audiences consist of individuals, who even when they share common viewing
> or reading experiences, use the media to satisfy their own particular purposes. A
> so-called "audience of fifty million" is a statistical amalgam that indiscriminately
> lumps together fifty million distinct individuals, each concerned with fulfilling
> his own needs, goals, and expectations (White 1971:18).

The reaction towards the notion of *the mass audience* has become increasingly influential both in mass media studies (Rosengren et al. 1985; Curran 1990) and in what is commonly called cultural studies (cf. Ang 1985; Carey 1988; Angus 1989; Jensen & Rosengren 1990). The notion of the mass audience is replaced by the notion of *the sovereign individual*, who instead of being a passive consumer is turned into an active and even creative explorer of the rich possibilities inherent in consumer culture.

> Young people learn about their inner selves partly by developing their outer
> image through clothes. They use style in their symbolic work to express and
> develop their understanding of themselves as unique persons, to signify who
> they are, and who they think they are (Willis 1990:89).

It seems to be very difficult to present a balanced description of how young people use mass produced cultural goods such as clothes, records and films. However, it is obviously not the case that all individuals use all the commodities they purchase in such a way as to develop their inner selves in a conscious and creative way. Nor is it the case that youth forms an easily influenced anonymous mass of consumers brainwashed by commercial mass media and the fashion industry.

The problem with the former perspective is that in arguing for people's capacity to express and form an identity of their own it runs the risk of forgetting the individual differences in wishes in ability to use cultural artefacts and images in such a way. The problem with the latter, on the other hand, is that it runs the risk of excluding the possibility of creative and conscious individual use of mass produced cultural elements. With all its negative connotations of conformity, passivity and anonymity, the term *mass culture* is thus not very useful (see also, Modleski 1986; Carey 1988). A much better term in this context is *popular culture*, which is the one we will use from now on.

In the next section we shall try to give a more balanced picture of how young people use and become influenced by popular culture. We will also deal with some of the more specific forms of popular culture important during the period of youth.

Popular Culture and Youth Culture

The intimate connection between such popular cultural elements as jeans, rock and pop music, scooters, movie stars or records and youth culture may be regarded as a post-war phenomenon (Chambers 1986; Snow 1987). Following Chambers we can talk about a historically new interplay between consumption and everyday habits and tastes. More so than other age groups, youth became associated with the consumption of certain types of mass produced artefacts and goods and specific types of popular culture, often connected with the expanding type of popular music generically called rock and pop music. Almost all subcultures of concern to youth researchers have been identitified with rock music — for instance, Teddy-Boys, Rockers, Mods, Skinheads, Punks, and so on.

Much of what has happened in the youth cultural area has also been reflected in the movies. Films like *The Blackboard Jungle* (1953), *Rock Around the Clock* (1956), *Jailhouse Rock* (1957), *Easy Rider* (1969), *Tommy* (1975), *Saturday Night Fever* (1978), *Hair* (1979) *Flashdance* (1983), *Dirty Dancing* (1987), and *Do The Right Thing* (1989), have mirrored the different types of youth cultures and their strong connections to rock and pop music. The films mentioned above picture specific youth or subcultures, but even in films not primarily concerned with youth culture, popular music is often an important part, especially if a film aims at a young audience. Since young people constitute the greatest part of the movie audience, this is the case for most films produced today.

The intimate connection between film, rock and pop music and youth culture is also to be seen in the impact which music video has exerted during the last decade (see, for instance, Kaplan 1987; Denisoff 1988; Grossberg 1989; Wicke 1990; Burnett 1990a; Lööv 1990). Many artefacts and symbols used in youth culture actually have their origin in the stylistic creations of artists displayed in music videos.

During the last decades there has been a tendency within youth culture research to concentrate on style. This tendency has probably been most accentuated in some of the works by representatives of the Birmingham School (see, for instance, Hall and Jefferson 1976; Hebdige 1979). This concentration on style has often resulted in a focus on specific, distinct and rather expressive subcultures such as mods, rockers, hippies, punks and skinheads. Since only a limited number of young people in a society can be said to belong to such distinct subcultural groups, the problem involved in this kind of approach is that the majority of youth are largely neglected. This neglect is further increased when the subcultural approach is combined with a exaggerated emphasis on the creative and conscious use of popular music and other artefacts used by youth. What is forgotten is that many young people do not use music in such an active fashion as is suggested by subculture researchers. As Wicke says:

> Yet in spite of the significance of such sub-cultural contexts in the development of rock music and its different stylistic forms, we must not overlook the fact that these contexts are only supported by a relatively small circle of active fans. Most teenagers only have a more or less playfull relationship with these, one which often changes from one sub-culture to another. Simon Frith is quite correct in pointing out that not every teenager is an active rock fan and not every teenager gives rock music such a binding status in his leisure behaviour (Wicke 1990:89).

Whereas a relatively limited number of youth subcultures have been examined very thoroughly throughout the years, other youth groups have been largely neglected. Such limitations are among other things due to the following:

a) the concentration on youth cultures defined in terms of genres of popular music;

b) the fact that the young people studied have been the most dedicated and conscious followers of a particular youth movement;

c) the fact that foucs being on male youth, *and*

d) the fact that these youth cultures have often involved some idea of protest, thus having been in one way or another identified as threats against the norm system of the society in which they occur.

It is easy, however, to identify other and probably equally distinct youth groups that have not gained any particular attention from youth culture researchers.

First, there are youth groups identified in terms of other music genres than rock and pop music — for instance, fans of different jazz styles, folk music and classical music.

Secondly, it is probably possible to distinguish an countless numbers of youth cultures based on other interests than music. Some arbitrarily chosen examples might be, say, stamp collectors, horror movie fans, hackers, football fans, horseback riders, travellers or fantasy addicts.

Thirdly, the youth cultures that originate among girls have been almost totally neglected in research, which, of course, does not mean that they are missing also in real life. An exception from this neglect is Angela McRobbie's studies of girls' culture (McRobbie & Garber 1976; McRobbie 1991).

Richard Middleton sums up these limitations within subcultural theory nicely:

> The theory neglects particularities and overemphasizes structural coherence, especially in class-determined forms; thus cross-overs, ambiguities and changes in group taste are often missed, along with the role of fashion, maverick enthusiasts and trend setters. Girls are another absence — their alternative uses and valuations of music would threaten the coherence of sub-cultural analyses, just as the absence of unspectacular subcultures (Irish music enthusiasts; old-style dance-band fans; and so on) is necessary to protect the over-simple equation of style and politics. The importance of mainstream commercial pop, where music is a "background" or a "game" rather than a coherent part of a "serious" culture, is played down — despite the fact that the subcultures' own self-definitions and styles are generated in part through a symbiotic relationship with media-disseminated images and broad cultural and social trends (Middleton 1990:167).

To say this, however, is not to say that subculture research is pointless or downwright wrong. This kind of research has provided us with indispensable knowledge about the groups in question. These groups are doubtlessly important parts of youth culture, also in a wider sense: as inventors and trend-setters. There is no denying, however, that youth culture is a much broader concept than subculture, and if one is interested in young people's lifestyles — as we are — the concept of subculture is far from sufficient (see also, Clarke 1981). For attempting to fully comprehend multidimensional youth culture, the concept of lifestyle is more adequate, since it covers not only extreme expressions of youth culture but also mainstream, as well as the not-at-all-spectacular dimensions of youth culture.

Youth culture has been, and still is, intimately connected with popular culture, although one should not forget that the use of popular culture does not exclude the use of legitimate culture (in Bourdieu's terms). The use of popular culture has always been seen as vulgar and blameworthy by the representatives of legitimate culture. Therefore (and hardly surprisingly), youth culture has always been subject to suspicion and condemnation. This condemnation has affected youth culture in different ways. (For instance, popular culture has been restricted in diverse ways, and has also been exposed to censorship). Such restrictions have been aimed particularly against those groups studied by the subculture theorists, but they have nevertheless had great impact also on less distinct youth cultures. In the next section we shall discuss briefly, therefore, what the British researcher Stanley Cohen has called folk devils and moral panics.

Youth Culture, Folk Devils and Moral Panics

> Some contend that rock and roll is bad for
> the body and bad for the soul
> bad for the heart bad for the mind
> bad for the deaf and bad for the blind
> makes some men crazy and then they
> talk like fools makes some men crazy
> and then they start to drool
> Unscrupulous operators could confuse
> could exploit and deceive the conditional
> reflex theories and change the probabilities
> it's crass and rockous crackass place with
> Pavlov on the human race it's a terrible
> illness it's a terrible case and usually
> permanent when it takes place
> it's a teenage nervous breakdown
> it's a nervous teenage breakdown
> it's a tenenerve nervetene
> it's a tennenervenerna
> whoa!
> (Lowell George, Little Feat, 1972).

The attitudes towards rock music ridiculed in the above Little Feat song *Teenage Nervous Breakdown*, have often been the attitudes of adults towards certain kinds of rock and pop music. The same negative attitude has also been directed at other kinds of popular culture, such as movies, videofilms, comics and clothes. In some cases these attitudes towards young people's culture have turned into strong fears, and youth culture has been interpreted as a sign of social breakdown and moral degeneration. Those who interpret youth and its different cultural expressions in this way often put the blame for the moral decline and social disorder they discern on a permissive and liberal attitude in society. They therefore argue for solutions based on control, censorship and prohibitions directed towards different media contents.

> Since the earliest days of the nickelodeon, moralists and reformers had agitated against the corrupting nature of the movies and their effects upon American youth, much as similar groups are concerned about the effects of television in our era. Powerful pressure groups, often working through religious organizations, had been formed to protect American audiences from the display of morally pernicious materials on the screen (Cook 1981/1990:227).

Such fears have occurred in different forms throughout the centuries. Geoffrey Pearson argues in his book *Hooligan. A History of Respectable Fears* (1983) that successive generations have expressed such fears of social and moral decline in contrast to the sound and disciplined order of the past as remembered in a nostalgic way.

> If this long, connected history of respectable fears tells us anything at all, then it is surely that street violence and disorder are a solidly entrenched feature of the social landscape. Hence, they are going to be much more difficult to dislodge than if we imagined that they had suddenly sprung from nowhere in the past twenty years or so; or since the war; or because of the black people in Britain; or because of recent changes in the law; or as a result of "new-fangled" educational philosophies, or television violence, or any other symptom of "permissive" modernity.
> Such commonplace formulae as these, which refuse to grapple with the problems that have exercised the minds and actions of generations before us, trivialise the problem (Pearson 1983:242).

An often quoted work on exaggerations of the negative effects of popular culture on young people and society at large is Stanley Cohen's book *Folk Devils and Moral Panics. The Creation of Mods and Rockers* (1972/1987). Cohen claims that mass media have paid excessive attention to certain youth groups thereby contributing to the creation of a mythology around these groups. These two groups — the Rockers and the Mods as they were labelled — were thus turned into representatives of the decline in moral standards of the younger generation. In Cohen's vivid terms, Mods and Rockers became *Folk Devils*, surrounded by a stock of oversimplified generalisations about young people in general and Mods and Rockers in particular. It is fear built upon such oversimplifications and exaggerations mainly provided by the mass media which Cohen labels *Moral Panics*. He writes:

> Moral panics depend on the generation of diffuse normative concerns, while the successful creation of folk devils rests on their stereo-typical portrayal as atypical actors against a background that is overtypical (Cohen 1972/1987:61).

By and large the overemphasis in mass media (and in youth research) on youth as a problem and on specific and distinct subcultures giving these problems a contour have led to a distorted and stereotyped picture of youth (Cohen 1972/1987; Marsh et al. 1978; Roe 1983; Hebdige 1988). One of the reasons for this stereotypification is the difficulty which can exist in understanding how young people use popular culture and what meaning and symbolic value they ascribe to cultural elements used and integrated by them. Very probably many of the artefacts and elements apprehended by the interpreters as dangerous and demoralizing, were used by youth either rather unreflectedly or as a symbol of something completely different as compared with how, for example, adults, teachers and journalists. conceive of them. In one empirical study Leming has shown that young people interpret rock lyrics in a totally different way than do adults (Leming 1987:378).

One of the main reasons why moral panics occur in a society is that someone or something seems to threaten the more or less commonly held and taken-for-granted values of the society. Few, if any, of the youth groups or subcultures identified as "folk devils" constitute a real threat, however. First, they very seldom challenge the most fundamental values in society, but merely some specific values which they find problematic, and even then not in a fundamental way. Secondly, these values are often aesthetic, which means that what is seen as scary is the way the members of these youth groups dress, the sound their music has and how their hair-styles look — not basic ethical or metaphysical conceptions they hold. Thirdly, the small core of such youth groups may perhaps express disagreement with more basic ethical and metaphysical values, but they are so few that they cannot constitute a real threat — only a symbolic one.

The reactions towards youth groups identified as folk devils depends on a small group of "moulders" who see it as their mission to save society from the folk devils. A suitable term for these groups (mainly teachers, religious groups, journalists and parents) would be *moral* or *social exorcists*. People with such extreme attitudes towards youth groups and popular culture are equally few in numbers, and they themselves constitute a subculture. In turn, the negative attitudes expressed by these moral exorcists may well create reactions among youth which strengthen the position of the "folk devils" being hunted. In their way, moral exorcists thus help create the very devil they themselves seek to exorcise.

Whereas it is only in extreme cases that youth culture and the subcultures generated within it can possibly be a real threat against the social and moral order of society, they may well — although in an extreme and exaggerated way — express more general tendencies within society or among youth.

One of the more problematical tendencies in youth research has been the fact that youth culture has seldom been seen as mere fashion and images, but is often viewed as a very complex system of meaningful symbols and signs. The truth is that it is both, and that there is no need to overstate either. It is also impossible, therefore, to give a definitive answer to the question posed in the title of the next section of this chapter: is youth culture conformist or creative?

Youth Culture — Conformism or Creativity?

It is important to remember that most elements in popular culture contain a strong commercial aspect (Frith 1978, 1983, 1985, 1988). Popular culture goods are produced in order to be sold in as many copies as possible. If a commodity does not sell, it will disappear from the market. This is especially the case for popular music, one of the most lucrative areas of popular culture. The commercial interests in popular music are enormous, which can be illustrated by the fact that a few large record companies control almost the entire Western music market; big record companies strive for global control over the music industry (Wallis & Malm 1984; 1990; Wicke 1990; Burnett 1990b). If an artist or group does not become a commercial success they disappear from the scene. Obviously, therefore, it is the product with a calculatedly high commercial potential that is put on the market. This may lead to difficulties for artists, bands, film makers, designers and the like judged commercially uninteresting. (And one should not forget that "commercially uninteresting" is not the same as artistically uninteresting.) No doubt commercial interests may constitute a threat to artistic creativity and consequently also against the individual's freedom to choose cultural products. This, however, only one side of the coin. As we shall see, there is also a more positive side of it.

Popular culture is produced for the masses. It may also be bought by the masses, but it is not always used by them. With these seemingly contradictory statements we want to say that although many people purchase a certain product (a record or a pair of jeans, for example), they may nevertheless make use of them in totally different ways. One person uses a pair of jeans as a practical piece of clothing for gardening, another because he wants to look young, and yet another because he or she wants to look tough. A pair of jeans makes sense in different ways for different people (Fiske 1989). The same goes for the mass media. As has been shown in a number of studies, people use it and interpret its content in different ways (Blumler & Katz 1974; Radway 1984; Ang 1985; Rosengren et al. 1985; Peterson 1987; Fiske 1989). That is where the creative part of the consumer culture lies.

Fiske (1989) holds that the use of popular cultural goods always contains a more or less creative moment. He also maintains that popular culture is strongly related to different power relations in society. Therefore, in order to be popular, popular cultural products must — in one way or another — be of relevance to the everyday life of its user. According to Fiske, this is the case, since for most people everyday life contains power relations in terms of class, gender, age or race, the use of popular culture being a way for individuals to cope with these power structures and increase their feeling of possessing and exercising power themselves, thus also becoming more self-confident and being able to create a positive image of themselves.

The answer to the question posed in the heading of this section is thus a simple "Yes"; youth culture is conformist and it is also creative, and both the creativity and the conformity are important for its user because, as we shall see, they are related to the different types of identity.

When youth culture researchers discuss the relation between identity development and popular culture they often refer to the creative aspects of youth culture only. However, we will argue that also the conformity aspect of youth culture has an important role to play in young people's identity development. This is because for young people it is as important to belong as it is to differ (cf. Simmel 1904/1971). By accepting the different elements of the culture of various groups, individuals become part of this culture, learning its values, rules, mores, language and symbols. Therefore, a positive attitude towards, say, a film, a pop artist or a song may be due more to the conformity, to the common code of behavior and attitudes of the group, than to the individual's own personal and unique taste. This in turn is explained by the need for the individual to have a social and cultural identity. These parts of identity are by definition conformist, if by the term "conformist" we refer to the mutual acceptance of certain values, attitudes and actions within a group. To say that something is conformist is not the same as to say, however, that it is passive, an insight well expressed by Riesman in the following:

> Most of the teen-agers in the majority category have an undiscriminating taste in popular music; they seldom express articulate preferences. They form the audience for the larger radio stations, the "name" bands, the star singers, the Hit Parade, and so forth. The functions of music for this group are *social* — the music gives them something to talk or kid about with friends; an opportunity for competiveness in judging which tunes will become hits, coupled with a lack of concern about how hits are actually made; an opportunity for identification with star singers or band leaders as "personalities", with little interest in or understanding of the technologies of performance or of the radio medium itself (Riesman 1950/1957:411).

As we have discussed earlier, however, in order to be an individual, one must also have something that makes one different from others; it is this part of identity which we call personal identity. It is in relation to personal identity that the creative aspect of popular culture becomes relevant. The individual's use of popular cultural elements and the meanings ascribed to them help one to enhance a sense of personal freedom, integrity, self-esteem and self-confidence, or — differently expressed — one's unique personal identity.

Different kinds of popular culture are used by different individuals to express and develop their personal identity. Not everyone is equally devoted to or interested in, say, clothes, music and film. Not everyone, therefore, makes active use of these popular cultural elements, which thus vary in how important they are to the individual's personal identity. No doubt for some young people their musical taste is particularly important, for others their clothes — but even this is not for all. We have already observed that for a wide range of young people such cultural activities as sport fishing, stamp collecting, parachuting, scuba diving, horseback riding, sewing, knitting, entomology, belly dancing, chess, travelling, wine tasting, and so on — all activities not very much discussed within youth culture research — constitute a more important part of their identity and lifestyle than do the more commonly discussed areas of music and fashion.

Nevertheless, the use of popular culture — of whatever kind — is of utmost importance for the socialization of the young individual in modern society. Through the use of popular culture he or she learns the roles, values, attitudes and norms of the different social groups to which he or she belongs, using popular culture for self expression, for the development of self and for coping with the different power relations in society and everyday life.

Popular culture, no doubt, is generally something to be looked upon as a positive factor of pleasure and meanings in people's lives (see for example, Jameson 1989; Fiske 1989), but some authors have put their finger on a crucial and important aspect of popular culture and lifestyle, namely its ability to conceal and disguise the real power relations in society. The most important concept in this respect is probably *symbolic democratization* as used by Stuart Ewen (1982; 1988; 1990). It is this concept that is the object of the next section.

LIFESTYLE AND SYMBOLIC DEMOCRATIZATION

To identify the social position of a person by means of what clothes he or she wears is not as easy today as it once was. Although still very unevenly distributed. In pace with the growing prosperity in Western industrialized societies, individuals' incomes have become more equal. There are still great differences, of course, in access to economic capital, both between and within different classes and status groups. However, the welfare state has given most people enough money to not only satisfy their basic needs, but also to consume for pleasure. Discretionary income has grown. Therefore, one way of labelling modern society is to describe it as a *consumer society* (Bell 1976; Featherstone 1990a, 1991b).

Style and fashion have become important matters for modern man, not least among youth, and the style market supplies one with an infinite number of images and symbols by means of which one can try to construct what one wants to be or to become. This is not always equivalent to what one actually is or can become, however.

> If the style market constitutes a presentation of a way of life, it is a way of life that is unattainable for most, nearly all, people. Yet this doesn't mean that style isn't relevant to most people. It is very relevant. It is the most common realm of our society in which the need for a better, or different way of life is acknowledged, and expressed on a material level, if not met. It constitutes a politics of change, albeit a "change" that resides wholly on the surface of things. The surfaces, themselves, are lifted from an infinite number of sources (Ewen 1988:16).

In modern society, style is a very complicated phenomenon, and it functions in differing ways. One way it functions is as a generator of illusory transcendence of class. Stuart Ewen calls this process *symbolic democratization*. Thus, by developing a certain style in clothes or other material objects the individual can create a sense of partaking in what is seen as a desirable style of life, as it is presented in the mass media (cf. Schudson 1986). By possessing the goods identified with the powerful, the free and the beautiful, the individual develops a feeling of having power, beauty and freedom. Prior to the consumer society, the symbols of power, beauty and freedom were possessed by only those who had actual power. In the modern consumer society, however, the very symbols, due to their mass production, have been made available on a mass scale to the common man. Real power, on the contrary, is still in the hands of an elite. Thus the increasingly equal distribution of power symbols does not correspond with a more equal distribution of actual power. In this sense symbolic democratization is a form of false consciousness.

According to our view, the process of symbolic democratization has two sides: on the one hand, it may create an illusion, an inhibiting factor on the individual's capability to analyze and influence his or her social and cultural position. The person may become an obedient, submissive, uncritical and conform citizen; on the other hand, symbolic democratization may help one to develop one's self-confidence, her personality and identity, which in its turn may generate an awareness of one's capability of influencing one's situation and in that way also to assume at least some degree of real power.

Featherstone (1990a,b 1991a,b) has analyzed similar aspects of modern consumer culture. He claims that the possibilities to develop and refine a lifestyle differ between different classes, status and age groups in modern consumer culture (Featherstone 1990b; 1991b). Featherstone (1991b) argues that besides the new middle class (for instance, managers, scientists and technicians) in modern consumer society there has also developed an expanding group which with Bourdieu he calls the *new cultural intermediaries*. He thus describes this group:

> These are engaged in providing symbolic goods and services that were referred to earlier — the marketing, advertising, public relations, radio and television producers, presenters, magazine journalists, fashion writers, and the helping professions (social workers, marriage councellors, sex therapists, dieticians, play leaders, etc.) (Featherstone 1991b:44; cf. Bourdieu 1979/1984).

Still following Bourdieu, Featherstone also calls this group *the new intellectuals*. They are important in the lifestyle discussion, because they may be regarded as a kind of professional lifestyle creators, constantly engaged in seeking new experiences. The group is therefore also called "the new heroes of consumer culture", depending on their making lifestyle into a life project.

> They are fascinated by identity, presentation, appearance, lifestyle, and the endless quest for new experiences (...). Indeed their awareness of the range of experiences open to them, the frequent lack of anchoring in terms of a specific locale or community, coupled with the self-consciousness of the autodidact, who always wishes to become more than he/she is, leads to refusal to be classified, with the injunction to assist fixed codes as life is conceived as essentially open-ended (Featherstone 1991:44).

The function served by these new intellectuals is to legitimatize for intellectual analysis such traditional non-intellectual areas as sport, fashion and popular music, in this way supplying new symbolic goods and experiences to adherents of the lifestyles of the new middle class audience which they themselves have partly helped to create (Featherstone 1987, 1991b).

Especially important in the theories launched by Ewen and Featherstone is the critical analysis of the relation between social class or status and the development of individual lifestyles.

The use of popular culture among youth makes the concept of symbolic democratization a useful one, especially in youth culture research. Contemporary youth can be said to have a common foundation in their use of popular culture. Most young people listen to the same pop and rock music, watch the same films and videos, wear the same jeans, etc. On the surface, therefore, they may seem to be quite a homogeneous group of the population (with the exceptions of some small but rather conspicuous subcultural groups.) However, even though most young people, independent of class and gender, use very much the same cultural symbols, they use them in differing ways and with differing awareness. The symbols also mean differing things to them. This is impossible to notice at the first glance, however. It presupposes an intimate knowledge of the subtle distinctions made by different youth groups and different individuals. As already mentioned, popular culture thus serves both as an integrating force (or as symbolic democratization), and as a means of distinguishing oneself or one's group from other ones. On the one hand, young people use popular culture to distinguish themselves from the generation of their parents and teachers, and on the other, to make distinctions between themselves.

These twin processes will be further examined in the empirical part of our book. Before turning to a presentation of the results of our studies of young people in two Swedish cities, we will summarize our theory of lifestyle and youth culture, drawing together all its different threads. That is the aim of the next chapter.

CHAPTER 10
ELEVEN THESES ON LIFESTYLES AND YOUTH CULTURE IN CONTEMPORARY SOCIETY

Thus far, we have discussed a number of different concepts and phenomena. We have also tried to relate the concepts to each other. For obvious reasons, however, it is not our intention, to declare our theory to be *the* theory of lifestyle and youth culture. What we have arrived at is rather *a* theory of youth culture and lifestyle, a theory which is in line with our views on the phenomena at issue.

The key concept in any theory of lifestyle is, no doubt, that of change. Not only do the lifestyles existing in a society constantly undergo alterations as time goes by, but also the lifestyle of the single individual develops and changes during the person's lifetime. This being the case, one of the purposes of this book is to study, theoretically and empirically, cultural change on different levels of analysis. We start with a number of assumptions concerning lifestyle in contemporary Western society which have grown out of our work during the past few years. Before turning to the presentation of the empirical results of the study, we shall briefly sum up various such assumptions. We will present them in terms of the theses listed below. In so doing, we want to draw attention to certain problematic areas within the lifestyle discourse, on the one hand, and to start off with these assumptions when presenting and analyzing our empirical results, on the other.

1) During post-war modernity *the process of individualization has deepened*. People's value orientations have changed from emphasizing such values as material welfare and physical security to increasingly emphasizing values such as psychological growth and self-realization. These changes concern the younger generations to a greater degree than the older ones.

2) Lifestyles are not determined solely by the social structure or by such positional variables as class, gender, age or education, but also to a considerable degree by *the individual's unique characteristics*, personality and identity. In order to understand the lifestyle phenomenon, it is necessary, therefore, to take into consideration the complex interplay taking place between social structure, the individual's position within it, and the unique characteristics of the individual.

3) During the course of their life, individuals often alter their position in the social structure. That is, they are mobile in various respects. Such mobility can be defined in terms of access to cultural, social or economic competence. In discussing lifestyle, the notions of cultural capital and mobility constitute the basic concepts, but obviously *cultural mobility* cannot be studied in isolation from *social mobility*.

4) Since an individual does not develop and form his or her lifestyle in a vacuum, but within certain structural frameworks and in relation to different groups of other individuals, the role of lifestyle is manifold. However important it may be for anyone to distinguish oneself from others and express one's uniqueness and individuality, it is equally important that one show one's belonging to different groups. Still another function of lifestyles is to help the individual to create an image, whether true or false, of oneself and one's status in relation to other people and groups of people in society. In this context, Ewen's concept of *symbolic democratization* provides a useful analytical tool.

5) In order to fully understand the anatomy of the lifestyle concept, one must realize that behind all the visible expressions and signs which we designate as lifestyle, there exist a number of fundamental values. If one does not understand the relations between the individual's fundamental conceptions — or values — and the ways in which the individual consciously or unconsciously makes use of his or her attitudes and actions to express and visualize these conceptions to others, lifestyles are, and will remain, patterns of pastiches which are incomprehensible and superficial. The lifestyles of individuals can thus be conceptualized as actions manifesting attitudes based on values. That is, to a higher or lesser degree, the seemingly superficial actions and artefacts constituting a lifestyle have their origins in *individual value structure*. This is not to say, however, that this order is perfectly predictable and that irrationality does not exist.

6) In order to understand lifestyle and identity it is not sufficient to consider the outer-directed values — material or aesthetical — basically related to social identity. Neither is it sufficient to consider only the inner-directed values — ethical or metaphysical — related to personal identity. It is in the complex interplay between personal and social identity, and between *inner-directed* and *outer-directed* values, that we must look for the cultural components of identity, and thus the lifestyle of the individual. It is also important to consider whether the function of the individual's values

are primarily to establish *security or* to promote *development.*

7) Though it does not constitute the entire identity, lifestyle is an important component of a person's identity. Basically, an individual's lifestyle is related to his or her *cultural identity*, but it is also influenced by the personal and social parts of the person's identity.

8) During what we have called socially and culturally defined youth, the individual becomes more and more autonomous and aware of his or her own cultural identity and lifestyle. Even though it never disappears totally, the influence and of parents, siblings and peer groups on such matters becomes less important. In short: during this period of youth, the individual becomes more and more aware of himself/herself as an *autonomous cultural being.*

9) Youth culture is *conformist* as well as *creative.* That is, it is just as important to express one's individuality and uniqueness as it is to define oneself as a member of different cultural and social groups.

10) Empirically and methodologically it is possible to quantitatively distinguish in several different ways between a number of different lifestyles of the people in a given society. Such patterns are by definition quite general and do not say much about the purely individual characteristics of a given lifestyle. However, such empirical quantifications may help us to achieve a preliminary *categorization of the lifestyles in a society.* They also help us to distinguish some general traits of lifestyles. To understand the equally important particular traits of lifestyle and how single individuals relate to the general patterns, however, one must also study how particular individuals construct and develop their lifestyle. Studies of both types are necessary in order to reach a full understanding of the concept and phenomenon of lifestyle.

11) No doubt mass media play a central role in shaping cultural identity and lifestyle during the period of youth. Especially tastes in popular music and film comprise important features of the lifestyle of youth. Therefore it is of utmost importance to study intensely and carefully relations between *popular culture* as mediated by the mass media on the one hand, and lifestyle, on the other.

PART THREE:

METHODOLOGICAL CONSIDERATIONS AND METHODS EMPLOYED

CHAPTER 11
MEASURING VALUE AND LIFESTYLE

MEASURING VALUE

A problem related to terminological and theoretical aspects of the value and lifestyle concepts is that of how the two phenomena can be made empirically accessible. Despite various attempts over the years to measure human values as well as lifestyles no great advances in this direction have been made and no completely convincing solutions have yet been obtained. In this chapter we will discuss a number of central problems related to the empirical measurement of lifestyles and values.

Three Ways of Measuring Values

Methodology is always closely related to theory. During attempts in the past decades to develop acceptable methods for the empirical measurement of human values, three theories have become particularly influential. These are the theories of Arnold Mitchell, Ronald Inglehart and Milton Rokeach.

The empirical methods founded on Mitchell's theories are generally referred to as *The Values and Lifestyle Program* (VALS) (Mitchell 1983). As already mentioned, in classifying Americans into nine different lifestyles Mitchell has employed Maslow's well-known hierarchy of needs as his theoretical starting point. Methodologically he has proceeded in the following way. He has asked his respondents to consider approximately thirty different statements of more or less general character. The attitudes towards these statements are used as indications of both the values and the lifestyles embraced by the respondents. The distinction between the value concept and the lifestyle concept becomes in this way completely blurred in Mitchell's terminology and methodology, the two concepts tending to be dealt with as more or less interchangeable. Mitchell's definition of value is also rather broad, covering a number of different phenomena usually distinguished from the value concept, such as attitudes, beliefs, opinions, hopes, fears, prejudices, needs, and desires (Mitchell 1983).

Mitchell's VALS-typology has had a rather strong influence internationally. Hans Zetterberg (1977, 1983), in particular, has adapted Mitchell's method to Swedish conditions.

Mitchell's way of using the value concept is completely incompatible with our theory of value. Mitchell is surely on the right track in stating that all phenomena covered by his definition of value are important in discussing lifestyles, but we are convinced that Mitchell, his predecessors and his followers make a serious mistake in using the term value as ambiguously as they do. Values are definitely something different from attitudes, prejudices, convictions and opinions, and the value concept is clearly not equivalent with that of lifestyle.

In addition, there cannot be said to be exactly nine lifestyles, or even ten, or fifteen, or a hundred. It is basically impossible to exactly define or identify the number of lifestyles in a society. How many and what kind of lifestyles one can empirically discern depends on the operationalization of the concept. The nine American lifestyles Mitchell discusses are simply constructs resulting from his way of operationalizing the lifestyle phenomenon.

There are also good reasons for questioning the naturalistic assumption that people's values and lifestyles are founded on human needs — something Mitchell's use of Maslow's theory of the relation between psychological growth and human needs suggests. The risk is that in such a theoretical framework both values and lifestyles are reduced to human needs. In order to adequately study the relation between human needs and human lifestyles it is necessary — just as when one studies the relation between value and lifestyle — to keep the concepts clearly apart.

Ronald Inglehart (1977, 1990), too, builds parts of his theory on Maslow's hierarchy of needs. He believes that values in Western societies have changed from emphasizing material wealth and physical comfort, to placing an increased emphasis on quality of life, a dimension encompassing both a material (instrumental) and a post-material (expressive) value orientation. Indicators of these two value orientations are obtained by presenting three lists to respondents, each of which contains four different societal goals: two of the goals indicating a material value orientation, and two of them a postmaterial value orientation. Respondents are asked to rank order the desirability of the four goals on each list. Much like Mitchell, Inglehart does not attempt to identify specific values ibut concentrates on the two value orientations he is concerned with. As is the case with Mitchell's empirical approach Inglehart's method of empirically measuring value-orientations has gained widespread international recognition (Gibbins 1989).

In Sweden it has been discussed and applied by Bo Reimer (1988, 1989) and Thorleif Pettersson (1988).

Rokeach, finally, has developed the most elaborate and clear-cut value theory and value definition of the three value-theoreticians referred to here. In *The Nature of Human Values* (1973), Rokeach defines values as enduring prescriptive or condemning idea in relation to a personally or socially desirable end-state (cf. Ball-Rokeach et al. 1984). Having their origin in culture, in society and its institutions, and in personality, values are nevertheless universal. According to Rokeach values are organized in what he calls value-systems.

Rokeach maintains that the total number of values embraced by any individual is always limited to about twenty, and that it is possible to identify and measure each of them. He endeavors to do so by having his respondents rank eighteen basic values which he identified earlier in a series of carefully designed preparatory studies. The resulting rank order is regarded as an indication of the value-system of the individual. This and similar value-measurements are usually referred to as *List of Values* (LOV).

The most important difference between Rokeach and the other two theoreticians mentioned is that Rokeach, unlike the other two makes no naturalistic assumptions about the nature of human values. Rather, his theory of value is subjectivistic. In addition Rokeach — unlike Mitchell and Inglehart — actually discerns and identifies a number of separate human values.

Some General Problems With Measuring Values

Certain difficulties affecting empirical value-studies have to do with the fact that there is theoretical disagreement about the very nature of human values. To be able to measure something, one must first know what it is one wants to measure. As mentioned in chapter 6 four basic types of theories about the nature of human values have been dominant throughout the history of the philosophy of value: objectivistic or deontological theories, subjectivistic or teleological theories, naturalistic theories, and emotivistic or nihilistic theories.

Without an extensive axiological discussion, which is beyond the scope of the present study it is of course impossible to judge which one of the theoretical orientations is most adequate. However, regardless of one's choice of value theory, the choice will by necessity also affect the empirical work. Most empirical attempts to study values within the social sciences seem to rest upon some more or less well elaborated naturalistic theory. This is the case, for instance, with Mitchell's and Inglehart's theories.

Another general difficulty which appears in empirical value studies has to do with the ranking technique employed (for instance, both by Inglehart and Rokeach). Ranking techniques presuppose that it is possible for an individual to mutually rank a given number of identified values, that is, to conduct a *value-calculation*. There are different types of values, and these may well be mutually incomparable. Is it possible, for instance, to compare an ethical value with an aesthetic? Is it possible to compare "the beautiful' with "the good' and to say which one is preferable to the other? Probably not, since the criteria against which we judge ethical phenomena are totally different from the ones against which we judge aesthetic phenomena.

Yet another difficulty tends to emerge within such empirical approaches as that of Rokeach's, where a number of values are identified and given to respondents to rank order. In most cases, these values are so abstract and equivocal that the terms used to designate them may well have partly or even completely different connotations for different individuals.

Given the importance of these very general problems, it is rather surprising that so scant attention has been paid to them within the social sciences. Even if it is impossible to solve these problems — or in the present context to even discuss them sufficiently — the value researcher should nevertheless bear them in mind, regardless of which empirical approach he or she actually applies.

LOV or VALS?

The methodology most often used in studies where both values and lifestyles are involved is the so called VALS-typology. As already mentioned, however, the problem with VALS is the weak distinction made between these two concepts, theoretically as well as empirically. The rather broad definition of the value concept constitutes another problem, since in this approach it embraces as divergent phenomena as needs, attitudes, prejudices, wishes and convictions. Furthermore, no specific values are identified within this tradition. Thus in using VALS it is difficult to study empirically the relation between lifestyles and values, since this would of courses presuppose that the two concepts be clearly distinguished from each other.

The method developed by Inglehart aims at determining the positions of individuals on a dimension extending from material (instrumental) to post-material (expressive) value-orientations. Inglehart does not identify any particular values. Instead, he uses individuals' attitudes towards a number of societal goals as indicators of what their positions are on the dimension in which he is interested — not of which values are important to them. This is the main reason why Inglehart's method is not sufficient for investigating the relation between values and lifestyles.

The obvious alternative to Inglehart, and to VALS, is LOV, and primarily Rokeach's Value Survey (RVS). This method is exclusively focused upon measuring values, and Rokeach also supplies a list of eighteen values founded on extensive theoretical and empirical study. Rokeach also provides a detailed and univocal definition of the value concept as distinct from all the concepts embedded in, for instance, Mitchell's definition of value.

The difference between LOV and VALS has been discussed by Kahle et al. (1986) with respect to each method's possibilities of expressing the relations between persons' values and their patterns of consumption. They conclude that:

> The results imply that LOV significantly predicts consumer behaviour trends more often than does the VALS scoring system... (Kahle et al 1986:409).

As previously indicated actions of realizing interests, and thus patterns of consumption (what one buys, leisure activities, etc.), are one of the four different types of actions based on material values and attitudes which form the basis for the lifestyle of an individual. Kahle's and his co-author's results thus constitute yet another motive for using the LOV method in a study focused on the relation between values and lifestyles.

The LOV strategy demands, however, that one decide whether, as Rokeach did one should use a ranking technique or if one should apply some sort of rating technique such as, for example, a Likert scale.

Ranking or Rating

There are at least two different ways of using the LOV method in order to measure human values: ranking and rating. In the former case, one lets respondents rank the values. In the latter case, one lets them consider each of the identified values without ranking them in relation to each other. The first method is called "ranking", while the second is called "rating" (cf. Munson 1984; Reimer 1985; De Casper & Tittle 1988). Discussions in the literature regarding method's advantages and disadvantages has not as yet led to any unequivocal answer as to which method is best.

The ranking technique demands that the respondent differentiate between the values she or he has to order. This means that one gets more variation in the distribution of the answers from each respondent than if a rating technique is used. This in turn means that in factor-analysing the answers one in most cases gets more and better factors than if the rating technique is applied (De Casper & Tittle 1988). Furthermore, in applying the ranking technique, the values tend for natural reasons to be negatively correlated with one another, wheras the rating technique tends to create positive correlations between the different values.

One of the arguments often used to support the ranking technique is that values by their very nature contain a comparative element. This assumption is by no means obvious, however. Within the philosophy of value the possibility of so-called value calculi has often been discussed and questioned. There are different types of values that just cannot be compared to each other. Such value calculations, therefore, run the risk of being empty constructs without any correspondence in reality. If a rating technique is used, however, the problem of different values' incomparability can be avoided. If, on the other hand, one uses a ranking technique, one may assume, for good reasons, that artificial contrasts between the different values will emerge (Alwin & Krosnick 1985).

This fact is a strong argument for using a rating strategy, but it is not the only one. Michael Munson gives at least five other reasons why a rating technique is preferable to the ranking technique in using RVS:

1. Rank order data provides less information than higher ordered interval or ratio-scaled data in that it forces values which may be viewed as equally important by the individual into separate ranked categories.

2. Ranking ignores differences in the intensity with which a particular value is held. Large differences in the importance attached to two consecutively ranked values cannot be distinguished from smaller differences. (...)

3. The ranking instructions (...) do not permit the individual to distinguish between the situationally induced need for the value and the ascribed status attached to the value. (...)

4. Rank order data preclude the use of more powerful parametric statistical procedures which many marketing and/or other problems in the social sciences require for their analysis.

5. Forced rank ordering which does not allow for ties (as used by Rokeach) can produce ipsativity in the data (Munson 1984, 19).

In using Rokeach's Value Survey there are thus several reasons for applying the rating instead of the ranking technique. It is thus this technique that has been used in the present study.

Rokeach Modified

The method used in this study is a modified version of Rokeach's method. The fact that the ranking technique has been abandoned in favour of the rating technique means that the empirical method employed has been made partly inconsistent with Rokeach's value theory. Rokeach holds that a value is by definition desirable for all humans, whereas the Likert-scale used in our 1988-survey covered alternatives ranging from "Not at all important" to "Very important". The fact that it is very difficult for an individual to consider as unimportant any of the eighteen values Rokeach identified, led to the variation between the answers of our respondents being rather small. Quite naturally, most respondents usually chose one of the alternatives expressing a positive attitude towards the values in question.

In the 1990-survey we tried to solve this problem by excluding the negative alternatives, instead using five positive alternatives with a Likert-scale. In this form the scale ranges from the alternative "Quite important" to the alternative "Absolutely necessary". This modification of the scale had positive results. Compared to the 1988-survey, the variation in the answers of the respondents increased (Miegel & Dalquist 1991).

The perhaps most significant difference between Rokeach's original method and the one used within the LOM-project, however, is that to the list of eighteen values have been added six new ones, each of which was considered to be as important as the values which Rokeach distinguished. The six new values are: *justice, power, wealth, a clean world, health,* and *technological development*. Unfortunately, one of the values (true friendship) originally included in Rokeach's list of values was lost by mistake in printing the questionnaire used in the 1988 survey. In order to maintain as high a comparability as possible in 1990, we decided to exclude this value in the second survey as well.

MEASURING LIFESTYLE

To Measure Lifestyle

Just as in the case of values, a number of different methods have been
suggested for the operationalizing and empirical study of lifestyles. The
method chosen depends on the discipline of the researcher, the aims of the
research, and/or its topic. It is would be quite natural, for example, in a
medical application of the lifestyle concept aiming at gaining an
understanding of the relation between lifestyle and, say, ulcers or obesity,
empirical efforts were concentrated on such things as alcohol, tobacco, food
and excercising habits (see, for example, Berardo et al. 1985). For the same
reason, it is not very surprising that market researchers interested in the
relation between people's lifestyles and their tendency to consume different
goods or services often operationalize lifestyle as actual consumption (see,
for instance, Pitts & Woodside 1984).

Such seemingly inconsistent empirical points of departure are actually
quite natural consequences of the researcher's interest in different aspects of
lifestyle. Thus these various alternatives can be seen as equally relevant as
lifestyle indicators — but as being applied in different ways and in different
areas. However, no one of them alone can account for the complete
phenomenon of lifestyle. This is due to the fact that the lifestyle of an
individual needs to be seen as a pattern consisting of at least four different
types of actions, each of them expressing a number of different attitudes
based on the fundamental material, aesthetic, ethical and metaphysical
conceptions which constitute the values of the individual. In this sense, each
one of these types of actions constitutes one aspect of an individual's
lifestyle. Only when taken together can they give a complete picture of that
lifestyle.

As a rule, the many attempts made hitherto within different fields of
reasearch to empirically study lifestyle have been based on just one or
possibly two of these types of actions, never on all four of them. To provide
a complete picture of people's lifestyles would be an almost impossible task
empirically. Even doing so for any one of the four different types of actions
constituting a given lifestyle would represent an impressive task indeed. As a
rule, therefore, the lifestyles distinguished by different researchers depend
on a) which of the four types of actions has been considered, *and* b) what
aspects of these types of actions the researcher has concentrated upon.

Expressed differently, the outcome depends on what lifestyle indicators have been used.

Lifestyle Indicators

To a considerable extent the various lifestyles found in different empirical studies are the product of the measuring instruments used. A measuring instrument represents an operationalizing of a concept considered to be an indicator of lifestyles. As lifestyle indicators, researchers in the area have as a rule used activities, actions and behaviors based on the individual's material and/or aesthetic attitudes and values. One reason for this is that a great deal of lifestyle research has in one way or another been related to different kinds of market research. Because of this, it is only natural to use persons' actual consumption, tastes, preferences and interests when classifying them into different lifestyles.

There are various other areas, however, in which the concept of lifestyle may be of relevance but where material and aesthetic indicators are of only limited interest. One can readily assume there to be a relationship, for example, between people's lifestyles and their political behaviour (in connection with, say, an election). Obviously if one were to study such a relation, ethically and metaphysically based lifestyle indicators would probably be of greater relevance than material and aesthetic ones.

It is probably also the case that different lifestyle indicators are differentially relevant to different groups in society. If one intends to study the lifestyles of teenagers, one probably has to use another measurement instrument than if one intends to study the lifestyles of senior people. In discussing on which grounds one wants to classify a group of people into different lifestyles, it is thus very important to consider positional factors: gender, age, class and education.

We have concentrated our empirical efforts on four areas which we consider to be crucial components in most young people's culture. Of these, three concern attitudes and one activities. Since we also measure values, we cover at least certain aspects of each of the three conceptual levels — value, attitude and action — which we use in order to understand how the lifestyle of an individual is structured.

In studying attitudinal level, we have considered only *taste* for music, film and clothes. This means we have operationalized phenomena basically founded on the aesthetic values of the respondents. However, other types of values influence the tastes of individuals too, but probably to a smaller degree. The implications of the concentration on basically aesthetic attitudes are that, just as many other lifestyle researchers, we are faced with the limitation of primarily capturing lifestyle components based on the outer-directed values, missing the equally important components based on inner-directed values.

Operationalizing, on the action-level involves the asking of a number of questions concerning how frequently respondents practice some fifty different leisure time activities. These operationalizations are not subject to the problems of measurements at the attitudinal level, since the leisure time activities considered range over a multitude of different areas, not just a few distinct areas, as is the case in our study of the attitude level.

This discrepancy between the results of our theoretical lifestyle discussions and our empirical efforts havequite natural explanations, however. The research project (LOM) on which we depend for our empirical material has a long theoretical and empirical tradition, reaching back more than a decade before we joined the project. The unique longitudinal design of LOM, its focus on the mass media, and its relation to its predecessor MEDIA PANEL, quite naturally have exerted considerable influence on the theoretical as well as the empirical design of the LOM project. We entered the project before having begun to fully develop the theory of lifestyle put forward in this book. Influenced as we were by previous lifestyle research in designing the LOM questionnaires, our lifestyle questions concerned primarily such typical youth culture phenomena as taste in film, music and clothes, and leisure time activities.

Furthermore, our concentration on variables such as values and taste in film, music and clothes which either were not used in the MEDIA PANEL project or were not as elaborated as in the LOM-questionnaires, have unfortunately made it almost impossible for us to take advantage of the possibilities inherent in longitudinal analyses. These possibilities, however, will be utilized by other researchers within the project on areas common to the MEDIA PANEL and the LOM projects.

The empirical problems referred to above originate from the fact that within a project of the size and range of LOM there are several individual researchers involved, each with his or her specific interests and theoretical and methodological perspectives. It is difficult, therefore, to completely satisfy the interests and cover the perspectives of each individual researcher within one project. On the other hand, there are also major advantages in working within a large project such as LOM. The access to previously collected data, the theoretical and methodological knowledge and experience of the research team and the work conducted by its present and previous members are just a few such advantages.

While such advantages are invaluable, the problems inherent in working within a larger research program can always be at least satisfactorily overcome by complementary data collections. This is one important reason for conducting a number of case studies, designed to fit our interests and theoretical perspective, and through which we can at least throw some additional empirical light on our theoretical assumptions.

Ideal Type Lifestyles and Individual Lifestyles

An important methodological distinction to be made in lifestyle research is between different levels of analysis. We will distinguish between two levels of analysis, the macro and the micro level (Lööv & Miegel 1989).

Lifestyles can be analyzed from both a macro and a micro perspective. On the macro level, lifestyles can be regarded as some form of ideal type cultural patterns. Such patterns are abstract theoretical constructions, consisting of a number of common characteristics, for various reasons judged to be important to an understanding of lifestyle phenomena.

On the macro level of analysis we are mainly concerned with different kinds of social and cultural structures and positionally distinguished social formations within the structures which, in a sense, set the framework for individual action and interaction. On this level of analysis at least two different types of observational data may be used: macro data such as historical documents, etc., and aggregated individual data.

The unit of study on the micro level, on the other hand, is the single and unique individual with distinctive features who has established more or less unique relationships with the various social and cultural conditions found on the structural and positional levels of determination.

According to the creator of the concept of ideal types, Max Weber, sociology should aim at understanding social action and the meaning which the individual ascribes to his or her behavior, actions, thoughts, etc. Weber also stressed that society and its structures are constantly developing and changing, and that in order to keep up with these changes, social science itself must change accordingly. The same goes for concepts used by social scientists as tools for reconstructing social actions and events. In this sense, concepts are constructs consisting of those features which the constructor chooses to regard as important for understanding the phenomenon at issue (Weber 1924/1968).

Making use of the notion of ideal types, one can discern a number of more or less clearly articulated lifestyle patterns within a society. Further theoretical refinement of the various patterns thus distinguished can allow them to be conceived in a gradually purer form, so that they finally represent as what we like to call *ideal types of lifestyles*.

Individuals within a society take on elements from several of these patterns; depending on which pattern is predominant for a given individual, one can locate him/her within one or more ideal types of lifestyles. Most individuals have characteristics which make them candidates for more than one — sometimes even contradictory appearing — lifestyles. The ideal types of lifestyles are aggregates consisting of individually determined characteristics, and are thus analyzed from a macro perspective. In fact, however, every individual has her or his own personal and unique lifestyle: what we call an *individual lifestyle*. In order to cope with this dilemma, we must move on to the micro level, where it is necessary to study aspects of the individual's personality and identity development.

It is quite possible to study forms of life and ways of living on both the macro and micro level. In our view, however, the micro level is especially well suited to the study of individual lifestyles. Individual lives are partly determined by structural and positional characteristics. However, within existing societal structures individuals also adopt their own specific lifestyles. We will therefore argue that the concept of individual lifestyles should be applied on the micro level of analysis. We will return to this question in more detail in discussing the empirical results of this study.

CHAPTER 12
SAMPLE AND METHOD

THE DESIGN OF THE PROJECT "LIFESTYLE AND MASS MEDIA CULTURE"

The project *Lifestyle and Media Culture* (LOM) has grown out of a long-term Swedish research program, the *Media Panel Program* (MPP), which is being carried out by a research group at the Department of Sociology of the University of Lund (Rosengren & Windahl et al 1989; Rosengren 1991a).

MPP consists of a number of panel and cross-sectional studies which since 1975 have been conducted on some 5,000 children, adolescents and young adults. The majority of these studies have been conducted in the cities of Malmö and Växjö (230,000 and 60,000 inhabitants) in the counties of Skåne and Småland, respectively. The Malmö-panel consists of a representative sample of the population under study, and usual tests of reliability and representativeness have been undertaken (Rosengren & Windahl 1989). The Växjö sample is made in a somewhat different way, and though this sample most probably are representative too, we must, in the name of honesty, give a brief description of how the different samples were made.

The study conducted within the LOM project involves three cohorts: individuals born in Malmö 1969 (M69), individuals born in Växjö 1969 (V69) and individuals born in Växjö 1963 (V63). Altogether, the sample for the LOM-project consists of 676 individuals, the Malmö panel consists of 229 individuals, the V69-panel of 228 individuals and the V63-panel of 219 individuals (Jarlbro et al 1989; Rosengren & Windahl et al 1989; Miegel & Dalquist 1991). However, the sample for the LOM-project differs from the original sample for the MEDIA PANEL-project, due among other things to panel mortality and various descicions made by researchers within the MEDIA PANEL-project. It is necessary, therefore, to say something about the two original samples used in this book.

The sample was constructed and the first data collection made in the M69-panel in 1975; thereafter, data from this panel has been collected on six other occasions. The two latest of these collections — 1988 and 1990 — have been carried out within the LOM-project. The individuals chosen for the initial data collection in 1975 consisted of a representative sample of 303 individuals, of which for various reasons 50 were excluded. Thus the original sample of the M69-panel consisted of 253 individuals. At the time of the first data collection within the LOM-project, 229 of these individuals were remaining.

The sample construction and first data collection for the V69-panel were made in 1978; thereafter, data has been collected on five different occasions (the two latest of these were carried out within the LOM-project). The original sample consisted of 250 individuals. The individuals were chosen from nearly all the schools in Växjö, but for practical reasons only a given number of classes from each school could be included. The reason for this was that the size of the sample were decided to include 250 individuals. The total number of the population were approximately twice as many.

Since the data collection was carried out during school time, it was most convenient, for the teachers as well as for the researchers engaged in the collection, to use all pupils in a number of classes rather than picking a number of individuals from all classes. Of the originally 250 individuals, some 228 remained at the time of the first data collection within the LOM-project.

The empirical data for this particular study (LOM), were collected on two different occasions: during the spring of 1988 and the spring of 1990. On both these occasions mail questionnaires were distributed to the individuals belonging to the three panels mentioned above.

Panel mortality is a problem, of course, but it has been possible to keep it at a fairly low level, and tests indicate that, even in the two latest panel waves, the individuals remaining do not deviate in any significant way from those in the original sample (Jarlbro et al. 1989; Dalquist 1991).

Taken together, the three panels of the LOM-project consisted of 676 individuals. On the first occasion, the spring of 1988, 486 individuals returned the questionnaire (72%). The response rate was 85% in Malmö, and 74% (V69) and 58% (V63) for the two groups in Växjö (Jarlbro et al. 1989). On the second occasion, the spring of 1990, 438 individuals returned the questionnaire (66%). The response rate was 72% in Malmö, and 70% (V69) and 57% for the two groups in Växjö (V63) (Dalquist 1991).

THE SAMPLE

The study presented in this book is primarily based on the two panels *Malmö-69* and *Växjö-69*. The reasons for excluding *Växjö-63* are the low response rate for the individuals in this particular panel and the advantages of having a homogeneous age group (cf. Miegel & Dalquist 1991).

Our study also builds on seven case studies of strategically chosen individuals. As previously mentioned, the questionnaires used within the LOM project contain a great number of lifestyle-related questions (musical taste, film taste, clothes, activities, etc.). On the basis of such items we constructed a scale for measuring gender specific cultural patterns or lifestyles.

The first cultural pattern identified consisted of individuals who liked romantic films, weeklies, disco music and the like. The second cultural pattern identified consisted of individuals who liked to read detective stories and thrillers, and to listen to heavy metal and heavy rock music.

The individuals chosen for case studies belonged to the statistically most typical representatives of each of the two "lifestyles". Altogether, we chose twelve persons, all of whom agreed to participate in our study. The initial interviews were made in the spring of 1988. On the second occasion, in the spring of 1990, five of these individuals either refused to participate or were impossible to locate (Lööv & Miegel 1991).

THE MEASUREMENT OF VALUES AND LIFESTYLES

In this section we will report briefly on the different instruments used to measure values and lifestyles. We will return to each of these in more detail in presenting the results.

We have used three different sets of questions for studying the values of our respondents. Two are well-known empirical instruments developed by Ronald Inglehart and Milton Rokeach, and one of them we developed ourselves.

In brief, Rokeach has identified eighteen values which he takes to cover the entire and universal value sphere. His technique is usually termed *List of Values* (LOV), It can be used in at least two different ways. Rokeach himself uses the ranking technique, which means that the respondents must arrange the eighteen values in order of preference. In this study we have, for reasons mentioned above, added additional six values and used a rating technique.

Contrary to Rokeach, Inglehart does not identify particular values, but uses what might be described as an indirect method of identifying the value orientation of respondents: he measures respondents' attitudes towards twelve concrete societal goals for the future. Like Rokeach he uses a ranking technique, whereas in this study we have employed a rating technique.

The last of our value measurements resembles Inglehart's, but we had our respondents rate their attitudes towards fourteen different goals for their own future, instead of using Inglehart's societal goals. In this measurement too, a rating technique is employed.

Two types of lifestyle indicators are used in this study. On the one hand, we have measured the individuals' attitudes towards music, film and clothes, and on the other, we have measured the relative frequency with which they pursue different leisure time activities.

METHODS

Statistical Methods

A number of analytical techniques from the statistical package SPSS/PC are employed in our study (Norusis 1988). Two of these techniques will be discussed here briefly: factor analysis and multiple classification analysis (MCA).

Factor analysis is a statistical technique by means of which it is possible to identify a number of factors, or patterns of relationsships, between a large number of interrelated items. The factors thus represent unifying constructs which characterize responses to related groups of variables (Norusis 1988:B-41).

The output of a factor analysis is a number of different factors which can serve to reduce and describe different empirical patterns in the material. Each factor can be used to construct an additive index which constitutes a new variable. A factor analytical technique thus helps to organize and structure a large set of variables into a relatively much smaller number of variables.

A choice of methods is to a large extent a theoretical question. In this study, factor analysis has been used to identify a number of different patterns of, for example, tastes in music, film and clothes, as well as leisure time activities. It should be remembered that factor analysis groups not individuals but variables. The technique does thus not allow one to categorize individuals according to a number of different lifestyles or taste patterns, but merely provides a hint of how the tastes for a variety of rather specific musical or film genres, for instance, tend to be related. It gives a general idea, so to speak, of how tastes and activities are structured among our respondents.

It is possible to interpret such factors as indicators of *ideal types of lifestyles*. On the basis of this method each individual can be assigned to *a number of different taste and activity patterns*. Each individual, to be sure, can and does use elements from different taste and activity patterns to construct her or his own, very specific *individual lifestyle*.

In the factor analyses, orthogonal rotation and Kaiser's criterion (Eigenvalue greater than 1) were employed. Cronbach's alpha was used to control the internal consistency of the variables included in the measurement scales (Kim & Mueller 1978; Norusis 1988).

Multiple classification analysis (MCA) is used due to its capacity to cope with certain basic problems encountered in our empirical analyses of values and lifestyles. The MCA technique is a powerful analytical tool (cf. Hedinsson 1981; Roe 1983; Norusis 1988). It allows for extensive control procedures, distinguishing between the independent or unique effects of each of a number of independent variables. Another advantage with this type of analysis is that it yields information concerning the linearity or curvilinearity of empirical relationships. Finally, it allows determination of overall explanatory power, that is, the additive effects of all the independent variables on the dependent variable.

In using an MCA technique it is also possible, and in fact necessary, to take account of interaction effects between the independent and dependent variables. If a strong interaction occurs, MCA scores become meaningless. It is thus recommended that checks be made as a routine. In our study we have tried to exclude the existence of multicollinearity by using an extensive controlling procedure. In short, we have checked the main effects of each of the independent variables and each of the background variables (including education, gender, city and class) after adjusting for all the other variables.

The SPSS/PC programme provides a test of significance for MCA-analyses. In the tables to be presented in later chapters, dealing with each of the independent variables, the significance value is indicated by means of asterisks in the last column of the tables. The following levels of significance are employed:

Number of asterisks	Level of significance
(*)	.10
*	.05
**	.01
***	.001

The numbers of cases in the different statistical analyses presented do not vary to any considerable degree (minimum 290 cases and maximum 314). Therefore, we have refrained from presenting the exact number of cases for the individual analyses.

Qualitative Method

Altogether, we met the seven young people included in the case study phase of this study on three different occasions. On the two first occasions we met them in their homes. On the third occasion we met them at different places in their home town of Malmö. The length of these interviews varied from two to three hours. The interviews were recorded on tape and transcribed in order to facilitate our analysis of the material. The interviews were based upon questions concerning the individuals' values, taste and leisure interests.

It is important to point out that we succeeded in establishing a very good relationship generally with these young people. Our interviews were thus characterized by a great deal of openness and trust.

In connection with each interview we asked the young person in question to choose a short piece of pop or rock lyrics, a piece which corresponded in one way or another to his or her own personal feelings, attitudes, wishes, etc.

Each case study also contained a *life plan*. The young persons interviewed try to reconstruct their lives, telling us about the persons and events that contributed to shaping their personality and lifestyle. They also provide us a short description of their future, that is, of how they would like their lives to be in a near future. We also asked them to imagine some alternative conceptions of their future.

The results of the qualitative study will be presented in the form of seven separate case studies. These young people's own way of expressing their ideas and of accounting for important events in their lives plays a central role in our presentation and discussion of the seven case studies. In order to make the actual quotations accessible to the reader we have combined quotations from different parts of the interviews. All such combinations are marked in the text. In order to protect these young people's integrity and ensure them anonymity, we have changed certain parts of their statements and given them fictitious names.

The case study method has several advantages especially when combined with other quantitative and qualitative methods. In a recent article, Randy Stoecker discusses the application and the advantages of the case study (Stoecker 1991). He argues that case studies may be used as a means of showing the specific processes involved both in general trends and in exceptions to such trends. In this manner the case study method can be used so as to make measurement instruments and predictions more specific.

The importance of having an elaborated theoretical framework in using case studies has often been stressed by social scientists (cf. Mitchell 1983; Stoecker 1991).

> In case studies statistical inference is not involved at all. Instead the inferential process turns exclusively on the theoretically necessary linkages among the features of the case study. The validity of the extrapolation depends not on the typicality or representativeness of the case study but upon the cogency of the theoretical reasoning (Mitchell 1983:207).

Although Stoecker (1991) argues that theory plays an important role in case studies, he also emphasizes the difficulties involved.

> Theorizing "idiosyncrasy" then, refers to bringing all possible theoretical perspectives to bear, and discarding and weighing each until we have built a valid and useful explanation. The difficulty involves determining the extent to which we rely on theory to guide us in choosing what to look for and how to explain what we find. Just how much to rely on theory, and thus risk missing important idiosyncrasies of particular cases, or restrain theory and thus risk overemphasizing the idiosyncratic, is a tricky question (Stoecker 1991:102).

In this book we have tried to solve this problem in three different ways. First, we have constructed a theory which is fairly "open", that is, a theory that takes account of the main contributions thus far to an emerging, overall theory of lifestyle. Secondly, we have introduced the distinction between ideal types of lifestyles and individual lifestyles. Thirdly, in discussing the more specific individual case studies we also draw on the results of the more general quantitative study which we present. This makes it possible to capture both general tendencies in young people's lifestyles and idiosyncrasis inherent in their more specific individual lifestyles.

In using the case study method the best validity check comes from the subjects themselves (cf. Stoecker 1991). Even if participants do not agree with the theoretical explanations provided by the researchers, they must agree that the behaviours, taste and attitudes we attribute to them are indeed their behaviours, taste and attitudes. Such a validity check was also made during the last interview. Our respondents read and commented on he descriptions based in the two first interviews (these descriptions are published in Lööv & Miegel 1991). Our descriptions coincided almost perfectly with the respondents' own view of their taste, attitudes, values, etc. The validity of our descriptions of these individuals may, therefore, be considered as high.

PART FOUR:

LIFESTYLES AS GENERAL PATTERNS OF CULTURE

Our inner life, which we perceive as a stream, as an incessant process, as an up and down of thoughts and moods, becomes crystallized, even for ourselves, in formulas and fixed directions often merely by the fact that we verbalize this life. Even if this leads only rarely to specific inadequacies; even if, in fortunate cases, the fixed external form constitutes the center of gravity or indifference above and below which our life evenly oscillates; there still remains the fundamental, formal contrast between the essential flux and movement of the subjective psychic life and the limitations of its forms. These forms, after all, do not express or shape an ideal, a contrast with life's reality, but this life itself (Simmel 1908/1971:352).

CHAPTER 13
AN EMPIRICAL PRELUDE

In this section of the book we concentrate on general patterns in the values, tastes and leisure time activities of the young people of our study. In the presentation and discussion of the quantitative part of our study we have tried to identify a number of rather abstract and general patterns concerning, on the one hand, the tastes in film and music among Swedish 21 year olds, and on the other, their leisure time activities. The presentation we provide of these cultural patterns are mainly descriptive, and it should be born in mind that the patterns identified to a certain degree depend on the measurement instruments. Thus, on the basis of the operationalizations we have selected for the examination of taste and of leisure time activities used, we have arrived at a number of music taste patterns, film taste patterns and activity patterns. Being aware of the relation between operationalization and empirical outcome, we do not claim to have identified the total number of taste and activity patterns in the age group at issue, but we believe that our categorizations and measurements of film and music genres and of activity patterns provide at least a rough picture of how tastes and activities are related and distributed in this particular age group of Swedish society.

The reasons for distinguishing such patterns are manifold. First, as just mentioned, they provide a rough picture of how these young people differ in these areas. Secondly, these patterns may be used in analyses of how individuals belonging to different social strata (class, status, gender, etc.), relate to the patterns in question. Thirdly, the patterns identified may be used as three different kinds of lifestyle indicators. Fourth, they make it possible to analyze how individuals embracing different values and possessing different value orientations relate to these various taste and activity patterns. Through analyzing these relations we can test some of the theoretical assumptions we have made concerning relations between lifestyles and different levels of determination, on the one hand, and between values and lifestyles, on the other.

In order to study the component of lifestyle determined by position in society, we have investigated how such variables as class, status and gender correlate both with the different taste and activity patterns and with the values and value orientations, examined in the study. Since we feel that values and value orientations constitute an important aspect of the identity of the individual, the relations of such variables as class, status and gender to the value variables give us a hint of the relation between positionally and individually determined levels of lifestyle. By keeping the impact of societal position on the values and taste and activity patterns constant when looking at the relationship between, values and value orientations, on the one hand, and taste and activity patterns, on the other, we can arrive at a rough picture of how individually determined characteristics of the individuals in our sample relate to the general and abstract lifestyle indicators.

In this part of the book we will concentrate upon three important questions in lifestyle research: the relation between different levels of determination concerning lifestyle, the relation between values, attitudes and actions and the function of popular culture in young persons' lives. The different empirical analyses presented here are thus related in one way or another to these theoretical questions. In the end of this section of the book we will thus turn once again to these theoretical questions and discuss briefly the relation between our empirical analyses and the more general theoretical questions underlying them.

CHAPTER 14
VALUES AND THE PROCESS OF INDIVIDUALIZATION

The process of individualization can be studied from several points of view. In this chapter, we will focus on a central dimension of this process, namely, the considerable change in values which have occurred in several Western societies, including the Swedish one. Empirically, these changes have been investigated extensively and in depth by Ronald Inglehart (1977, 1990). In short, Inglehart maintains that when society and its structures change, individuals' values and skills change accordingly. These changes lead, in turn, to consequences for society and its structures.

Inglehart indicates that in post-war Western societies a gradual shift in value-orientations is taking place. The earlier emphasis on material welfare and physical security has decreased, greater attention being paid to such phenomena as self-fulfillment, self-realisation and personal growth. This shift from a material to a postmaterial value-orientation can also be described in terms of a process of individualization.

The changes at the system level described by Inglehart have led to changes on the individual level as well, not only in the needs and values of individuals, but also in their special competences and skills for coping with politics, and their increasing inclination to call in question political decisions and social institutions (cf. Habermas 1975; Giddens 1991). In short, Inglehart states that in contemporary society individuals have not only become more able to influence their own lives, but also put higher value on self-development, personal growth, life-satisfaction and the like. In no longer having to put as much effort into the mere satisfaction of fundamental biological and material needs, contemporary Western man has become increasingly preoccupied with self development.

Inglehart thus charts a process which has been of major interest within sociology since the days of the classics. One of his main points, however, is that this process has accelerated during the post-war period, due to, among other things to the economic and technological developments, the rising level of education, the expansion of mass communication, and the like (cf. Habermas 1981/1984; Bellah et al. 1985; Beck 1986).

Inglehart distinguishes empirically a dimension reaching from a material value orientation to a postmaterial one. Inglehart's method has become widely used and has been applied in studies within many Western societies, including Sweden (cf. Reimer 1988, 1989; Pettersson 1988; Miegel & Dalquist 1991). Also in the empirical data employed in the present context this dimension is evident.

In Table 1 results of a factor analysis of the twelve societal goals which Inglehart identified is presented.

Table 1. Factor Analysis of Inglehart's Societal Goals.

	F1	F2
Factor 1		
Seeing that the people have more say in how things get decided	.63	.16
Trying to make our cities and countryside more beautiful	.67	.08
Giving the people more to say in important government decisions	.55	.02
Protecting freedom of speech	.49	.10
Progress toward a less impersonal, more humane society	.70	.00
Progress toward a society where ideas are more important than money	.71	-.16
Factor 2		
Maintaining a high rate of economic growth	-.18	.68
Maintaining order in the nation	.09	.70
Fighting rising prices	.26	.62
Maintaining a stable economy	.14	.66
The fight against crime	.14	.66
ALPHA	.71	.69
EIGENVALUE	2.8	2.4
PCT OF VAR	23.5	19.6
Dropped variable		
Making sure that this country has strong defense forces	-.32	.52

In principle, Inglehart's time-series study clearly indicates a "silent revolution" to be going on in the Occident. Our empirical data, on the other hand, cannot provide any direct support for this change, since they do not allow a time-series analysis to be carried out. We do have evidence, however, supporting his assumption of the existence of the dimension as such.

Inglehart's empirical results thus provide strong support for his thesis of a considerable value-shift occuring. It is against the background of such structurally determined changes that we must also analyze the value changes occurring on the positional and individual levels. Inglehart's methodology, however, is neither designed for studying individually determined value changes nor sufficient for this task. In order to understand how the structural value changes Inglehart and others discuss are expressed on an individual level, one must, therefore, use other measuring instruments.

We have developed a set of questions by means of which it may be possible to capture Inglehart's dimension on the individual level. Wheras Inglehart asks his respondents to state their opinions about the importance of a number of societal goals, we ask in a similar way about the importance to them which they attach to a number of goals. Needless to say, we do not claim that these questions cover all different aspects of young persons' personal value orientations. One could probably find many other personal goals which it would be possible to incorporate into our set of questions. Just as in almost all analyses of this type, one should bear in mind that the patterns distinguished depend on the scale employed. That goes both for Inglehart's measuring instrument and ours.

Our analysis of these questions resulted in five different personal value orientations which can be discussed in relation to Inglehart's materialist/postmaterialist dimension (Table 2).

The five personal value orientations which we have discerned can probably be interpreted in a number of different ways. From our theoretical point of view, however, Inglehart's dimension, which is located on a structural level, is not sufficient for an analysis at an individual level. Although the process of individualization is often described as involving a continuous, one-dimensional development towards greater individual freedom, this is only partly true. The relatively linear patterns and directions of development distinguishable on the structural level are often found to be much more complex when they are studied on an individual level. In studying personal value orientations, therefore, we need to also consider the individual's identity — as we argue throughout this book.

In studying these five personal value orientations we have been able to identify an interesting dimension extending from security at the one pole to development at the other. Emphasis on security or on development here encompassed three different areas or functions.

Table 2. Factor Analysis of Personal Goals for the Future

	F1	F2	F3	F4	F5
Factor 1, Material security					
Earning money	.73	.15	-.05	.01	.17
Having a safe job	.49	.49	-.11	.02	.18
Haing an own car	.73	.13	.04	-.28	-.05
Working full-time	.57	.22	-.22	.18	.01
Looking young	.57	.08	.44	-.06	.02
Factor 2, Personal security					
Having a stable relationship	.20	.78	-.13	.02	-.03
Having children	.10	.81	.05	.04	-.03
Factor 3, Personal development					
Travelling a lot	-.10	-.06	.75	.11	.17
Living abroad	-.01	-.24	.66	.36	-.01
Having an exciting job	.16	-.12	.46	.38	.31
Factor 4, Material development					
Investing in education	-.21	.09	.01	.69	.03
Making career	.50	.08	.11	.62	.11
Factor 5, Social security					
Having a job that suits me	.12	.17	.03	.12	.48
Having many good friends	-.02	.20	.40	-.08	.61
ALPHA	.69	.73	.68	.36	.31
EIGENVALUE	3.7	2.8	1.4	1.2	1.2
PCT OF VAR	18.6	14.1	7.1	6.2	5.8
Dropped variables					
Having an own home	.14	.60	-.04	-.09	.21
Staying in my home town	.31	.31	-.22	-.39	-.03
Trying different professions	-.04	.05	.48	-.06	-.07
Moving to a bigger city	.21	-.22	.40	.39	-.29
Moving to a smaller city/countryside	.01	.27	.27	.00	-.68
Living a healthy life	.26	.30	.23	.01	.36

First, there are the functions of *material security* and *material development*. For the category of material security, personal goals aimed at maintaining a stable social position, such as having a safe job, a stable income, and certain material welfare, are involved. For the category of material development, the aim not of security and stability but of increasing material and economic welfare is involved. The personal goals here of investing in education or succeeding in one's career — contain strong elements of the acqustion of high social position or status. There is a definite resemblance with Inglehart's material value-orientation in that material goals are stressed, but in contract to that, emphasis on security is lacking, and there is a strong element of individual development and of striving for economic power and social recognition.

Secondly, there are the functions of *personal security* and *development*. The goals included in the category of personal security are those of creating a safe and secure social environment, basically in terms of family life, through establishing a marriage or partner relationship and having children. The personal development function, on the other hand, is characterized by an emphasis on new experiences and impressions. Stress is placed on personal goals such as travelling, living abroad and having an exciting job. Individual development and progress are viewed as more important than security and social status.

Thirdly, we have the category of *social security* characterized by an emphasis on job satisfaction and having good friends. This category could be interpreted as an extension of the category of personal security in its stressing of the importance of secure relations, also outside the private sphere.

Since an instrument for measuring personal value orientations is not yet fully developed, we have not succeeded in identifying the specific components of a social development category. However, such a category should probably include such personal goals as those of becoming acquainted with other people, of gaining new friends, of trying out different jobs, and the like.

What appears to be the most important dimension in this respect, however, is one that encompasses both security and development. This dimension is clearly related to identity development. The individual has a need and desire, on the one hand, to establish safe and secure personal, social and cultural points of reference and, on the other, to broaden his or her views and to develop personally, socially and culturally. However, the need for development or security may vary from one individual to another, and for a given individual from one time to another.

The five categories referred to above are therefore not mutually exclusive but may be combined in various ways. It is thus possible at one and the same time to possess security, to pursue developmentally oriented personal goals for the future, and to emphasize the personal, social and cultural components of identity (cf. Mitchell 1983; Bellah et al. 1985). To understand the complexity of these relations it is necessary to investigate more closely how lifestyles are constructed and expressed on an individual level, concentrating not only on the values and value-orientations of the individual, but also to consider the individual's attitudes as well as actual behavior in different areas. As we have argued already values are expressed and manifested in a variety of attitudes and actions.

In order to comprehend the relations between values, attitudes and actions in the context of lifestyle, one must obviously distinguish between these three concepts. This distinction is somehow blurred in Inglehart's measurements of societal goals, as well as in our measurement of personal goals. Thus, neither we nor Inglehart focus on specific values; in studying personal value orientations, we consider attitudes towards more or less well established conditions.

Milton Rokeach's value study clarifies the distinction between values, attitudes and actions. He also distinguishes between a number of specific values in his empirical measurements. He is less interested in finding basic dimensions for trends or value shifts in Western societies. Rather, he argues that the values of the individual are enduring and universal. What changes from one time to another, is, in his view, their importance in the individual's value system. Rokeach is interested in how values are related to and affect other components in the total belief system of the individual. For studying the phenomenon of lifestyle, therefore, Rokeach's approach toward measuring individual values is more useful than is Inglehart's approach. That is so, due to Rokeach's empirical method's allowing us to study the influence of a particular value on a particular attitude or action.

What Inglehart has shown is that there is a continuing process of value change going on in the Western world. It is against the background of these cultural changes at a structural level that we should understand relations between the values, attitudes and actions of the individual in contemporary Western societies. We also believe that in studying personal value-orientations, the patterns of interests are more complex than Inglehart maintains. In analyzing how the values of Swedish youth of today influence their attitudes and actions and thus their lifestyles, we will mainly make use of Rokeach's method for measuring values since this method considers value as a central aspect of the total belief system of an individual. Thus, Rokeach and his followers aim at understanding the complex interplay of, and relations between, values, attitudes and actions. In addition to Rokeach's more specific procedures of value mesurement, however, we will also employ Inglehart's approach to measuring societal and our approach to measuring personal goals. Inglehart's dimension provides us with a general understanding of young people's attitudes towards developments in the society of which they are a part, more specifically, whether they prefer a societal development directed towards increasing material wealth and security or towards increasing individual freedom and non-material life satisfaction.

Table 3. Values and Value Orentations Related to Sex, Class, City and Education (Pearson's Correlations).

	Sex	Class	City	Education
Material security	-.14	-.07	-.03	-.14
Personal security	.15**	-.07	.04	-.10
Social security	.19***	.04	.03	.02
Personal development	.11	.15**	-.04	.08
Material development	-.08	.20***	.06	.20***
Material	.02	.04	-.01	-.08
Postmaterial	.35***	-.04	-.12	-.02
A clean world	.18**	-.05	.00	-.07
Technological developm	-.39***	.15	.04	.08
A comfortable life	.11	.04	-.09	-.15
An exciting life	.05	-.04	-.04	-.11
Sense of accomplishment	.14	.03	.06	.00
Peace	.30***	-.07	-.11	-.14
A world of beauty	.22***	-.08	-.10	-.23***
Equality	.39***	-.14	-.17**	.11
Family security	.30***	-.07	-.10	-.08
Freedom	.16**	.06	-.03	-.07
Happiness	.30***	-.02	-.16**	-.10
Inner harmony	.24***	.06	-.08	-.01
Love	.27***	.00	-.10	-.12
National security	.02	.00	.10	-.03
Pleasure	.09	-.09	-.09	-.16
Salvation	-.02	-.03	-.08	.00
Self-respect	.09	.15	-.02	.18**
Social recognition	-.08	-.04	.03	-.10
Wisdom	-.04	-.01	-.12	.07
Justice	.26***	.03	-.09	-.06
Power	-.23***	.03	.02	-.07
Health	.10	.03	-.07	-.07
Wealth	-.22***	.06	-.01	-.08

Our own approach to measurement provides a general assessment of the predominant function of the values embraced by the individuals (that is whether they stress security or development). In Table 3 the measurements of values and value orientations are presented in their totality as well as in relation to class, education, city and gender.The table provides a general picture of the relation between the positional variables and the three different measurements of values and value orientation. The positional variable best explaining variations in values or value orientations is clearly gender, although there are also some correlations of interest between class, city and education, on the one hand, and values and value orientations, on the other.

First, there are various correlations of note between social class and personal value orientations. Both personal and material development are positively related to class; young people from a middle class background are more inclined to emphasize the developmental function of their values than are those from working class backgrounds. There are no significant correlations between any other value or value orientation and class, which suggests there to be no relations between young person's class background and their values.

Secondly, there are several correlations of interest between educational level and certain values and value orientations. The personal value orientation towards material development is positively correlated with education level. Young persons of high education tend to value material development higher than do those of low education. Furthermore, the Rokeachean values of a beautiful world and of self-regard are positively correlated with education.

Thirdly, there are several correlations of interest between values and value orientations and gender. It seems reasonable, therefore, to talk about some values and value orientations as either *female or male oriented*. The positive correlations between two personal value orientations, those being personally and socially secure, respectively, indicate that women tend to emphasize the security function of values more than men. Moreover, women also tend to emphasize postmaterial values to a higher degree than men do. In examining Rokeachean values we can distinguish between a number of female oriented values — a clean world, peace, equality, family security, freedom, happiness, inner harmony, love and wisdom — and a number of male oriented values — technological development, power and wealth. All in all, these results indicate that women tend to emphasize the security function of values and the postmaterially oriented values more than men, whereas men emphasize material values more than women do.

Before discussing these values in greater detail, we need to account for the concepts of attitude and action. In the next two chapters we will, on the one hand, present young people's attitudes towards various youth cultural phenomena, specifically, popular music and films, and on the other hand, report on their actions as evident in their leisure activities.

CHAPTER 15
TASTE — CULTURAL BACKGROUND OR INDIVIDUAL CHOICE?

SOME INTRODUCTORY REMARKS

In discussing young people's lifestyles the most common point of departure is probably their tastes in different areas of popular culture, such as music and film. In analyses of young people's tastes in these areas it is often suggested that variations in taste are mainly determined by the individual's class, gender or ethnicity (cf. McRobbie & Garber 1976; Willis 1977; Hebdige 1979; Brake 1980; Christenson & Peterson 1988). From our theoretical view, we can partly agree with this perspective, since we argue that positions of individuals in society affect their individual choices.

However, position does not explain the entire range of variations in taste among contemporary youth. We argue that much variation is better explained by relating it to the values of the individual (and then not simply to the material and aesthetic values, but also to the metaphysical and ethical ones).

It is thus necessary to keep in mind that when we speak of aesthetic values as the basis for taste, we do this in a very simplified way. We do not take into consideration here the complex relations existing between the different types of values constituting the entire value system of the individual.

Furthermore, we believe that tastes of individuals to also be related to the way they look upon development in society, and whether they emphasize security or developmental function in their values. That is why Inglehart's material/postmaterial dimension and our security/development dimension are also important for an understanding of the relation between values and the individual's attitudes towards music, film and clothes.

In sorting young people into different categories on the basis of their musical taste, one makes the theoretical assumption that music plays a such a central role in young people's lives that it can serve as the core of their lifestyle. The resulting categorizations also depend on how musical taste is operationalized empirically, as well as on the musical categories employed in the measurement. Lifestyle thus becomes operationally defined in terms of taste in music, which means that neither attitudes based on other aesthetic values, nor attitudes based on other types of values — material, ethical and metaphysical — are included in the definition of lifestyle. Consequently, in identifying patterns of taste in one area or another statistically, we consider only a very limited segment of the lifestyle patterns in society. Actually, it would be more accurate to call these patterns *taste patterns*, rather than lifestyles. In order to reach a more thorough understanding of the individual's entire lifestyle, one must consider a wide range of attitudes and actions based on all the different types of values embraced by the individual.

What we intend to do is to distinguish between a number of such taste patterns based on different popular cultural forms, such as music and film. In the next chapter we will also distinguish between a number of patterns of action based on leisure activities. All these patterns can be seen as possible and very likely components of young people's lifestyles. However, to really understand these aspects of lifestyle we must also — insofar as possible — study their relations to the values of the individual. In this way, we can arrive at a general understanding of how various aspects of lifestyle among young people in Sweden are structured in terms of different taste and activity patterns.

Whereas such general patterns may be very useful for understanding major trends in the ifestyles of youth culture, we believe they do not tell us very much about the way particular individuals build their own individual lifestyle. For arriving at such an understanding, intensive studies of a number of single individuals are called for. This is, of course, best seen against the background of more general trends. We will end this empirical presentation, therefore, with seven such case studies.

Somewhat metaphorically, the general patterns of taste and activities distinguished below can be said to constitute a cultural map on which we can locate the individuals and follow their moves in different directions over time.

PATTERNS OF MUSICAL TASTE

By means of music the passions enjoy themselves (Nietzsche 1886/1990:46).

During the last decades interest in popular forms of music has increased considerably (see, for instance, Frith 1978, 1983; Middleton 1990; Wicke

1990; Roe 1990; Shepherd 1991). Music has also become more intimately connected with the selling of images and the packaging of lifestyles (Frith 1988). Even though musical taste may not be sufficient to discriminate between different lifestyles, there is no doubt that music is one of the most powerful and influential components of contemporary youth culture.

> Music is a passionate sequencing of thoughts and feelings that express meaning in a manner that has no parallel in human life. It is a universally recognized synthesis of the substance and style of our existence — *a blending of personal, social and cultural signification* (italics added) that is confused with no other variety of communication (Lull 1987:10).

During the 1980s one has witnessed several different attempts to categorize music into different taste patterns (see, for example, Shepherd 1986; Christenson & Peterson 1988; Nylöf 1990; Roe 1990).

One of the reasons why music is such an attractive starting point in discussions of young people's lifestyles is that it is an area in which young people make very clear distinctions. Although music plays different roles for different individuals, everyone listens to music and everyone makes judgements of taste concerning it. Music is probably also the area within youth culture which is most rapidly developing and changing. New musical styles and categories are constantly entering the popular musical scene. During the 1980s and 1990s we have witnessed a constant flow of new forms and mixtures of both old and new categories of popular music. Hip hop, rap, acid house, speed metal, trash metal, death metal, and mixtures of heavy metal and modern dance music are only a few examples.

This constant development has implications, of course, for empirical attempts to distinguish and categorize taste patterns in popular music. If one is interested in studying developments in young people's tastes over time — as we are — it is necessary to constantly upgrade measurement instruments in order to insofar as possible capture the developments whioh occur in the cultural phenomena themselves. Thus, from one data collection to another, one must both remove and add several items.

The matter is complicated further by the fact that the categories seldom are pure, but often contain elements of other categories. The intricate play between tastes and distastes is visible not only between different music categories, but also within the empirically distinguished categories.

Table 4. Music Taste, Distaste, Indifference and Ignorance (means and percentages).

	X̄ (1990)	1988 %				1990 %			
		Taste	Distaste	Indiff	Ignorance	Taste	Distaste	Indiff	Ignorance
Pop	4.2	82	6	12	-	84	3	13	-
Disco	4.0	81	8	11	-	75	10	15	-
Modern Rock	3.9	82	7	11	-	70	7	23	-
60's Rock	3.7	40	27	32	1	63	9	28	-
Folk Pop	3.6	55	18	25	2	59	13	27	1
50's Rock	3.4	43	22	35	-	50	16	35	-
FM-Rock	3.4					57	7	26	10
Guitar Rock	3.3					49	16	30	5
Reggae	3.3	49	24	26	1	44	25	31	-
Funk	3.3					48	20	29	3
Rock Poets	3.2					45	19	33	4
Hard Rock	3.2	55	26	19	-	45	29	26	1
Classical Music	3.1	36	43	19	1	41	26	32	1
Protest Music	3.0					38	25	34	3
Musicals	2.9					34	17	37	12
Popular songs	2.9	44	27	29	-	32	36	31	-
Troubadours	2.8	18	51	28	3	32	33	34	2
Soul	2.7	24	40	22	14	29	22	36	13
70's Hard Rock	2.7	32	44	23	1	29	44	26	1
Glam Metal	2.7					33	33	27	7
Blues Rock	2.6	23	38	30	9	26	24	38	12
Synth	2.6	35	39	25	2	20	44	35	1
Blues	2.5	14	56	18	12	24	30	31	14
Symphonic Rock	2.5					29	21	30	20
Hip Hop / Rap	2.4					23	48	27	7
Opera / Operetta	2.4					16	49	33	2
Heavy Metal	2.3	19	63	17	1	21	53	25	1
Country	2.3	10	57	30	3	10	50	38	2
Pub Rock	2.3					24	18	33	24
Traditional Jazz	2.2	16	63	15	6	15	51	26	8
Acid House	2.1					20	43	21	16
Dance Orchestras	2.1	11	64	22	1	12	63	24	1
Avant Garde Rock	2.0					15	27	33	25
Punk	1.9	12	68	17	3	10	68	19	3
Folk Rock	1.9					17	22	27	34
Modern Jazz	1.9	8	63	15	14	10	54	23	13
Modern Country	1.8	6	50	26	18	6	43	31	20
Swedish Folk Music	1.8					5	64	22	8
Post Punk	1.6	9	31	18	42	11	34	21	34
Jazz Rock	1.6	14	61	17	8	10	45	18	28
Glam Rock	1.6	13	35	21	31	9	33	23	34
Rockabilly	1.5	8	33	20	39	9	27	25	39
Garage Rock	1.5	12	33	17	38	11	32	19	38
Am Southern Rock	1.5					15	18	18	48
Speed/Trash Metal	1.4					6	61	11	22
Bebop Jazz	1.4	7	43	14	36	6	25	25	43
World Music	1.3					11	17	19	53
Salsa	1.1	3	28	6	63	6	25	15	54
Industrial Rock	1.0					4	27	15	54
Art Music	1.0	4	37	9	52	4	28	13	55
Fusion	0.9					3	32	9	56
Avant Garde Jazz	0.9	5	47	6	42	3	31	11	56
Hard Core	0.7					2	21	11	67
Folk Music	-	10	73	15	2	-	-	-	-
Afro Rock	-	5	30	13	52	-	-	-	-

In Table 4 we can see the respondents' attitudes towards a number of different music styles, as of 1988 and 1990. We have used four categories — taste, distaste, indifference and ignorance — to illustrate how general attitudes towards these musical categories have developed among our respondents between the two years in question.

The first conclusions to be drawn from Table 4 concern the variations which occur in pop and rock music, which are the most popular musical types among the young people in our sample. Such categories as folk music, different types of jazz, art music, classical music, and country, do not seem to attract people in this age group very much. Certain artists and musical categories are accepted and enjoyed by a vast majority of the nineteen to twenty-one year olds. It is thus possible to discern a number of musical genres that may be described as mainstream. This goes, for example, for pop (Roxette, Eurythmics and Bangles, etc.), disco (Michael Jackson, Whitney Huston, etc.), and modern rock music (Bruce Springsteen, Bryan Adams and John Cougar Mellencamp, etc.). Most young people express a positive attitude towards these artists, and only few dislike them. These artists and genres are frequently represented in hit lists, music videos, etc., and they sell a large number of records. In a way they constitute a basic popular musical taste pattern embraced by most young people.

Apart from such general taste patterns we can identify a variety of more specific and distinct taste patterns consisting of such musical genres as folk music, heavy metal, punk, country, speed and trash metal, and different forms of jazz music. The attitudes towards these musical taste patterns are characterized by *distaste* on the part of most young people. These are also the musical genres often related to various subcultural groups. The young people expressing a positive attitude towards the more distinct and narrow musical categories are probably in general more interested in music than are those who primarily listen to the mainstream genres. Their musical taste is probably also a more important element, and sometimes even a substantial one, in their lifestyle.

To say this is not, however, to claim that listeners of mainstream music are passive and conformist consumers of popular culture. No doubt, pleasure and enjoyment can be equally great, whatever one's musical preferences are. Nevertheless, musical tastes, have different functions for different individuals with respect to their lifestyles.

As we have seen, most young people have a positive attitude towards mainstream music, but there are also those who have developed and incorporated additional and more distinct musical genres into their taste. For the listeners of basically mainstream music there are probably often other types of cultural activities that are more important in terms of their lifestyles, but for those who have developed more distinct tastes, music is probably an area in which they express their individuality. We will return to this discussion later.

Comparing the respondents' attitudes towards the different musical genres at the age of nineteen with their attitudes at the age of twenty-one, one can observe a general tendency. Attitudes towards mainstream genres remain rather stable, whereas attitudes towards more distinct categories tend to become less negative. This fact can be explained in different ways.

First, the music industry, like the fashion industry, develops different trends from year to year. During the two years we have studied these young people, certain types of music have increased in popularity and others have diminished. We have witnessed a blues revival, for instance, and a renewed interest in the music and fashions of the 1960's. These trends have left traces in our material, and between 1988 and 1990 we can notice a considerable increase in young people's expressing of positive attitudes towards 1960's rock music and blues, and a corresponding decrease in negative attitudes towards such music.

The second explanation of the tendency to express less negative attitudes towards most musical genres is that it probably has to do with maturation. During the teenage period, identity gradually becomes more stable, and in the early twenties the young person is more sure about his or her identity. Musical taste and distaste must therefore be interpreted differently depending on the person's age. During the psychologically defined period of youth identity is constantly undergoing changes, the need to identify oneself in relation to certain groups being more important than during the socially and culturally defined period in which the individual has reached a more stable identity. Therefore, the individual is also more inclined to make categorical statements about his or her musical preferences in order to clearly express to which groups he or she belongs and does not belong.

Table 5. Factor Analysis of Music Taste

	F1	F2	F3	F4	F5	F6	F7	F8	F9	F10	F11	F12
Factor 1, Jazz												
Traditional Jazz	.83	.13	-.02	.08	-.06	.03	.11	.07	.20	.07	-.04	-.08
Modern Jazz	.89	.01	.02	.09	-.06	.04	.15	.04	.11	.10	-.09	.00
Jazz Rock	.89	.09	.07	.17	-.01	.02	.08	.02	.11	.00	.03	.01
Fusion	.89	.19	.15	.09	.01	-.09	-.01	.03	.08	.00	.16	.08
Avant Garde Jazz	.91	.05	.10	.03	-.10	.00	-.01	-.02	-.05	.08	.11	.12
Factor 2, Post Punk												
Post Punk	.16	.77	.05	.05	-.13	-.03	.07	.03	.14	.04	.06	-.02
Glam Rock	.19	.72	.28	.20	.12	-.05	-.05	.11	.07	.04	.14	.06
Garage Rock	.15	.75	.15	.16	-.21	-.09	-.01	.15	.00	.17	.00	.12
Rockabilly	.23	.66	.19	.19	.06	.15	-.06	.13	-.17	.16	.01	-.05
Hardcore	.11	.68	.16	-.22	-.15	.10	.25	.10	.16	-.07	.14	.16
Factor 3, Heavy Metal												
Heavy Metal	.03	.12	.89	-.01	-.05	.05	-.01	.08	.05	-.12	-.01	-.05
70's Hard Rock	.15	.13	.78	.17	-.20	-.08	-.01	.24	.00	-.03	.07	.03
Hard Rock	-.09	-.07	.73	-.04	.34	.16	-.10	-.01	-.09	.09	-.02	.10
Speed/Trash Metal	.05	.35	.63	-.16	-.15	.18	.04	.00	-.03	-.26	-.10	.01
Glam Metal	.02	.19	.77	.19	.07	.05	.08	-.07	-.06	.06	.18	-.04
Factor 4, Folk & Rock												
Folk Pop	.13	.09	-.10	.70	.23	.13	.10	.07	.20	.09	-.14	.08
Modern Rock	.12	.05	.16	.58	.38	.11	-.16	.19	-.07	-.11	.23	.11
Folk Rock	.14	.49	.02	.50	-.28	.01	-.03	.05	.14	.40	.10	.08
Guitar Rock	.15	.17	.11	.48	-.06	-.03	-.06	.22	-.10	.04	.44	.21
Rock Poets	.16	.06	.14	.77	-.08	.02	.00	.08	.10	-.07	.09	.13
Factor 5, Mainstream												
Pop	-.09	-.15	-.01	.17	.79	.03	.02	.07	.03	-.01	.04	.01
Disco	-.08	-.23	-.08	-.07	.74	.07	.36	.00	.10	.07	-.03	.12
Factor 6, Country												
Country	.03	.01	.07	.14	.00	.92	.00	.12	.00	.04	.01	.03
Modern Country	.17	-.01	.07	.13	.02	.89	.06	.08	.00	.02	.09	.08
Factor 7, Modern Dance												
Acid House	.06	.09	-.01	.03	.09	.06	.88	-.11	-.11	-.03	.03	.02
HipHop/Rap	.11	.04	.05	-.09	.05	.07	.88	-.05	-.10	-.01	-.05	-.04
Factor 8, 50's and 60's Rock												
50's Rock	.03	.16	.11	.03	.27	.28	-.05	.76	-.01	-.05	-.05	-.05
60's Rock	.08	.20	.09	.30	-.08	.02	-.09	.67	.24	.04	.02	.14
Blues Rock	.38	.22	.24	.21	-.23	-.07	.06	.51	.00	.16	.17	.14
Factor 9, Opera/musicals												
Opera/Operett	.56	.10	-.07	-.04	.05	-.06	.00	.13	.60	.01	.02	.05
Musicals	.25	.06	-.05	.15	.16	.10	-.07	.05	.76	.07	.09	.07
Factor 10, Ethnic Music												
Salsa	.38	.09	-.11	-.20	.19	.19	.08	.02	-.01	.68	.23	.06
World Music	.35	.31	-.13	.23	-.06	-.11	.08	.12	.15	.65	-.18	.06

	F1	F2	F3	F4	F5	F6	F7	F8	F9	F10	F11	F12
Factor 11, Symphonic and Southern Rock												
Symphonic Rock	.09	.12	.18	.23	.13	-.02	-.04	.00	.40	.09	.63	-.09
Southern Rock	.19	.23	.42	.37	.01	.19	-.05	.27	.00	.14	.43	-.18
Factor 12, Socially Conscious												
Reggae	.10	.00	.05	.14	.11	.14	.26	.32	-.05	.21	-.15	.54
Protest Music	.03	.16	.00	.24	.14	.20	-.05	-.04	.08	-.03	.11	.75
ALPHA	.96	.86	.86	.79	.76	.92	.90	.69	.72	.62	.64	.52
EIGENVALUE	12.2	4.9	4.5	3.0	2.6	2.5	2.0	1.6	1.4	1.2	1.1	1.1
PCT OF VAR	23.0	9.2	8.4	5.6	4.9	4.7	3.7	3.1	2.7	2.3	2.2	2.1
Dropped variables												
Punk	.14	.40	.30	.08	-.41	-.11	-.01	.26	-.10	-.23	.10	.21
Popular Songs	-.14	.01	.04	-.15	.57	.48	.01	-.04	.17	-.03	-.12	.30
Synth	-.06	.13	-.03	.02	.08	.01	.22	-.06	.14	-.06	.07	-.06
Classical	.53	.10	-.10	.08	-.09	-.14	.02	.11	.51	.13	.13	-.03
Swedish Folk Music	.58	.19	.03	.18	.10	.33	-.16	-.10	.19	.18	-.03	.07
Be-Bop Jazz	.70	.32	-.05	.02	.02	.20	.09	.11	-.10	.11	.06	-.01
Blues	.54	.09	.06	.10	-34	-.03	.11	.36	.10	.30	.13	-.01
Soul	.44	-.04	-.15	.05	-.01	-.03	.31	.31	.09	.30	.33	.02
Troubadours	.32	.27	-.05	.28	-.06	.15	-.06	.13	.12	.16	-.02	.38
Dance Orchestras	-.12	.02	.15	-.25	.39	.62	.02	-.02	-.06	-.10	-.04	.24
Art Music	.41	.24	.03	.03	-.19	-.05	-.10	-.16	.27	.49	.23	.09
Funk	.15	-.02	-.06	.11	.15	-.16	.62	.16	.33	.17	.06	.10
Pub Rock	.29	.17	.30	.36	-.05	-.12	.30	.14	-.20	.21	.13	.03
Avant Garde Rock	.40	.17	.32	.35	-.20	-.11	.09	.11	-.07	.23	.20	.15
FM-Rock	.11	.46	-.02	-.23	-.14	.16	.14	-.20	.04	-.06	.37	-.08
Industrial Rock	.03	.16	.00	.24	.14	.20	-.05	-.04	.00	.05	.57	.21

In the early twenties, that is in the beginning of the socially and culturally defined period of youth, the individual is more self-reliant and more ready to accept inconsistencies and contradictions as natural parts of his or her identity. The need to belong to a certain peer-group and to share in the taste and style of this group is now replaced with an increased ability to develop and maintain one's own personal attitudes, preferences and values. The desire to belong to a certain group is now combined with a stronger desire to be regarded as a unique person within this group.

During this period, the young person leaves school, starts working, moves away from home, finds a partner, and so on. This involves having to play different roles, and consequently becoming influenced by the increased number of different groups to which one has to relate. To cope with the expectations of different roles one must develop an own cultural identity which makes it possible to function satisfactorily within different types of groups. To do this, one must basically rely on oneself and one's own competences, rather than on the conformity to the group. The need to express distaste of tastes which characterize other groups thus also becomes weakened, since one no longer identifies primarily with the group, but rather defines the group in relation to what one sees as one's own unique person.

In order to gain a rough idea of how young people's taste in popular music is structured, we asked our respondents about their attitudes towards some fifty different music genres. To make this material more manageable, we have employed factor analysis to arrive at a number of taste patterns, as we like to call them (Table 5.). These taste patterns may be interpreted as a number of quite general patterns of musical taste towards which responents relate in differing ways depending on their class, gender and education, and also on which values they hold.

Even though the patterns distinguished in the factor analysis presented in Table 5 are not altogether consistent and homogeneous, they can nevertheless be considered meaningful, since they indicate roughly how musical taste is structured among nineteen to twenty-one years old persons in two Swedish cities.

These patterns are used as a basis for creating twelve additive indices, each of which constitutes a new variable which can be used in further statistical analyses. Since the patterns distinguished are far from mutually exclusive and homogeneous, we will not examine the relations within and between these patterns in any great detail.

In the theoretical parts of this book we have discussed the relation between values and lifestyle, arguing that musical taste can be used as an indicator of the lifestyles of young people. In the rest of this section we intend to discuss empirically the relation between values and taste in music, on the one hand, and the influence of social class, gender and education, on both musical taste and values, on the other.

Table 6. Music Taste Related to Positional Variables, Values and value Orientations (Pearson´s Correlations).

	Jazz	Post Punk	Heavy Metal	Folk & Rock	Main-stream	Country	Modem Dance	Opera/ Musical	Ethnical	Symph/ Southern	Socially Consc	50's & 60's Rock
Sex	-.09	-.19***	-.20***	-.07	.13	.05	-.10	.19***	-.09	-.24***	.26***	-.08
City	-.05	-.08	.05	-.10	.13	-.09	-.01	-.01	-.05	-.09	-.15**	-.13
Class	.06	.08	-.03	.11	-.05	-.18**	.04	.15**	.01	.02	-.09	-.01
Education	-.01	-.08	-.27***	.03	-.08	-.15**	-.01	.28***	-.03	-.04	-.12	-.10
Material security	-.08	-.16**	.09	-.23***	.29***	-.05	.03	-.18**	-.12	.00	-.09	-.19***
Personal security	.01	-.14	-.08	-.13	.31***	.07	-.07	-.07	-.13	-.03	.00	-.08
Social security	.06	-.06	.00	.01	.20***	-.02	.12	.12	.01	-.03	.11	.01
Personal developm	.19***	.09	-.08	.14	-.01	.01	.25***	.23***	.20***	.02	.10	.04
Material developm	.13	.05	-.11	.08	.04	-.04	.13	.19***	.07	.12	-.02	-.03
Material	.01	-.16**	.02	-.09	.31***	-.09	.07	-.01	-.01	.02	-.03	-.10
Postmaterial	.19***	.04	-.09	.20***	-.02	.01	.05	.24***	.13	-.01	.18**	.12
A clean world	.08	-.04	-.09	.18**	.09	-.01	-.05	.17**	.10	.04	.14	.14
Techn development	.17**	.06	.06	-.03	.10	-.08	.14	.04	.06	.12	-.18**	-.04
A comfortable life	.03	-.04	-.03	-.00	.13	-.04	.02	.05	-.08	.07	.04	-.04
An exciting life	.14	.01	.01	.07	.02	-.09	.09	.08	.10	.09	.01	-.00
Accomplishment	.16**	.02	-.11	.11	.09	-.14	.08	.19***	.11	.07	.02	.04
Peace	.02	-.15	-.07	.07	.26***	.04	.03	.08	-.02	-.09	.23***	.07
A world of beauty	.13	.02	-.00	.04	.13	.07	.05	.07	.16**	-.00	.23***	.07
Equality	.03	-.10	-.10	.02	.06	.00	-.01	.09	.02	-.12	.17**	.06
Family security	.01	-.16**	-.07	-.00	.28***	.11	-.01	.10	-.10	-.04	.12	.00
Freedom	.00	-.15	-.13	-.01	.21***	.03	.08	.01	-.01	-.12	.06	.02
Happiness	-.00	-.05	-.07	-.02	.14	.07	-.06	.01	-.05	.00	.10	-.03
Inner harmony	.10	.02	-.03	.09	.12	-.04	.08	.18	.03	.06	.15**	.07
Love	.05	-.05	-.07	.09	.20***	.08	-.08	.10	-.03	.03	.21***	.06
National security	.01	-.12	.01	-.09	.28***	-.02	.10	-.04	.04	-.00	-.09	-.15**
Pleasure	.08	-.06	.03	-.05	.20***	.01	.02	.01	.01	.04	.09	-.04
Salvation	.07	-.01	.02	-.11	.12	.05	-.02	.03	-.03	-.09	.01	-.05
Self-respect	.13	.09	-.01	.14	.11	-.10	.08	.24***	.18**	.14	.05	.14
Social recognition	.03	.02	.01	-.7	.18**	.06	.01	-.10	.08	.05	-.02	-.04
Wisdom	.18**	.14	-.04	.10	-.07	-.09	.02	.22***	.15**	.05	-.03	.09
Justice	-.01	-.09	-.15**	-.05	.16**	.06	.02	.04	.03	-.08	.11	.07
Power	.09	.10	.00	-.11	.08	.03	.09	-.07	.11	.07	-.15**	-.10
Health	-.06	-.11	-.03	-.01	.25***	-.05	-.02	.02	-.09	.02	.07	.00
Wealth	.02	.04	.07	-.11	.11	-.07	.16**	-.11	.05	.12	-.16**	-.09

The empirical results presented in Table 6 may be regarded as providing a rough and preliminary indication of how young people's lifestyles are constructed. In a great deal of the contemporary lifestyle literature taste, attitude, or activity patterns are used to categorize and label different lifestyles (see, for example, Zetterberg 1977; Berardo et al. 1985; Donohew et al. 1987). According to our theory, lifestyle is to be understood as a complex system of relations between the individual's values, attitudes and actions. The aim of this book is not primarily to identify or distinguish a number of different lifestyles among Swedish young people, but to endeavor to comprehend the complex interplay between values, attitudes and actions through which individuals develop and construct their lifestyles. The results presented in Table 6 can be interpreted in a variety of ways and analysed from different points of view.

First, we can discuss the different taste patterns in relation to social status and cultural capital, taking Bourdieu's theoretical perspective as a point of departure. On the one hand, there is the taste pattern we call *Opera/Musicals* which is closely related to what Bourdieu calls educational or cultural capital. On the other hand, we have the taste patterns of *Country* and *Heavy Metal* which are related to possessing a low degree of educational capital.

Secondly, taking either Blumer's or Zablocki and Kanter's theoretical perspective we can interpret the results as indicating a differentiation of lifestyles not necessarily related to such positional variables as class, status or gender. Thus, several of the musical taste patterns show no significant variation along the dimensions of socio-economic status, education or gender. This means that if we wish to explain differences between individuals' musical tastes, it is necessary to also look for other factors than those of social class and gender.

From our theoretical point of view it is more interesting to look at the relations between individuals' specific values and musical taste, on the one hand, and the positional variables, and value and taste patterns, on the other.

First, using Inglehart's material/post-material value orientation, we note that the musical pattern of *Mainstream music* is related to a material value orientation and that the musical patterns *Jazz, Folk and Rock, Opera/Musicals* and *Socially conscious* are related to a post-material value orientation. That is, young people expressing positive attitudes towards societal developments directed at an increased emphasis on quality of life rather than at economic and material stability or development, are more inclined to express positive attitudes towards these genres.

Secondly, taking the results of our own attempt to measure personal value orientations, we note that the musical pattern of *Mainstream music* is related to the personal value orientations of material, social and personal security. The musical patterns of *Jazz* and *Modern dance music* are related to the personal value orientation directed at personal development. The musical pattern of *Opera/Musicals* is related to personal value orientations of personal and material development. Finally, *Ethnic* music is related to the personal value orientation of security on a social level.

Thirdly, using Rokeach's value measurement we note that ten of the twelve musical patterns are related to at least one of Rokeach's terminal values. We will not discuss all of these relations here, but we note, for example, that *Jazz* is related to the values of technological development, self realization and wisdom; *Mainstream* music is related to such basic and commonly held values as peace, family security, love, social recognition, health and justice.

Thus far, we have pointed out some of the relations possible to identify in Table 6, but what do these correlations actually mean? A multitude of different interpretations are possible, and we will present some of them.

The first interesting observation is that it is possible to interpret the musical taste pattern of *Mainstream* as indicating the existence of a common popular cultural base for young people in Sweden. As has already been shown in Table 4 above, very few individuals express negative attitudes towards the musical genres constituting the *Mainstream* pattern. Furthermore, no relationship is found between this musical taste pattern and any of the positional and structural variables used in our analysis.

This interpretation of the *Mainstream* musical pattern obtains further support when we note in Table 6 that this common musical taste pattern is related to a number of very basic and commonly held values such as peace, family security, freedom, love, national security, social recognition, justice and health. It is also positively correlated with Inglehart's material value orientation, and with our personal value orientations of material, social and personal security. Inglehart and Mitchell argue that it is only when the needs tied to a material value orientation are satisfied, that the individual develops needs based on what Inglehart calls postmaterial and Mitchell outer-directed values. Following their argumentation we conclude that the *Mainstream* musical pattern is a taste pattern primarily based on values having to do with security.

The reason why almost all our respondents express a positive attitude towards mainstream music is probably that it constitutes a common popular culture sphere to which everyone can relate. The taste for mainstream music thus contribute to a sense of cultural security and belongingness, a feeling of sameness and integration. This interpretation is further strengthened by the fact that the *Mainstream* musical pattern is the only one that is positively correlated with the value of social recognition. Following Kamler's view, positive attitudes towards mainstream music can be considered to be based on values held by the individual *because of* what other people think of his or her values. Thus, these are the kind of values we call outer-directed.

The fact that most young people in our sample express positive attitudes towards mainstream music implies that it does not primarily serve to differentiate between Swedish young people. The desire to distinguish oneself, to be unique and authentic is to be found in the attitudes towards other music genres than the ones constituting the *Mainstream* musical pattern. These attitudes are probably based to a higher degree on other types of values than outer-directed ones. To comprehend differentiation within youth culture it is thus necessary to also discuss ethical and metaphysical values in relation to musical taste. In line with this, we will discuss three rather distinct musical taste patterns: *Jazz, Opera/musicals,* and *Socially conscious.*

These three patterns are all correlated positively with Inglehart's postmaterial value orientation, which suggests that they are based on other values and attitudes than the *Mainstream* musical pattern. Furthermore, the musical genres constituting the three patterns in question are characterized by wide variations in respondents' attitudes towards them. This implies that these taste patterns are used as means of differentiation and distinction rather than of belonging and showing sameness. It is reasonable to assume, therefore, that positive attitudes towards these taste patterns are based on values held not only because of what other people think, but more importantly *irrespective of* what other people think.

The first musical taste pattern we will discuss is *Jazz.* Of the twelve patterns this is one of the most distinct. It is related to the values of technological development, a sense of accomplishment, wisdom and the personal value orientation of personal development. These values all express progress and development in different areas. In contrast with the values and value orientations related to the *Mainstream* pattern, they have nothing to do with security in either the personal or the social sphere. The taste for jazz music is probably mainly based on aesthetical, but probably also to a certain degree on ethical and metaphysical values. Many great jazz artists have been influenced by Eastern religions and mysticism, but also by Western religions. Many classical pieces within jazz history are actually devoted to metaphysical contemplation. One of the most famous is probably John Coltrane's album from 1964 *A Love Supreme*, dedicated to God.

During the year 1957, I experienced, by the grace of God, a spiritual awakening which was to leave me to a richer, fuller, more productive life. At that time, in gratitude, I humbly asked to be given the means and privilege to make others happy through music. I feel this has been granted through His grace. ALL PRAISE TO GOD (John Coltrane 1964).

The other taste pattern we shall deal with here is *Opera/musicals*. This taste pattern can be characterized as high cultural. It correlates positively with level of education, and it is mostly women who express a positive attitudes towards this kind of music genres. The *Opera/musicals* pattern is mainly related to the values of a clean world, a sense of accomplishment, inner harmony, wisdom and self-regard, and the personal value orientations of personal and material development. Like the *Jazz* pattern, this taste pattern is related to personal and social development, albeit in a somewhat different way. It is related not only to aesthetic, metaphysical and ethical values, but also to material values. Inner and personal development here are thus intimately related to the quest for a high status position in society.

Finally we will discuss the taste pattern we call *Socially conscious*. This taste pattern is strongly related to gender; girls tend to express positive attitudes towards the musical genres included in this pattern more than boys. Furthermore, it is related to the values of peace, equality, and a world of beauty, inner harmony and love. It is also negatively correlated with the values of power and wealth. Positive attitudes towards this musical taste pattern seems to be related to an interest in ethical and political issues. The values lying behind the taste pattern in question differ from the values related to the *Jazz* and *Opera/musicals* patterns in that they are not basically related to personal development and satisfaction, but to social development — values which could properly be described as idealistic. Using Arnold Mitchell's terminology, we may speak of socially conscious individuals.

Our discussion of the empirical relations between values, positions and taste patterns is necessarily somewhat schematic and general. Nevertheless, the empirical results presented and analyzed hitherto provide us with a basic picture of how music may serve different functions within youth culture. However, to arrive at a more profound understanding of how individuals' values are related to their tastes in music or in other areas, it is probably necessary to study how the single individuals integrate the different parts of their identity so as to constructs their own lifestyle. For this reason, we will return to these relations in more detail in discussing and analysing the seven case studies.

From the simple correlation matrix presented in Table 6 we cannot gain insight into the complex relations between values, societal position and tastes. Thus, we have conducted a number of MCA-analyses in order to arrive at a more thorough knowledge of the empirical relations between these different variables.

In order to carry out a complete analysis of the relations between societal position, values and musical taste patterns, we would have to conduct an MCA-analysis for all the thirty values and value orientations concerning their relation to each of the twelve musical taste patterns, a total 360 MCA-analyses. No attempt will be made to present all these analysis here. Rather, we have chosen two analyses in particular in order to exemplify the relations in which we are interested. Our basic concern is with the relations as such and not with the way in which a particular taste pattern is influenced by a certain value or a certain positional variable. We will endeavor to demonstrate that those complex relations to be found between structure, position and lifestyle which we have discussed in the theoretical parts of this book may indeed be found in empirical reality.

We first present two musical taste patterns, *Mainstream* music and *Opera/musicals*. We could have chosen any two of the twelve musical taste patterns, but we wished to contrast the more general mainstream pattern with a more distinct taste pattern. We located, for each of the two taste patterns, the value showing the strongest correlation with it. This was to be able to see whether the correlation remained after the influence of the positional and structural variables had been controlled for.

In Figures 7 and 8 we account for each positional variable's unique influence on a value, on the one hand, and a musical taste pattern, on the other. In the same figures we also account for the unique influence of a specific value on a specific taste pattern. Each figure is based on nine single analyses in which the relation between two variables was investigated while the influence of the other relevant variables was kept constant. Our intention was primarily to analyze empirically the complex relations between the influence of structural, positional and individual variables on musical taste.

Figure 7. MCA-Analysis of the Relations Between Positional Variables, the Value of Wisdom and the Music Taste Pattern of Mainstream.

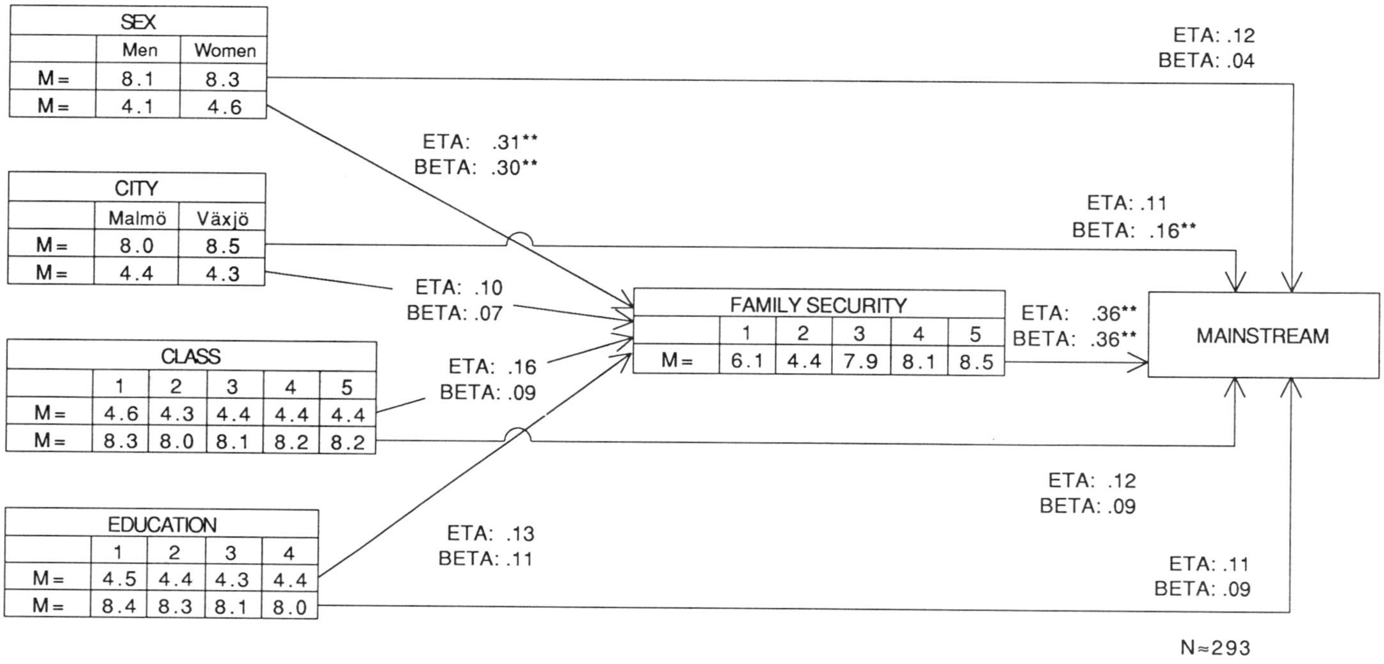

SEX

	Men	Women
M =	8.1	8.3
M =	4.1	4.6

ETA: .31**
BETA: .30**

CITY

	Malmö	Växjö
M =	8.0	8.5
M =	4.4	4.3

ETA: .10
BETA: .07

CLASS

	1	2	3	4	5
M =	4.6	4.3	4.4	4.4	4.4
M =	8.3	8.0	8.1	8.2	8.2

ETA: .16
BETA: .09

EDUCATION

	1	2	3	4
M =	4.5	4.4	4.3	4.4
M =	8.4	8.3	8.1	8.0

ETA: .13
BETA: .11

FAMILY SECURITY

	1	2	3	4	5
M =	6.1	4.4	7.9	8.1	8.5

ETA: .36**
BETA: .36**

ETA: .12
BETA: .04

ETA: .11
BETA: .16**

ETA: .12
BETA: .09

ETA: .11
BETA: .09

MAINSTREAM

N≈293

Figure 8. MCA-Analysis of the Relations Between Positional Variables, the Value of Wisdom and the Music Taste Pattern of Opera/Musicals.

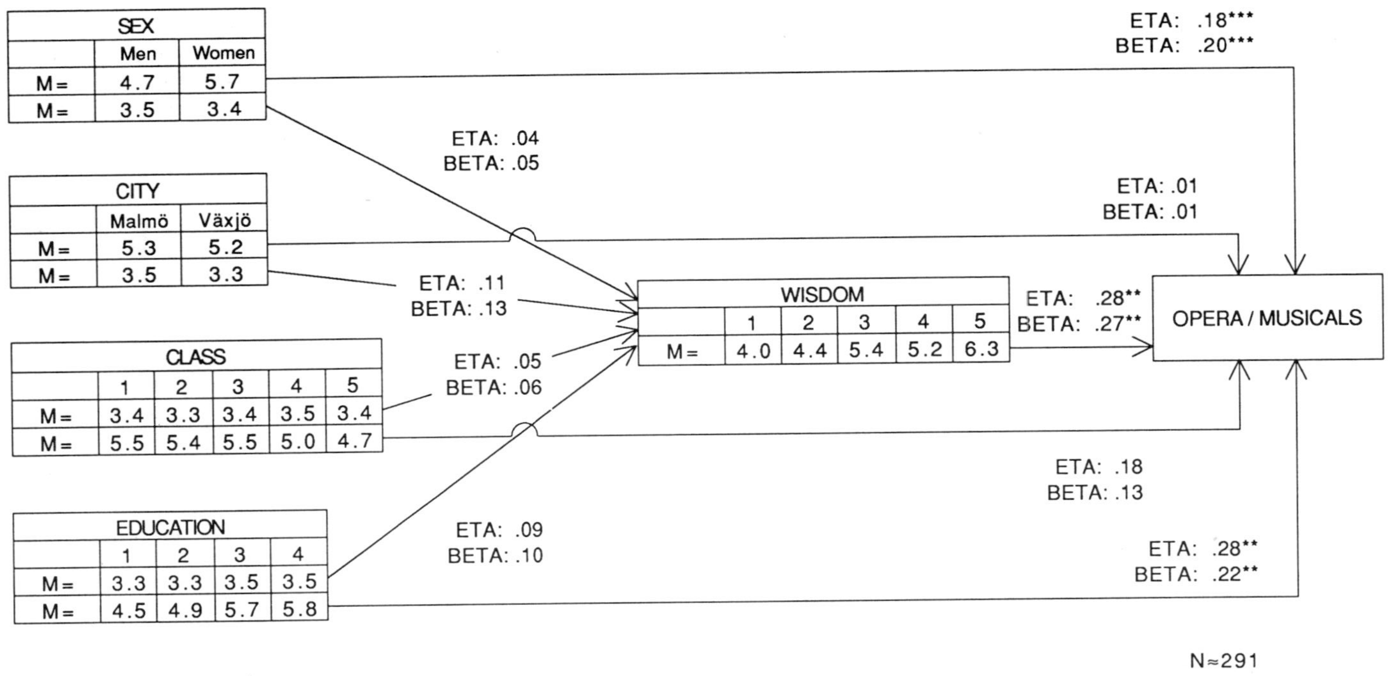

ETA: .18***
BETA: .20***

ETA: .01
BETA: .01

ETA: .28**
BETA: .27**

ETA: .18
BETA: .13

ETA: .28**
BETA: .22**

OPERA / MUSICALS

WISDOM

	1	2	3	4	5
M =	4.0	4.4	5.4	5.2	6.3

ETA: .04
BETA: .05

ETA: .11
BETA: .13

ETA: .05
BETA: .06

ETA: .09
BETA: .10

SEX

	Men	Women
M =	4.7	5.7
M =	3.5	3.4

CITY

	Malmö	Växjö
M =	5.3	5.2
M =	3.5	3.3

CLASS

	1	2	3	4	5
M =	3.4	3.3	3.4	3.5	3.4
M =	5.5	5.4	5.5	5.0	4.7

EDUCATION

	1	2	3	4
M =	3.3	3.3	3.5	3.5
M =	4.5	4.9	5.7	5.8

N=291

Since musical taste can be used as one indicator of lifestyle, such an analysis constitutes a possible way of arriving empirically at an understanding of how lifestyles are influenced by structural and positional features as well as by individual ones. In the models presented the unique influence of value on the taste pattern provide an indication of the strength of the individual influence, whereas the influence of gender, class and education indicates the strength of positional influence, and the influence of place of birth indicates the strength of the influence emanating from structure.

In analysing the relation between the family security value and the *Mainstream* musical pattern, our hypothesis about mainstream music as an expression of a common culture based on security values and the desire to belong rather than to differ receives further support. Although the value of family security shows a strong correlation with gender, this correlation does not explain the total variation in the dependent variable. The very strong influence of the value of family security on the taste for mainstream music remains intact even when gender and the other positional variables are held constant.

The rather strong correlation between the value of family security and the mainstream music pattern can be explained in different ways. Since family security is one of the most commonly held values identified by Rokeach, one can pose the question of the extent to which structure explains the relation in question. Family security can be seen as a value commonly agreed upon among Swedish young people, just as mainstream music seems to be a commonly liked popular musical genre. This implies that both this particular value and the musical taste pattern are part of the common value and taste structure among Swedish youth. This is not to say, however, that the value and the taste patterns are totally determined by structural factors, only that the individuals within this structure are more likely to incorporate both the family security value and the *Mainstream* musical taste pattern, than other values and taste patterns. There are also positionally determined explanationswhich can be given here: females emphasize the family security value to a higher degree than males. Furthermore, individually determined explanations to the relation between family security and mainstream music can be given, as indicated by the fact that the taste for mainstream music is independent of gender, and that the impact of family security on mainstream music remains intact even when gender is controlled for.

In cases where a commonly held value is correlated with a commonly liked taste pattern, one can note complex relations between the three determining factors: structure, position and individual. As already discussed, the taste for mainstream music is probably not primarily based on developmental values, but rather on values related to the need and desire to feel secure. Family security is obviously a value expressing such needs and desires, and it is thus not surprising that it is positively correlated with the musical taste pattern representative of the common youth culture. However, this does not mean that there no individual choice is involved in embracing security values and *Mainstream* musical taste. As already indicated, the need and desire for belonging and for sameness constitute one aspect of the identity of the individual. It is quite natural that the *Mainstream* musical taste pattern is positively correlated with a number of very basic and commonly held values relating to security such as peace, family security, love, national security, justice and health. Furthermore, not everyone likes mainstream music, and not everyone embraces the values of security in an equally strong way, there being considerable variations between individuals in this respect.

We now turn to the next example of the relations between value and musical taste (see Figure 8). This relation differs from the former in that the attitudes towards the value concerned — wisdom — are more differentiated among the respondents than was the case with family security. Also, the attitudes towards the musical genres constituting the taste pattern — *Opera/musicals* — are considerably more distinct than in the case of mainstream music. Furthermore, the values related to this musical taste pattern are not primarily security values, but are instead related to Inglehart's postmaterial value orientation and to those Rokeachean values expressing personal development: wisdom, a sense of accomplishment, inner harmony and self-regard.

The taste for *Opera/musicals* is thus not primarily a function of the individual's needs and desires to feel sameness and cultural security. Contrary to the *Mainstream* taste pattern, the taste for *Opera/musicals* is to a large extent held regardless of what other people think. Through a taste for *Opera/musicals* individuals distinguish themselves from other groups and individuals. This becomes obvious when one notes that the taste for *Opera/musicals* is correlated with education and thus with the degree of cultural capital. Through the attitudes towards musical genres constituting this taste pattern, the individual can express his or her social and cultural status. The pattern in question is also correlated, however, with gender; women favors this type of music more than men. The taste for *Opera/musicals* is thus partly determined by the individual's social and cultural position — but not entirely.

The value of wisdom shows no relation with any of the positional variables, which indicates that the value is held irrespectively of class, education or gender. There is a rather strong positive correlation, however, between wisdom and the musical taste pattern *Opera/musicals*. This correlation remains strong even when the positional and structural variables are controlled for. This indicates that the element of individual determination is considerable in the case of *Opera/musicals*. It is also probable that the taste for *Opera/musicals* is primarily based on other types of values than the security oriented ones.

There are probably several different explanations of the individual impact of the attitudes towards *Opera/musicals*. One could expect, for example, that the taste for this type of music would relate to social and cultural mobility. That is, individuals interested in career and status listen to this type of music in order to increase their cultural capital. This is also indicated by the fact that the taste pattern in question is positively correlated with the personal value orientation of material development. However, one could also assume that the taste for *Opera/musicals* is related to cultural mobility without being related to the status dimension. This hypothesis is supported by the rather strong positive correlation between the personal value orientation of personal development and the taste pattern in question.

As mentioned several times before, the complex system of values, attitudes and actions which we call a lifestyle is determined by a variety of structural, positional and individual phenomena. In this section we have analyzed the relation between the value and the attitude levels of lifestyle, on the one hand, and the relation between structural, positional and individual influences on these relations, on the other. Before proceeding to a general theoretical and analytical discussion of these different relations, we will consider empirically both relations between value and another set of taste patterns, that of film taste, and the relation between value and the action level of lifestyle in relation to the three levels of determination.

PATTERNS OF FILM TASTE

The second popular culture area which we shall discuss which is important to youth culture is film. Just as with music, film is something almost all young people nowadays are in contact daily with. Ever since film ceased to reside in the movie theatres only and moved into people's homes via TV and video, it has become an increasingly common component of young people's everyday life. Accordingly, it has increased in importance as a component in young people's lifestyles.

According to Featherstone (1991a), Hollywood film has played an important role in the creation of new standards of appearance and of bodily presentation. Film stars and lifestyles have been created and been packaged for audience consumption. Hollywood has marketed stars as "personalities", along with ideals of how to look and behave. The present-day perception of the body has been highly influenced by the wide array of images and stars provided both by the motion picture and the advertising industries.

The influence of the movies and its stars on people is complex, however, and it should not be simplified and be regarded merely as creating a desire or wish to be like, or even resemble, its characters. Rather, the movies supply its viewers with images by means of which they can maintain, transcend and develop their conceptions of themselves, regardless of the class or status boundaries of the real world. In this manner movies can contribute to what Ewen (1988) calls an illusory transcendence of class. Robert Sklar (1985) puts this point neatly in his study of the role of American movies, *Movie-made America*.

> But it would be a mistake to conclude that the popularity of American movies overseas was based on the desire to look or talk or live like Americans. People who changed their appearance or behavior following the modes of American movies did not hope to become someone else so much as they wished to be more like their conception of themselves. Hollywood gave the world images of personal felicity that directly denied the barriers and prerogatives of class. Girls could get their boys, and boys their girls, no matter what their income or social station; right could triumph over wrong no matter what forces of power or privilege stood in its way. The happy ending was a formula invented by neither Americans nor movies, but for several decades in the first half of the twentieth century no other medium or national culture could create visions of love and social satisfaction in the glamorous, confident, compelling manner of Hollywood (Sklar 1985:227).

Against the background of this it is reasonable to conclude that the increased availability of films through TV and video has increased the importance of films as a major influential force in contemporary identity and lifestyle development among youth.

A thoroughgoing analysis of the star phenomenon is to be found in Richard Dyer's book *Stars* (1986a) Following the writing of this more theoretically oriented work, Dyer wrote *Heavenly Bodies* (1986b), in which he provided a detailed account of three different stars: Marilyn Monroe, Paul Robeson and Judy Garland. According to Dyer (1986a,b), the most interesting aspect of the star phenomenon is not the characters portrayed by the stars, but rather the whole business of their constructing, performing and being a certain "character".

> Stars articulate what it is to be a human being in contemporary society; that is, they express the particular notion we hold of the person, of the "individual". They do so complexly, variously — they are not straight forward affirmations of individualism. On the contrary, they articulate both the promise and the difficulty that the notion of individuality presents for all of us who live by it (Dyer 1986:8).

Stars thus articulate and help to clarify fundamental cultural issues such as the self-versus-others distinction, in what ways individuality can be expressed, how identity can be handled, and the like. Stars have probably had different functions in different historical periods, as well as for different individuals living in the same society.

Dyer (1986a) maintains that it is meaningful to distinguish between two different and historically determined functions of stars: their being embodiments of *ideal ways of behaving*, and being embodiments of *typical ways of behaving*. During the period prior to the 1930s, stars were treated more or less like Gods and Goddesses or as heroes. After the 1930s stars became identification figures in the sense of being "people like you and me".

No doubt, the star still has an important role in young people's attitudes towards different film genres. This becomes obvious when one considers Table 7, which summarizes our respondents' attitudes towards some forty different film genres.

The most popular genres consist of films in which the lead character is played by Anglo-Saxon or Swedish contemporary film actors or actresses who are widely recognized, for instance Harrison Ford, Julia Roberts, Jack Nicholson, Sean Connery, Donald Sutherland, Kim Basinger, Mel Gibson, Gösta Ekman, Lasse Åberg, Eddy Murphy or Meryl Streep.

The less popular genres, on the other hand, consist of films in which the lead characters are played either by non-Anglo-Saxons, non-Swedes or less widely recognized Anglo-Saxons, such as in the films of Fassbinder, Jarmush, Tarkovskij, Wajda and Kurosawa.

Table 7. Film Taste, Distaste, Indifference and Ignorance (means and percentages).

Film genre	$\overline{X}$	% Taste	% Distaste	% Indiff	% Don't know
Action comedy	4.5	94	2	5	-
Swedish comedy	4.3	86	3	11	-
Adventure	4.2	82	6	12	-
Farce	4.0	74	7	19	-
James Bond	4.0	75	8	17	-
Thrillers	3.9	75	8	16	-
Dance film	3.8	66	15	19	-
Gangster film	3.8	67	10	22	1
Agent film	3.7	71	6	23	6
Police film	3.7	64	9	24	3
Satire	3.6	61	21	18	-
Romantic film	3.6	56	12	31	2
Youth film	3.6	57	13	29	1
Relation film	3.5	56	10	27	6
Animated film/cartoons	3.5	54	9	35	3
College film	3.5	40	10	25	5
Mini series	3.5	57	16	25	1
War film	3.5	56	16	27	-
Erotic film	3.5	55	10	30	5
Western	3.4	53	20	26	1
Classic Hollywood	3.3	45	10	42	3
Horror	3.2	47	27	25	1
Tragicomic film	3.0	37	24	36	3
Science fiction	2.9	31	40	28	-
Future film	2.6	30	20	33	17
Situation comedy	2.6	25	11	46	18
Fantasy	2.6	32	28	24	16
Historic film	2.5	26	16	38	20
Documentaries	2.5	28	18	34	20
Splatter and gore	2.5	28	29	27	16
Classical masterpieces	2.3	22	14	38	26
Karate and ninja	2.2	14	57	28	1
Socially conscious film	2.1	21	15	30	33
Pornography	2.0	10	55	26	9
Psychological films	1.9	12	44	26	19
Poetic film	1.6	9	38	21	32
Underground	1.2	6	23	18	52

Although the star phenomenon can be considered as part of the explanation of why young people favour certain film genres and ignore others, there are other explanations as well.

First, films which for one reason or another are not socially accepted and are often even condemned on basically moral grounds do not find acceptance among our respondents. Among this type of films we find hard-core pornography, karate films, splatter and gore films, etc., that is, films containing or even concentrating on extremely explicit portrayals of either sex or violence or a combination of both. The films in question are the same ones which has been subject to moral condemnation and discussion in the mass media (cf. discussion of moral panics in chapter 9).

Secondly, our respondents are not especially attracted by films primarily made, not to entertain or amuse people, but to deal with more or less controversial, existential, social and/or psychological problems (for instance, documentaries and political films). For young people film is primarily a means of entertainment and amusement. However, from this does not follow that young people are uninterested in existential, political, social or psychological questions; they may use other media and channels for involvement in such issues.

Thirdly, the majority of our respondents express distaste or indifference towards experimental films or films which have abandoned the traditional narrative rules, such as underground films and poetic films. In these films the plot is not always the central component; often the visual aesthetics and method of telling the story are put in the foreground instead. One reason why this type of film is not very popular among our respondents may be that these films require certain cineastic knowledge and competence of its audience, that is, a certain type of popular cultural capital to a high degree.

To obtain a general and more manageable overview of our respondents' film tastes we present a factor analysis in Table 8. The analysis resulted in nine different factors or taste patterns: *Romantic films*, *Poetic/psychological* films, *Socially conscious* films, *Science fiction/fantasy* films, *Horror* films, *Porno & violence* films, *Agent* films, *Comedy* films, and *War/gangster* films.

Table 8. Factor Analysis of Film Taste

	F1	F2	F3	F4	F5	F6	F7	F8	F9
Factor 1, Romantic									
Classic Hollywood	.66	.18	.24	-.02	-.12	.02	.06	.06	-.18
Miniseries	.81	-.17	-.03	-.08	.03	.06	-.03	.15	-.08
Relation Film	.71	.04	.25	-.21	-.05	-.15	.00	.01	.05
Romantic Film	.81	-.08	-.10	-.03	-.05	-.04	.03	-.01	.06
Dance Film	.79	-.15	-.06	.08	-.01	.07	-.07	.07	.05
Youth Film	.58	-.02	-.28	.10	-.05	.08	-.02	.23	.33
Factor 2, Poetic/Psychologic									
Poetic Film	-.04	.77	.35	.00	-.13	-.03	-.05	-.15	.03
Underground	-.18	.76	.33	-.04	.05	.08	-.20	-.10	-.09
Psychologic Film	-.04	.78	.26	-.03	.06	-.07	-.01	-.12	-.08
Factor 3, Socially Conscious									
Historic Film	-.03	.16	.65	.19	-.27	-.10	-.05	-.02	.09
Documentaries	.02	.15	.72	-.06	.08	-.11	.02	-.07	.13
Socially Conscious	.05	.36	.61	-.16	-.15	-.15	-.09	-.13	-.02
Classic Masterpieces	.00	.41	.62	.12	-.04	-.07	.00	-.02	.03
Factor 4, SF/Fantasy									
Science Fiction	-.19	-.06	-.06	.74	.10	.27	.07	.06	.05
Fantasy	.02	-.12	-.10	.72	.22	.33	-.10	.06	-.07
Factor 5, Horror									
Thrillers	-.15	-.11	.05	.03	.75	-.01	.17	.03	.22
Horror	-.08	-.07	-.15	.12	.81	.15	-.05	.07	.14
Splatter and Gore	.04	.01	-.12	.25	.74	.20	.05	.17	-.05
Factor 6, Porno and Violence									
Karate and Ninja	.11	-.12	-.13	.29	.11	.65	-.01	-.03	.03
Police Film	.09	-.23	-.09	-.03	.30	.55	.37	.27	.14
Western	-.04	.04	-.10	.05	.05	.65	.32	.25	.01
Pornography	-.02	.09	-.29	.07	.27	.48	.13	.00	.35
Factor 7, Agent									
James Bond	.00	-.11	-.10	.15	.05	.17	.84	.09	.03
Agent Films	-.12	-.04	.10	.09	.05	.16	.84	.02	.16
Factor 8, Comedy									
Farce	.26	-.21	-.17	.13	.18	.16	.15	.68	.00
Swedish comedy	.22	-.12	-.30	.06	.10	-.11	.42	.42	.07
College Film	.38	-.17	-.14	.14	.21	.29	.01	.52	.08
Action Comedy	.13	-.32	-.11	.12	.19	.28	.31	.44	.08
Factor 9, War and Gangster									
War Film	-.16	-.17	.11	.04	.03	.54	.08	.06	.57
Gangster Film	-.09	-.11	.23	-.09	.19	.16	.22	.13	.66
ALPHA	.85	.87	.76	.75	.78	.70	.81	.76	.62
EIGENVALUE	7.3	4.6	3.4	1.9	1.8	1.4	1.3	1.2	1.1
PCT OF VAR	19.8	12.5	9.2	5.1	4.8	3.8	3.5	3.1	3.0
Dropped Variables									
Satire	-.52	.25	.13	.20	-.01	-.02	.05	.46	.24
Tragikomic Film	-.13	.63	.02	-.02	-.29	-.17	-.04	.31	.18
Future Film	-.31	.30	.10	.61	.07	.03	.10	.01	.02
Situation Comedy	-.03	.11	.50	.00	.02	.08	-.01	.51	.07
Adventure	.03	-.39	.03	.38	.25	.22	.25	.23	-.07
Erotic Film	.32	.26	.02	.16	.19	-.04	.03	-.10	.58
Animated Film / Cartoons	.16	.07	.16	.67	.02	-.24	.17	.13	.11

The purpose of our distinction between different film taste patterns is primarily to identify some general categories which are possible to use in the analysis of relations between young people's film taste, their social and cultural background and their values. In Table 9 we present an overview of the relations between these variables.

Table 9. Film Taste Related to Positional Variables, Values and Value Orientations (Pearson´s Correlations).

	Romantic	Poetic/ Psycho	Socially Consc	SF/ Fantasy	Horror	Porno & Violence	Agent	Comedy	War & Gangster
Sex	.55***	-.01	-.02	-.30***	-.30***	-.40***	-.33***	-.15**	-.31***
City	.04	-.10	-.07	-.07	-.04	-.01	.15**	-.06	-.03
Class	-.15**	.01	.09	-.04	-.05	-.19**	.09	-.12	.00
Education	-.15	-.01	.01	-.19**	-.29***	-.34***	.00	-.26***	-.10
Material security	.20***	-.26***	-.20***	.25***	.24***	.37***	.26***	.46***	.19***
Personal security	.33***	-.14	-.08	.04	-.02	.05	.06	.20***	-.04
Social security	.24***	.01	.03	-.04	.01	-.09	.05	.14	-.04
Personal develop	.06	.23***	.23***	-.01	.02	-.14	-.03	-.09	-.04
Mat develop	-.02	.05	.12	-.05	-.01	-.03	.15**	-.01	.11
Material	.24***	-.22***	-.12	.06	.18**	.18**	.16**	.37***	.15**
Postmaterial	.18**	.20***	.22***	-.11	-.17**	-.24***	-.10	-.11	-.14
A clean world	.14	-.03	.08	-.06	-.13	-.16**	-.06	-.01	-.07
Techn developm	-.13	-.04	.02	.19***	.21***	.22***	.30***	.15**	.23***
Comfortable life	.22***	-.06	.05	-.01	.01	.07	.09	.25***	.01
Exciting life	.01	-.17**	.17**	.00	.10	-.01	.08	.00	-.01
Accomplishment	.10	.08	.21***	-.04	-.02	-.03	.15	-.01	.03
Peace	.29***	-.03	.05	-.07	-.02	-.06	-.10	.16**	-.07
World of beauty	.22***	.10	.15**	.04	.09	.03	.00	.11	.01
Equality	.25***	.15	.16**	-.04	-.10	-.18**	-.23***	.00	-.10
Family security	.33***	-.07	.01	-.04	.02	.01	-.02	.20***	.00
Freedom	.16**	.06	.09	-.06	.02	-.04	-.01	.09	.00
Happiness	.29***	.01	.02	-.04	.00	.03	-.02	.22***	-.08
Inner harmony	.18**	.07	.14	-.03	-.03	-.06	.03	.01	-.04
Love	.30***	.02	.07	-.08	-.06	-.07	-.02	.16**	-.04
National security	.19***	-.12	-.04	.11	.12	.22***	.22***	.23***	.24***
Pleasure	.25***	.00	.05	.04	.08	.19***	.16**	.26***	.13
Salvation	.07	-.05	-.04	.07	-.05	.06	.03	.7	-.05
Self-respect	.08	.10	.23***	.10	-.02	-.04	.21***	-.01	.13
Social recognition	.08	.00	-.02	.14	.11	.24***	.25***	.17**	.19***
Wisdom	-.15**	.15**	.21***	.06	-.07	-.13	-.04	.15**	-.05
Justice	.17**	.04	.13	-.06	-.05	-.08	-.08	-.02	.05
Power	-.09	.01	.01	.14	.20***	.31***	.27***	.14	.20***
Health	.17**	-.05	.00	.05	.05	.03	.02	.25***	-.02
Wealth	-.01	-.01	-.05	.20***	.27***	.28***	.24***	.27***	.21***

The first striking observation concerning our respondents' film tastes is that they are much more closely related to social status and gender than is the case with musical taste. The most influential of the positional variables is gender. All but two of the film taste patterns are related to this variable. However, each of the film patterns is also related to at least two of Rokeach's values, and in most cases to Inglehart's value-dimension, and to one or more of the personal value orientations, as well.

Of the nine taste patterns, only one is female-oriented, whereas five are clearly male oriented. It is noteworthly that the female-oriented film pattern (*Romantic*) is the one with the strongest relation to gender. This pattern contains films which basically concern the relation between a women and a man, dealing with such traditional female themes as family relations and romantic love. Such films include Hollywood melodramas (*Gone with the Wind* (1939), *From here to Eternity* (1953)), Romantic love films (*The Blue Lagoon* (1980), *An Officer and a Gentleman* (1982)), Relations films (*Children of a Lesser God* (1986), *Falling in Love* (1984), *Kramer vs. Kramer* (1979)), Mini-series (*Lace* (1984), Dance films (*Flashdance* (1983), *Dirty Dancing* (1987)), and Swedish youth films (*PS — sista sommaren* (1988), *Ingen kan älska som vi* (1988)).

It is not surprising, therefore, to find that this film pattern is likewise related to a number of Rokeach's values previously identified (Table 3) as primarily female: equality, family security, happiness, love, peace, and the like. It is also related to the security oriented personal value orientations of material, social and personal security. The *Romantic* film pattern is also related to both of Ingelhart's value orientations, but most strongly to the material orientation. Since in Inglehart's terms females are more postmaterial than males (Table 3), these results suggest that gender provides a more important explanation of the respondents' attitudes towards the romantic film pattern than their value orientation does. That is, women like such films irrespective of their postmaterial or material orientation. The romantic film pattern can be said to be a mainstream female taste pattern.

As indicated previously, no less than five of the nine film taste patterns distinguished are clearly male-oriented. These are: Science fiction/fantasy (*Star wars* (1977), *Conan the Barbarian* (1982)), Horror (*Frantic* (1988), *The Shining* (1980), *Evil dead* (1983)), Porno & violence (*Foxy Lady*, *The Good, the Bad and the Ugly* (1967), *Sudden Impact* (1983), *Game of Death* (1978)), Agent (*Eye of the Needle* (1981), *A View to a Kill* (1985)), and War/gangster (*Platoon* (1986), *The Godfather* (1972)).

Characteristic of most of these films is that they contain traditional male elements such as violence, male heroes, power, crime, physical strength, and the like. The main characters portrayed in these films are, of course, male and many of them are individualistic. Whereas romantic films deal basically with problems and questions experienced by the majority of girls in everyday life, the male-oriented film patterns primarily deal with extraordinary matters. And while the heroes and heroines of female-oriented films cope with conflicts and problems in a basically verbal and emotional way, the heroes of the male oriented films let their muscles, fists and guns talk.

Just as the female taste pattern is related to typically female values, the male taste patterns are related to typically male oriented Rokechean values such as technological development, power and wealth. Furthermore, they are related to the personal value orientation of material security and to Inglehart's material value orientation. Whereas the female taste pattern was positively correlated to both Inglehart's value orientations, the male taste pattern was either negatively correlated or was not related at all to a postmaterial value orientation. Since in Inglehart's terms males are less inclined to be postmaterial (Table 3), this result provides further support for the hypothesis that film taste is clearly related to gender.

These results should be interpreted against the background of the traditional gender roles of Western society. Boys and girls are socialized in very different ways. There are thus great differences between boys' and girls' in their biological, psychological, social and cultural development. Whereas mothers tend to identify more with daughters and to provide them less in differentating, they identify less with their sons, who are pushed towards differentiation and the taking of a male and more individualistic role in society (Chodorow 1974, 1978; Miller 1976, 1984).

I would suggest that a quality of embeddedness in social interaction and personal relationships characterizes women's life relative to men's. From childhood, daughters are likely to participate in an intergenerational world with their mother, and often with their aunts and grandmother, whereas boys are on their own or participate in a single-generation world of age mates. In adult life, women's interaction with other women in most societies is kin-based and cuts across generational lines. Their roles tend to be particularistic, and to involve diffuse relationships and responsibilities rather than specific ones. Women in most societies are *defined* relationally (as someone's wife, mother daughter, daughter-in-law; even a nun becomes the Bride of Christ). Men's association (although it, too, may be kin-based and intergenerational) is much more likely than women's to cut across kinship units, to be restricted to a single generation, and to be recruited according to universalistic criteria and involve relationships and responsibilities defined by their specificity (Chodorow 1974:57f).

Although film tastes seem to be strongly related to gender, and the film tastes of our respondents suggest very traditional gender roles and tastes, there is nevertheless considerable individual variation in taste. This is shown by the fact that two taste patterns could be identified which were not at all related to gender (*Poetic/psychological* (*Stalker* (1979), *Down by Law* (1986), *The Seventh Seal* (1957)), and *Socially Conscious* (*Danton* (1982), *Koyaanisqatsi* (1983), *Man of Marble* (1977), *Potemkin* (1925)), and one pattern only slightly male oriented (*Comedy* (*Police Academy* (1984), *The Adventures of Picasso* (1978), *Porky's* (1981), *Beverly Hills Cop* (1984)).

It is interesting to note that the film taste patterns *Poetic/psychological* and *Socially conscious* are not related to any of the positional variables. Our respondents' attitudes towards these film patterns seem to be primarily related to their values and value orientations. Both patterns are positively correlated with Inglehart's postmaterial value orientation and the *Poetic/psychological* pattern is also negatively correlated with his material value orientation. Both taste patterns are positively correlated with the personal value orientation of personal development, and negatively correlated with that of material security. These results imply that preferences for these film genres are related to values stressing personal development and personal growth. This assumption obtains even more support when one notes that the taste patterns in question are positively related to the Rokeachean values of an exciting life, wisdom, self-regard, a sense of accomplishment, and the like. These taste patterns cut across the gender, class and status dimensions.

In in an attempt to provide a more detailed understanding of relations between the positional variables, values and film taste, we will present and discuss three MCA-analysis. The first of these concerns the female *Romantic* taste pattern, the second the male-oriented *Porno & violence* taste pattern, and the third the *Socially conscious* taste pattern (unrelated to gender).

Figure 9. MCA-Analysis of the Relations Between Positional Variables, the Value of Family Security and the Romantic Film Pattern.

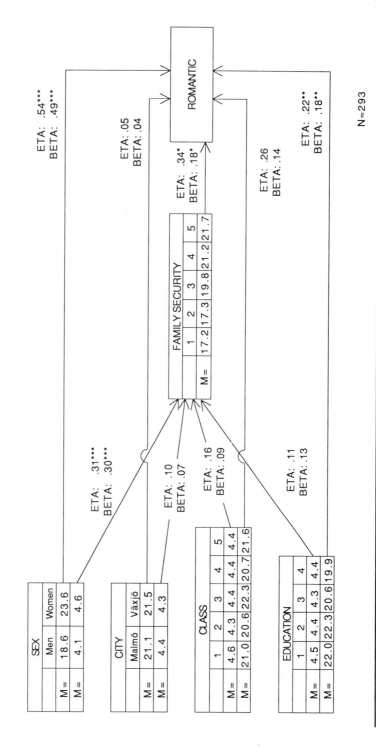

Figure 10. MCA-Analysis of the Relations Between Positional Variables, the Value of Power and the Film Taste Pattern of Porno & Violence.

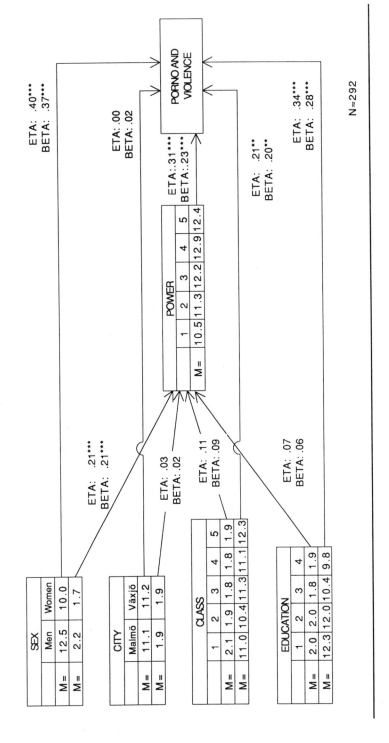

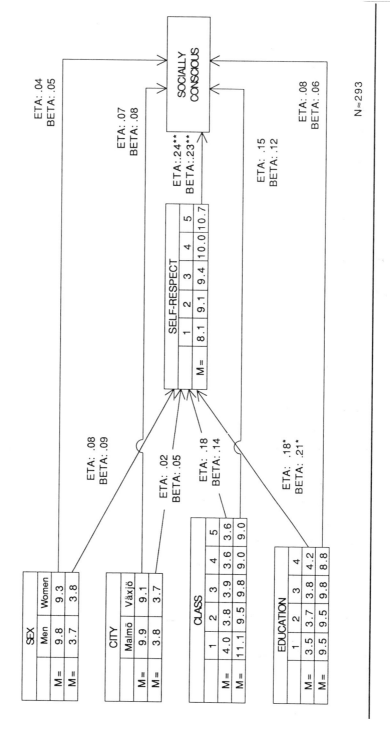

Figure 11. MCA-Analysis of the Relations Between Positional Variables, the Value of Self-Respect and the Socially Conscious Film Taste Pattern.

The relation found between gender and the *Romantic* film pattern obtains further support in Figure 9. As evident in this figure, gender shows the strongest correlation with the film pattern in question, even when the other variables are held constant. We also note that education shows a relatively strong correlation with the *Romantic* film pattern. These results suggest that it is predominantly women of low education who like romantic films. This, however, is only part of the truth. A moderate correlation is also found between the family security value and this film pattern, which indicates there to also be non-positional explanations here.

The results reported on in Figure 9 can be interpreted in at least two different ways. On the one hand, the strong relation between gender, education, the family security value and the *Romantic* film pattern, suggests the existence of traditional gender roles among youth in Swedish society. This clearly illustrates the importance of the structural framework within which the positional and individual variations take place. The reason why gender constitutes the major explanation of a taste for romantic films thus appears to be that these films deal with areas located historically within the female value sphere (cf. Drotner 1991). What is commonly seen as traditional feminine concerns such as care, family, matrimony, strong emotional expressions, and the like, still appeals to a majority of our female respondents. However, this does not necessarily mean that traditional gender roles are unchanged. It is more likely that females have added other values, concerns and interests to these traditional cultural patterns, without abandoning the old ones. The relationship shown in Figure 9 between low education and a taste for romantic films indicates that it is among the lower educated or working class women that the traditional female role is most clearly maintained. However, the extraordinarily strong impact of gender goes far beyond the impact of education, which means that women of both low educational level and high like romantic films.

Although gender constitutes a major explanation of the taste for romantic films, the impact of the family security value evident when the other variables are held constant indicates that non-positional explanations can also be valid. Thus, regardless of either gender or education, our respondents held positive attitudes towards romantic films *if* they valued family security highly. This supports our assumption that the values held by the individual influence her or his tastes. Thus, the relationships shown in Figure 9 illustrate well the complexity inherent in the relations between the structurally, positionally and individually determined aspects of taste and thus of lifestyle.

The results presented in Figure 10 also indicate the existence of a strong relationship between position and film taste. It is scarcely surprising to note that preference for the *Porno & violence* pattern shows relatively strong correlations with gender, education and social class. It is mainly men of low education and low social class who find these kinds of films appealing.

It is also interesting to note that there is a strong correlation between the power value and the film pattern at issue. Power is a value men tend to honor more than women. Whereas the *Romantic* film pattern was typically female, the *Porno & violence* pattern definitely is typically male. It involves films dealing with phenomena and attitudes traditionally related to male culture: virility, authority, power, strength, domination, violence, and the like (cf. Willis 1977). Just as the female *Romantic* film pattern is representative of a traditional female culture, the *Porno & violence* pattern does the same for the traditional male culture.

However, even when holding the positional variables constant, there is a rather strong correlation between the power value and the *Porno & violence* film pattern. That is, irrespective of gender, social status and education, people for whom power is an important value tend to have positive attitudes towards these films. Thus there are also individually determined variations in attitudes towards the film pattern in question.

Although class, social status and above all gender explains a great deal of the variations in film taste, there are also strong individual elements active in the development of taste. This is quite strikingly illustrated in Figure 11, in which the value of self-regard constitutes the strongest explanation of our respondents' attitudes towards the *Socially conscious* film pattern. No positional variables are significantly correlated with this film pattern.

Within the films constituting this film pattern the gender stereotypes inherent in romantic or porno & violence films are often called in question or are simply put aside in favour of other themes. Within this specific film category we find films dealing with such subjects as equality, oppression, racism, sexism, and a diversity of other moral and social issues. Whereas the two patterns previously discussed involve films which are basically consumed for their entertainment value, the socially conscious films aim to a higher degree at educating, discussing, commenting and reflecting on moral and social conditions. Whereas the characters portrayed in the romantic and porno & violence films often are one-dimensional caricatures, being unrealistic, beautiful, and often superhuman, the characters in socially conscious films are multi-dimensional, realistic, ordinary looking, and human.

Different films probably serve different functions for the individual. It seems reasonable to assume that women watching romantic films obtain an image of the *ideal woman*: beautiful, caring, loving, desirable, intelligent, sensitive, and the like. In the same way, in watching porno & violence films, men are supplied with images of *masculinity*: virility, strength, power, self-sufficiency, smartness, toughness, and the like.

Films of the respective types thus provide men and women with archetypical images of gender and of gender roles. Although the male consumers of films probably do not totally identify with Rambo, Dirty Harry, Bruce Lee or John Holmes, they can use them as stereotypes of certain typically male traits and characteristics, useful in the development of a more complex male identity. The same goes for the female consumers of romantic films. It is hard to believe they completely identify with Julia Robert's character in *Pretty Woman*, Scarlet O'Hara or Lace. Rather than being objects of identification, the characters of the typically male and female films, burlesque and exaggerated as they are, may be regarded as fascinating representatives of traditional gender roles.

Recently, however, female Hollywood stars such as Laura Dern, Linda Hamilton, Susan Sarandon, Glen Close and Ellen Barkin have tended to transgress the traditional distinctions between male and female ways of behaving and acting, expressing a more aggressive and self-conscious femininity. This type of female star thus calls in question — often in a dramatic way such as in the film *Thelma and Louise* — the traditional boundaries between masculinity and femininity (cf. also American film noir, Kaplan 1988). This tendency however, has been difficult to capture in our study in that these female stars also transgress the distinctions between the different genres used here.

The characters in socially conscious films are often easier to identify with, since they more closely resemble ordinary people with their complex personalities and characteristics. These films often deal with real life dilemmas and with phenomena most people have experienced. One could also state that watching romantic films and porno & violence films contains a dominant element of escaping everyday life and reality for an hour or two, whereas socially conscious films make the audience confront the problems of reality during such a period more intensely than in everyday life.

We are thus dealing with two rather different phenomena and functions. On the one hand, there are films which provide the public with portrayals of archetypical men and women, extraordinary and fantastic events, happy endings, etc. These kinds of films make it easy for young people to escape from the problems and routines of everyday life and to experience something extraordinary and exciting. (We should mention that by escape we do not mean passivity, but simply a desire most young people have now and then to relax and fantasize. Obviously this can be a very active behavior.)

On the other hand, there are films which provide the public with portrayals of morally and socially conscious characters, thus giving them the means of understanding and relating to both themselves and society. Such films help the audience to confront themselves with important social issues and to obtain a deeper understanding of the causes of these problems, as well as different ways of solving them. The lack of relationship between liking such films and the variables of gender, class, and education, as well as the rather high correlation between self-regard and the film pattern in question, indicates that individual values and attitudes and an interest in the matters discussed in socially conscious films better explain why certain young people find these films attractive than do the more general features of gender, class and education.

In the next section we will sum up and discuss the empirical results presented in this chapter.

VALUES, MUSIC AND FILM

The major aim in the empirical parts of this book is to illustrate and if possible test our theoretical assumptions about the complex relations between values, attitudes and actions, on the one hand, and the importance of structure, position and individual in the making of lifestyles, on the other. Our aim here is not to describe a number of actual lifestyles, but rather to distinguish various taste patterns relevant to the lifestyles of young people. This aims in turn at providing a general understanding of certain important mechanisms in contemporary youth culture. As has been shown, music and film taste patterns depend not only on social class, education and gender, but also on individual choice, based on individually held values.

In classic as well as contemporary works on lifestyle there has been a tendency to exaggerate either the influence of class or status on lifestyle, or the individual freedom to develop or change to whatever lifestyle one wants. It may well be that one can explain a great deal of the variance in the lifestyles of a population using class or status. It may also be possible to empirically support the thesis that the individual has lost his or her earlier ties to culture and its values and has become more individualistic. Stressing the one perspective too hard leads to determinism, and stressing the other too much leads to an extreme form of individualism. Either outcome is unsatisfactory.

What must be kept in mind is that an increased freedom of the individual to form his or her life and lifestyle always takes place within certain structural and positional frameworks to which the individual cannot remain unrelated. The individual must know and honor certain commonly held values, codes of behavior and norms of society. Otherwise he or she will be put in jail or in a mental hospital. The individual must also come to honor the commonly held values, norms, attitudes and roles of his or her class, status group, gender and ethnic group. Otherwise the person will lose his or her cultural and social identity and either become forced to change to another group and adopt its norms and values, or become more or less isolated.

In this chapter we have shown empirically that in the areas of music and film some people make very clear and subtle distinctions of taste, while others adopt a more or less commonly held and general taste. This partly reflect the fact that music and film are not equally important to everybody. For some persons it is a dominant interest through which they can define, express and develop their lifestyle, whereas for others it is one interest among other, and perhaps more important, interests. Therefore, it seems natural that within most areas of popular culture we often find both some mainstream tastes and some very distinct and specific tastes.

To achieve an adequate understanding of taste in these areas it is necessary to understand what kinds of values can be found behind the attitudes shown towards different film and music genres. It is not surprising to find that the taste patterns we refer to as mainstream are primarily related to values of security, whereas the more distinct tastes are primarily related to developmental values.

As argued previously, mainstream music and film tastes constitute a common popular cultural base to which most young people can relate. Thus, one important function of mainstream culture is that it supplies a common frame of reference within the areas of popular film and music. Mainstream culture attracts most young people, since it constitutes the most easily accessible part of the various popular cultural areas. It is the music that gets most air time, and it is the big motion pictures starring the most popular actors and actresses which constitute the lowest common denominator of youth culture. The fact that this music and these films are so widely recognized make them incarnations, so to speak, of the needs and desires to belong and feel secure as a contemporary young person. This is probably the main reason why young people relate to the values and value orientations of security.

Other, less popular and less recognized film and music genres probably have other functions for its consumers than the mainstream genres have. Since the narrower and more specific music and film genres are not as easily accessible, they call for more active effort on the part of the consumers. The willingness to put effort into finding films and music with content and qualities not usually present in mainstream culture, expresses a dissatisfaction with what mainstream tends to offer, as well as a need and desire for new and different experiences. Thus, it represents a desire to develop and transcend the framework of common culture. This may be the reason why the music and film genres in which tastes differ considerably among our respondents often relate to developmental values and value orientations.

In most popular cultural phenomena there exists a mainstream, expressing the values of security and belonging, and a number of more specific and distinct tastes expressing the values of transcendence and development. Whereas it is quite possible to emphasize mainstream taste in most areas without putting to much effort into it, it would take much energy and time to transcend the boundaries of common culture in all specific popular cultural areas. Therefore, most young people choose some areas for development and transcendence, and in most other areas they stick to mainstream culture. This insight regarding the double function of popular culture in relation to lifestyle is very central indeed. It suggests that it is not sufficient to use the taste shown in one single popular cultural area in order to distinguish between the lifestyles of youth generally, since the individuals identified as mainstream in one area most certainly make their basic lifestyle distinctions in other areas.

Just as the need and desire to feel secure and to be part of common youth culture is common to most young people, the need and desire to develop and distinguish oneself from mainstream culture is also a common need and desire. In studying taste empirically in any particular popular cultural area, one is likely to find indications of most individuals' need and desire for security, but of only some individuals' need and desire for development. This is because in order to be recognised as being part of one's society and culture one must have a basic knowledge and awareness of its fundamental values, norms, mores, language, and so on, whereas being recognized as a distinct individual requires that one develop and transcend common taste, competence and knowledge in at least some area or possible in several.

Problems of lifestyle are thus complicated by the fact that the individual has a need not only to express individuality and a belongingness in relation to others, but also — quite apart from the role of others — to develop his or her own identity and self. Besides values expressed in attitudes and actions, not only in popular culture but also in other areas, we also possess a number of values which are not as easily made explicit or visible in attitudes and actions. Values of the former type — outer-directed values — become evident and explicit in the consumption of a variety of primarily aesthetic or material goods. Values of latter type, in contrast — inner-directed values — are not as easily observed in either the attitudes or the actions of the individual. This is because these values pertain primarily not to the qualities of objects or artefacts, but to the ethical and metaphysical qualities of various types of actions, ideas, conceptions and convictions. These values, to be sure, influence and are influenced by material and aesthetic values, but are basically of a different kind.

Just as with material and aesthetic values, ethical and metaphysical ones are of course expressed in a variety of attitudes and actions. However, such attitudes and actions cover much broader areas of the individual's life, since it is through ethical and metaphysical conceptions that one shapes one's philosophy of life, and one's views of the nature of reality, and of what is good and evil, right or wrong, true or false, etc. Obviously it is much more difficult to identify a number of clear-cut areas of actions and attitudes based on metaphysical and ethical values, than is the case with material and aesthetical attitudes and actions. There are no such distinct metaphysical and ethical phenomena are not as distinct as are aesthetic (music, film, literature and arts) and material ones (the consumption of goods and services).

Although we cannot empirically distinguish in a satisfactory way between outer-directed material and aesthetic values and the inner-directed ethical and metaphysical values, we can nevertheless find indications that these differing value types do indeed relate to differing taste patterns. Although we cannot ascribe exclusively to one of the four value types any one of the preferable end-states of existence that were identified by Rokeach as values, some of them are more likely to be desired on ethical grounds, others on metaphysical grounds, and so on.

Wisdom, for instance, with its connotations of a broad understanding of life and reality, is likely to be predominantly based on metaphysical values. The same goes for *salvation*, *equality* and *justice*, referring to preferable or ideal relations between the rights and obligations of people, which usually are probably mainly based on ethical values. *Wealth* and *technological development*, expressing the desirability of money and material objects, are probably based to a high degree on material values. *A world of beauty*, relating to the desirability of beauty in nature and in the arts, is probably mainly based on aesthetic values. However, the individual may find one and the same end-state of existence desirable on material, aesthetic, ethical *and/or* metaphysical grounds. Therefore, we have to basically rely on our own interpretations of each of the empirical relations between a value and a taste pattern, in identifying a taste pattern as being primarily based on one or another of the four value types. Whereas taste in music and film almost always is based on some kind of aesthetic judgements, and thus on aesthetic values, the other types of values may nevertheless be quite important for the individual's distinctions in taste.

It seems reasonable, for instance, to interpret the relation between wisdom and taste for jazz as being based on aesthetic and metaphysical values. On the one hand, jazz is a relatively distinct taste pattern so the attitudes towards it are likely to be based on rather subtle aesthetic distinctions; on the other hand, jazz music often contains strong religious, mystic and meditative elements. Hymns and other religious music have often been used as themes in jazz improvisations. Furthermore, jazz music is a transcendent musical form in its constant quest for expanding its possibilities and of incorporating elements from music of different ethnic origin, and often from "primitive" cultures. Charlie Parker, Dizzy Gillespie, Thelonius Monk, John Coltrane, Miles Davis, Pharoah Sanders, Chico Freeman, Wayne Shorter and Keith Jarett are just a few examples of musicians representing these tendencies within jazz from the bebop era and onwards.

> Bebop differed from swing and rythm & blues not just musically but in the players' attitude towards their audience. Cool, self-assured, and, despite widespread drug use among its stars, often dignified in appearance, beboppers made it plain they really didn't care if people — black squares as well as white — understood what they were playing. This was musicians' music, first and foremost. ... Gillespie, like Parker, Monk, and the others, took his music seriously and considered it art as high-minded and elitist as the Western classical music he both envied and despised. ... These musicians were less secular stars than quasi-religious figures, and their fans often referred to them with godly reverence (George 1988:24ff).

It also seems reasonable to interpret the relation between the *Socially conscious* music pattern and the values of peace and equality as being a relation based to a high degree on ethical values. Since the themes of a wide number of so-called protests songs have to do with pacifism, international and ethnic solidarity and inequalities in the world we live in, it is reasonable to assume that its listeners find the ethical gospel of the lyrics congenial.

The relation between the technological development value and film genres such as science fiction, agent and war films are probably at least partly explained by the material values of the viewers. Science fiction often portrays advanced technological equipment of the future. In watching a James Bond film, viewers are often curious about what technological novelties M equips 007 with, and in war films the advanced weapon technology may impress the audience.

It is obviously almost impossible to identify exactly what kind of values lie behind a particular attitude towards a genre or pattern in music or film. Despite this, there are often a number of indications of such relations. The relations involved should be interpreted with care, however, and one should remember that the different types of values here are interrelated in complex ways. This complexity has implications, of course, among other things for the way empirically identified relations between values and taste patterns are to be interpreted.

After considering in the next chapter relations between values and activities, we will return to a more thorough discussion of relations between values, attitudes and actions, and of the relations of these to lifestyle.

CHAPTER 16
STRUCTURING EVERYDAY LIFE

INTRODUCTION

Thus far we have been mainly occupied in the empirical work we have presented with the attitudinal level of lifestyle. In this chapter we will concentrate on the action level. As we have argued earlier, the values of the individual lie at the basis of his or her attitudes. In order to express and visualize these values and attitudes, however, the individual must act. The individual's rather abstract and fundamental conceptions which represent his or her values, and the more concrete specifications of these values, which we refer to as attitudes, become materialized and externalized in the individual's actions (cf. Berger & Luckmann 1966/1987). Thus, it is in the actions of the individual that we actually can observe his or her lifestyle.

We are well aware of the fact that young people have attitudes towards a multitude of social and cultural phenomena other than music and film, but these are two rather general areas in which most young people engage, more or less actively. Therefore, they are useful in empirical research aimed at discerning general patterns of attitudes inherent in most young people's lifestyles. We are equally aware of the fact that work and school are important parts of young people's lifestyle, but we concentrate here on their leisure time activities. That is because of their having the greatest possibilities to freely choose what they do in their leisure time.

Although to a certain extent individuals choose their leisure time activities freely, there are certain limitations. They are constraint, for example, by the social and physical environment. More important, however, are constraints related to limitations in time. A relatively large part of our time is occupied by things we must do: work, sleep, eating, and so forth. The remaining hours are at the individual's disposal, and it is during these hours the individual can develop his or her own specific interests. What the individual then chooses to do, of course, is partly influenced by situational constraints and stimuli, but mainly by what values he or she embraces.

Since identity comprises emotions, beliefs, and attitudes, it is a prime motivator of action. Identity directs action. This is not to deny the importance of situational constraints and stimuli in determining behaviour. It is simply to reaffirm their meaning through interpretation within the individual system of beliefs and values. Their implication for purposive action rather than unintended behaviour are, therefore, mediated by identity (Breakwell 1986:43).

ACTIVITY PATTERNS AND VALUES

Although it is empirically impossible to include all possible leisure time activities in one and the same instrument of measurement, one can theoretically identify a number of such activities which at least roughly provide a general picture of young people's different areas of leisure time interests. This is what we have tried to achieve. In Table 10 we present an overview of the 56 activities included in our study.

As can be seen in the table, the list reaches from very generally practiced activities to more specific ones. Most young people read books and magazines, meet their parents, siblings and partners, watch video, go to the movies, go to parties and discos, visit pubs and restaurants, exercise, buy clothes and liquor, and so on. Looking at these activities we get what would appear to be a fairly representative picture of young people's cultural activities. These activities do not distinguish among various young people, but rather express their common culture.

Looking at the bottom of the list we find the more specific and individual activities such as brewing beer and making wine, acting, stamp and coin collecting, singing in choirs, playing in bands, studying the Bible, carpenting, fishing, hunting, painting, drawing, working on cars, and so on. Thus — just as there is common culture in various areas of music and film, there is also a common area of leisure time activities. Just as there are distinct specific and distinct film and music tastes, there are also specific and distinct leisure time activities.

The existence of both a common culture and more specific and distinct culture in all these popular cultural areas shows clearly the double function of youth culture and lifestyle. Common cultural tastes and leisure time activities express the importance of conformity, belongingness and integration. The more specific and distinct cultures, on the other hand, express the importance of uniqueness and individuality.

Table 10. Leisure Time Activities (means).

Leisure Time Activities	$\overline{x}$
Reading journals and magazines	3.0
Being with parents and siblings	2.9
Being with boyfriend/girlfriend	2.8
Watching video	2.7
Going to discotheques	2.6
Going to partys	2.6
Reading books	2.6
Reading weeklies	2.6
Visiting pubs	2.5
Going to the movies	2.4
Buying clothes	2.4
Going to restaurants	2.3
Excercising	2.2
Buying things for the home	2.2
Buying liqour	2.1
Visiting hairdresser	2.1
Individual sport	1.9
Working overtime	1.9
Discussing pålitics	1.8
Going to the countryside/forest	1.8
Reading comics	1.7
Inviting people to dinner	1.7
Team sports	1.6
Film, photo, video	1.6
Travelling abroad	1.6
Visiting solarium	1.5
Visiting the library	1.4
Body-building or workout	1.4
Betting on horses, soccer or lottery	1.4
Visiting sports events	1.3
Working extra	1.2
Writing diary or lyrics	1.1
Visiting museums or exhibitions	1.0
Going to rock concerts	1.0
Attending courses	0.9
Praying	0.9
Playing a musical instrument	0.8
Sailing, motorboating etc	0.8
Painting, drawing etc	0.8
Car or motorcycle mechanics	0.7
Going to the theatre	0.7
Needlework	0.7
Visiting church	0.6
Using personal computer	0.6
Hunting or fishing	0.5
Buying and selling stock shares	0.4
Carpeting	0.4
Going to jazz or blues concerts	0.3
Playing classical music/singing in choirs	0.3
Reading the Bible	0.3
Acting	0.2
Playing in jazz, blues or rock bands	0.2
Going to classical concerts	0.2
Coin, stamp etc collecting	0.2
Brewing beer and making wine	0.1
Attending political meetings / demonstrating	0.1

In order to arrive at a more general and manageable picture of young people's leisure time activities we have conducted a factor analysis which has resulted in eleven factors or patterns of activity: *Culture, Party, Music, Sports, Domestic, Fashion, Religious, Hunting & fishing, Exercise, Media,* and *Travel* (see Table 11).

These factors or patterns of activities will be used in a series of analyses of relations between structural and positional variables, values and actions. We start by presenting in Table 12 a correlation matrix displaying these relations.

Just as was the case with the attitudinal patterns of music and film taste, several patterns of leisure time activities are related to class, education and gender. In most cases they are related to one or more of Rokeach's values, to Inglehart's value orientations and to the personal value orientation. Thus, just as with taste, the choice of leisure time activities is tied to structure, position and to the individual.

The *Cultural* activity pattern — made up by such activities as attending the theatre or rock concerts, going to museums, exhibitions, or libraries, reading books, discussing politics and carrying on drawing and painting — can be characterized as female oriented and as being related to high education and class. The fact that an activity pattern is female oriented and is related to high education and to class, does not mean, of course, that men and less educated young persons do not engage in these activities, but merely that females and those of higher education and class are more inclined to spend their leisure time in such activities.

More interesting are the correlations of the *Cultural* activity pattern with certain kinds of values and value orientations. To begin with Inglehart's value dimension, it is obvius that being engaged in cultural activities is based on a postmaterial value orientation. The *Cultural* actvitity pattern shows a positive correlation with a postmaterial value orientation and a negative correlation with a material value orientation. The character of the pattern stands out as even more obvious when one notes that it is negatively correlated with the Rokeachean values of technical development, national security, social recognition, power and wealth, and is positively correlated with wisdom and a sense of accomplishment. Furthermore, the *Cultural* activity pattern is related to the developmental personal value orientations of personal and material development, but shows a strong negative correlation with the material security value orientation.

Table 11. Factor Analysis of Leisure Time Activities

	F1	F2	F3	F4	F5	F6	F7	F8	F9	F10	F11
Factor 1, Culture											
Going to the theatre	.64	.15	.30	.04	.16	.06	.14	-.07	.08	-.14	.04
Going to rock concerts	.49	.34	.21	.18	-.02	-.05	-.02	-.09	-.23	.00	.02
Museums/Exhibitions	.73	.03	.07	.07	.15	-.05	.07	.06	-.10	-.01	.21
Reading books	.57	.11	.01	-.18	.06	.15	.05	-.12	.28	.15	-.16
Visiting the library	.68	.00	.07	-.02	-.08	.01	.11	.04	.07	-.17	.09
Discusing politics	.46	.07	.11	.06	-.05	.12	.02	.16	-.01	.00	.09
Painting/Drawing	.41	-.22	.10	-.13	.12	-.05	.05	.10	.09	.32	.32
Factor 2, Party											
Buying liqour	-.05	.76	.03	.10	.08	-.13	-.04	.11	-.05	.13	-.04
Visiting pubs	.18	.81	.08	.03	.01	-.08	.04	-.06	-.01	.04	.14
Going to parties	.17	.72	.01	.08	.15	.27	.09	.10	.06	-.01	-.04
Going to discoteques	-.02	.75	-.11	.16	-.12	.22	.02	.05	.26	-.01	.15
Factor 3, Music											
Musical instrument	.01	-.04	.77	-.03	-.03	-.01	.16	-.01	.08	.10	.06
Jazz/Blues/Rock band	.04	.05	.73	.05	.14	-.11	-.09	-.04	-.10	-.03	.03
Classical music/Choir	.09	-.04	.65	-.08	-.07	.09	.27	-.02	.08	.03	.00
Jazz/Blues concerts	.36	.16	.57	.01	-.01	-.06	.03	.03	-.10	-.05	-.03
Classical concerts	.21	-.02	.68	-.05	-.10	.01	.15	.04	-.03	-.11	.11
Factor 4, Sports											
Individual sports	-.05	.04	-.01	.70	-.10	-.04	.02	-.02	.22	-.11	.10
Team sports	.03	.08	-.01	.71	.00	-.08	.02	.11	.02	.13	.08
Visiting sports events	.05	.18	-.07	.77	.05	.13	.05	.07	.10	.13	-.07
Factor 5, Domestic											
Inviting people for dinner	.22	.09	.08	.07	.70	.20	.22	.08	-.03	-.03	.07
Buying things for home	.11	.10	-.12	-.10	.59	.41	.10	.01	.00	.09	.02
Handworking	.04	-.11	.03	-.21	.42	.28	-.07	.06	.20	-.04	-.20
Boyfriend/Girlfriend	-.11	-.01	-.05	.04	.73	-.05	.04	-.06	-.01	.20	.01
Film/Photo/Video	.29	-.07	.10	-.08	.44	.21	.01	.25	-.05	.09	.23
Factor 6, Fashion											
Visiting hairdresser	-.07	.12	.11	.07	.02	.60	.16	.00	.04	.04	-.15
Buying clothes	.07	.26	-.04	.09	.23	.64	.08	-.03	.12	-.02	.14
Parents/Siblings	.13	-.18	-.08	.01	.12	.57	.12	-.07	.00	-.05	.09
Reading weeklies	.00	.12	-.18	-.20	.18	.50	.06	-.03	.18	.29	.07
Factor 7, Religious											
Visiting church	.07	.02	.15	.02	.06	.15	.77	.11	-.13	.03	.00
Praying	.06	.02	.02	.00	.15	.10	.73	-.05	.10	-.06	.03
Reading the Bible	.12	.04	.20	.04	.01	.10	.81	.10	.01	.09	-.01
Factor 8, Hunting and fishing											
Sailing/Motorboating	.03	.28	.04	.14	.11	-.21	.13	.57	.24	-.09	.05
Hunting/Fishing	-.10	.11	-.07	.09	.05	-.14	.15	.72	.00	.04	-.01
Factor 9, Excercising											
Excercising	.17	.03	-.03	.22	-.01	.11	-.03	.09	.74	-.13	-.07
Bodybuilding/Workout	-.03	.16	.00	.14	.00	.18	.01	-.06	.65	.05	.21

	F1	F2	F3	F4	F5	F6	F7	F8	F9	F10	F11
Factor 10, Media											
Watching video	-.24	.19	.03	.09	.21	.21	-.16	.04	.08	.64	.13
Reading comics	.07	.03	-.02	.09	.07	-.06	.13	.07	-.12	.74	-.06
Factor 11, Travelling											
Travelling abroad	.21	.15	.08	.28	.12	.15	.11	-.13	.03	-.21	.54
Working extra	.08	.14	.07	-.06	.04	-.02	-.04	.15	.05	.06	.63
ALPHA	.74	.82	.75	.71	.66	.59	.74	.70	.66	.52	.34
EIGENVALUE	6.94	4.30	3.28	2.90	2.26	2.11	1.76	1.64	1.52	1.48	1.26
PCT OF VAR	12.4	7.7	5.9	5.2	4.0	3.8	3.1	2.9	2.7	2.6	2.3
Dropped variables											
Countryside/Forest	.25	-.13	-.07	.01	-.04	-.09	.13	.57	.22	.12	-.06
Going to the movies	.39	.31	.12	.23	-.09	.23	-.06	-.01	.09	.14	.23
Going to restaurants	.19	.42	.02	.05	.36	.17	.03	-.06	.02	.17	.36
Attending courses	.33	-.02	.25	.11	.11	.30	-.01	.06	.13	-.09	-.09
Visiting solarium	-.01	.34	-.01	.02	.40	.18	-.03	-.23	.25	-.09	-.02
Betting	-.23	.18	-.03	.45	.13	.11	-.05	.14	-.14	.43	-.14
Stockshares	.06	.02	.08	.42	.13	.05	-.09	.09	.00	-.29	.04
Diary/Lyrics	.38	-.04	.08	-.23	.16	.01	.27	-.10	.21	.01	.25
Working overtime	.08	.30	.06	.16	.33	.14	.01	.16	-.01	.01	.21
Car or MC mechanics	-.21	.10	-.03	.12	-.15	.24	-.06	.51	-.42	.08	.08
Carpenting	.00	-.03	.11	.08	.01	.15	.17	.64	-.27	.03	.10
Brew beer/make wine	.01	.19	-.08	.01	.09	-.05	.13	.00	-.09	.03	-.05
Political meetings	.20	.01	.06	.02	-.02	.03	.05	.10	.12	.08	.15
Journals/Magazines	.45	.04	-.05	-.12	-.01	.21	-.10	.08	.07	.01	-.24
Personal computer	.08	-.16	.06	.01	.04	-.04	.03	.09	-.10	.15	.06
Acting	.09	.03	.33	-.02	.08	-.04	.10	.01	.12	.05	.09
Coins/Stamps	.17	-.18	.00	.12	.06	.07	.08	.17	-.25	.07	.11

Although education, class and gender partly explain why people engage in the activities of the *Cultural* pattern, one can assume that it is the values of individuals that provide the fundamental and most important explanation here. In looking at the individual activities in the pattern at hand, one can readily see that they serve the purpose or function of enhancing the social and cultural experience, knowledge, and the competence of the individual. As with the values lying behind them, the activities here are thus oriented towards personal, social and cultural development rather than towards security, and similarly towards aesthetic and cognitive experience rather than material wealth, and towards engagement rather than consumption.

Table 12. Leisure Time Activities Related to Positional Variables, Values and Value Orientations (Pearsons´s Correlations).

	Culture	Party	Music	Sports	Domestic	Fashion	Religious	Hunting/Fishing	Excercise	Media	Travel
Sex	.24***	-.10	-.04	-.34***	.40***	.38***	.11	-.22***	.18**	-.20***	.09
Class	.17**	.01	.18**	.21***	-.15	-.13	-.02	.07	.05	-.11	.14
City	-.06	.09	-.01	.17**	-.13	-.07	-.07	.18**	.06	-.05	-.08
Education	.29***	-.02	.16**	.12	-.11	-.04	.03	.01	.10	-.25***	.17**
Postmaterial	.26***	-.12	.17**	-.21***	.20***	.09	.07	-.17**	.03	-.11	.19***
Material	-.24***	.10	-.12	.10	.07	.19***	-.05	-.01	.07	.05	-.10
Material security	-.43***	.06	-.18**	.10	.10	.19***	-.08	.08	.05	.26***	-.12
Personal security	-.10	-.05	-.13	.00	.29***	.26***	.09	.08	-.01	.09	-.05
Social security	.08	.14	.07	.09	.15***	.28***	.07	-.04	.19***	.10	.14
Personal developm	.29***	.19***	.14	.07	-.03	.03	.03	.10	.26***	-.04	.41***
Material developm	.20**	.18**	.10	.17**	-.02	.06	.01	.13	25***	-.10	.18**
A clean world	.12	-.14	.07	-.09	.12	.05	.08	-.06	.03	.06	.02
Techn develpment	-.17	.02	.06	.18**	-.11	-.02	.01	.08	-.06	.12	.01
A comfortable life	.03	.10	.00	.05	.26***	.21***	.10	.02	.13	.06	.01
An exciting life	.14	.20***	.10	.03	.05	.07	.07	.13	.16**	.07	.20***
Accomplishment	.19***	.13	.02	.04	.11	.05	.05	.05	.10	-.10	.16**
Peace	.05	.02	-.01	-.02	.22***	.21***	.12	-.05	.12	-.01	.12
A world of beauty	.02	.08	-.01	-.12	.26***	.20***	.15**	-.03	.08	.16**	.17**
Equality	.14	-.02	-.01	-.15**	.28***	.19***	.15**	-.11	.09	-.02	.15**
Family security	.03	.01	-.10	-.14	.34***	.30***	.18**	-.02	.10	.04	.07
Freedom	.03	.00	-.04	-.09	.06	.14	.04	-.02	.09	-.01	.03
Happiness	.03	.02	.01	-.07	.32***	.18**	.07	.06	.18**	.05	.11
Inner harmony	.14	.02	.08	-.10	.23***	.12	.13	-.02	.11	-.06	.10
Love	.09	.00	.00	-.07	.30***	.20***	.08	.05	.11	.08	.05
National security	-.21***	.12	-.12	-.01	.05	.22***	.08	.06	.09	.10	.02
Pleasure	-.12	.11	-.07	.01	.24***	.12	.07	.12	.13	.11	.07
Salvation	.05	.02	.10	.03	.15	.14	.64***	.02	.08	.19***	.02
Self-respect	.15	.14	.07	-.03	.07	.09	.12	-.01	.06	.01	.12
Social recognition	-.20***	.05	-.12	.00	.05	.10	.01	.00	.05	.16**	.02
Wisdom	.24***	-.08	.19***	-.06	-.03	-.08	.16**	-.01	.07	.02	.09
Justice	.10	-.04	-.06	-.04	.20***	.17***	.11	.01	.13	-.01	.04
Power	-.17**	.12	-.16**	.09	-.04	.03	-.14	.11	.01	.16**	.03
Health	-.04	.03	-.11	.02	.16**	.13	-.01	-.03	.04	.10	.08
Wealth	-.21***	.15**	-.13	.13	.02	.08	-.16**	.14	.07	.24***	.05

Among the patterns identified, the *Party* activity pattern is probably the most mainstream or common one. It consists of a number of activities which most young people engage in: going to pubs, parties, and discotheques and consuming alcohol. Partying is a fundamental component of youth culture. Therefore, it is not surprising to find that this pattern is totally uncorrelated with class, education and gender and is neither postmaterially nor materially oriented. The *Party* pattern shows rather weak correlations with the personal value orientations of personal and material development. Its strongest correlation is with the Rokechean value of excitement. This pattern concerns simply having fun when not working or studying. It concerns what Tom Waits describes in his song *(Looking for) the Heart of Saturday Night*.

And you comb your hair, shave your face
trying to wipe out every trace
of all the other days in the week
you know that this will be the Saturday you're
reachin' your peak (Tom Waits 1974).

The activity patterns we call *Music* consists basically of activities of musical performance and consumption of live music: playing musical instruments, playing in pop, rock, jazz and blues bands, singing in choirs, and attending jazz, blues and classical music concerts. This pattern shows a weakly positive relation to class and education, to Inglehart's postmaterial value orientation and to the Rokeachean value of wisdom. It is negatively correlated with the personal value orientation of material security and the Rokeachean value of power. The activity pattern in question is rather specific and distinct. It is clearly oriented towards aesthetic expression and development. Just as with the *Cultural* pattern, the *Music* pattern is neither material nor security oriented, but is clearly aesthetically and developmentally oriented.

Hardly surprising is the finding that the activity pattern of *Sports* is clearly male oriented. This can be partly explained by the fact that the examples used to exemplify sport activities were rather male oriented: tennis, golf, squash, soccer, indoor bandy, and the like. The more female-oriented sports — horseback riding, swimming, and the like — were unfortunately not included in our examples. The *Sports* pattern is also middle-class based. The fact that it is a male-oriented pattern becomes even more evident when one notes that it is negatively related to a postmaterial value orientation and the Rokeachean value of equality, and is positively related both to the personal value orientation of material development and the Rokeachean value of technological development.

The *Domestic* activity pattern is a typically female activity pattern, based on the kinds of values and value orientations we have identified earlier as female oriented (see Table 3): postmaterial value orientation, the personal value orientations of social and material security and the Rokeachean values of peace, a beautiful world, equality, family security, happiness, inner harmony, love, and justice. This pattern once again confirms the impact of gender roles in lifestyle creation.

Just as with the *Domestic* activity pattern, the *Fashion* pattern is clearly female-oriented. The two patterns differ, however, is the values and value orientations behind them. Whereas the *Domestic* pattern is positively correlated with a postmaterial value orientation, the *Fashion* pattern is positively related to a material value orientation. The *Fashion* pattern is also more positively related to the three security oriented personal value orientations than is the *Domestic* one. Furthermore, even though the *Fashion* pattern is correlated with basically the same Rokeachean values as the *Domestic* one, these correlations are generally weaker and in some cases even absent. The former activity pattern is also rather strongly correlated with national security, a value not at all related to the *Domestic* pattern.

There is thus an interesting difference between these two female oriented activity patterns. The *Domestic* one shows basically the same correlations with the values and the value orientations as the female-oriented film and music patterns. The *Fashion* pattern, on the other hand, is opposed to the other female-oriented taste and activity patterns, is not related to the postmaterial value orientation, but is only related to the material one.

This is interesting since it clearly indicates the importance of a material component also in female lifestyles. This component has not been as visible in other female taste and activity patterns. The reason for this is probably that the other patterns have concerned areas in which women do not make as clear distinctions as men. The *Fashion* pattern, on the other hand, concerns an area in which women do make such distinctions. If men make distinctions and express their individuality through tastes in film and music to a higher degree than women, fashion is an area where women express themselves and their individuality more strongly than men. Therefore, clothes, fashion magazines, and the like, are more important material objects for females than for men, whereas records and films are more important to men.

In order to shed some empirical light on the similarity between the functions of fashion, music and film for men and women, respectively, we have studied what our respondents find important concerning clothes. In the same way as in the case of music and film, we have distinguished between a number of taste patterns within the fashion area. The factor analysis of 14 different items resulted in five different factors or taste patterns (this table is available from the authors). Of these factors, two are of particular interest, one of them male and one a female oriented pattern. The male pattern involves items such as high quality, gender typical, the brand and indifference towards costs, whereas the female-oriented pattern stresses the importance of clothes being unusual and personal.

In Table 13 we present an overview of the relations between the structural and positional variables, the values and value orientations, and the fashion patterns.

Table 13. Fashion Patterns, Positional Varibales, Values and Value Orientations (Pearson´s Correlations).

	High quality	Personal unusual	Fashionable tough colorful	Classical discrete	Comfortable
Sex	-.39***	.24***	.14	.11	.12
Class	.06	.02	-.13	-.05	.01
City	.03	-.14	-.07	-.08	-.04
Education	-.04	-.07	-.19***	.01	.02
Post Material	-.14	.19***	.02	.26***	.29***
Material	.19***	.03	.23***	.04	.16**
Material security	.33***	-.04	.36***	.04	.06
Personal security	.09	-.01	.17**	.08	.18**
Social security	-.07	08	.15**	.02	.23***
Personal development	.07	.25***	.17**	.13	.01
Material development	.25***	.11	.09	.10	.14
A clean world	-.05	.15	.06	.21***	.26***
Techn development	.36***	-.03	.05	.08	.06
A comfortable life	.14	.15**	.17***	.13	.32***
An exciting life	.20***	.28***	.20***	.20***	.17**
Accomplishment	.16**	.29***	.14	.24***	.28***
Peace	-.03	.11	.20***	.12	.21***
A world of beauty	.11	.24***	.18***	.21***	.18**
Equality	-.13	.24***	.14	.20***	.19***
Family security	-.03	.12	.18**	.15**	.18**
Freedom	.03	.20***	.14	.10	.14
Happiness	-.00	.24***	.21***	.04	.17
Inner harmony	.00	.22***	.06	.12	.32***
Love	-.01	.21***	.14	.08	.28***
National security	.27***	-.01	.22***	.01	.11
Pleasure	.19***	.14	.31***	.12	.19***
Salvation	-.05	-.00	-.00	.01	-.01
Self-respect	.09	.08	-.03	.10	.18**
Social recognition	.31***	.09	.27***	.18**	.07
Wisdom	.11	.14	.01	.21***	.10
Justice	.01	.28***	.17**	.17**	.10
Power	.42***	.14	.27***	.07	.00
Health	.04	.05	.15**	-.07	.10
Wealth	.37***	.03	.22***	.06	-.07

Significant differences between the values and value orientations of the fashion patterns for the males and females are evident. The male pattern is positively correlated with a material value orientation, the personal value orientations of material security and material development, and such Rokechean values as technological development, national security, social recognition, power and wealth. The female fashion pattern is positively correlated with a postmaterial value orientation, the personal value orientation of personal development, and such Rokeachean developmental values as a sense of accomplishment and inner harmony, and the more typically female values of, for example, equality, love and happiness.

This indicates a basic difference between men's and women's use of popular culture. Men tend to place higher importance on *expressing* and *claiming their material and social status and their individuality*, whereas women seem to put more importance on *developing their individuality without abandoning their values of security and concern for others* (cf. Miller 1976; Chodorow 1978; Miller 1984).

Already discussed (chapter 2), fashion seems to serve a double function in the making of lifestyles. On the one hand, it is used to express sameness, group affiliation and belonginess, and thus basically social and personal security. At thesame time, it is also used to express individuality, uniqueness and particularity, representing basically personal growth and development (cf. Simmel 1904/1971; Blumer 1969). The variability of styles in modern dress combined with the motto *No clothes are right for a particular occasion*, means that clothes and fashion represent a cultural field in which it is possible to express and develop the representation of self in everyday life (Back 1985). It could well be that fashion in clothes represents for many the most appropriate way of showing both one's individuality and one's group identity. This could explain fashion being the area in which women express and experiment with their personal and cultural identity particularly.

One reason why women have often been neglected or even forgotten entirely in youth cultural research may be empirical and theoretical concentration there has been on popular cultural areas in which men make more distinctions than women, such as music and film. The truth, however, is that women also make clear taste distinctions — although particularly in other, equally important popular cultural areas (cf. McRobbie 1984; Carter 1984; Drotner 1991).

Returning to the results presented in Table 12, one can note that the *Religious* activity pattern is not related to any of the positional variables. It does not show any appreciable correlation with Inglehart's value orientations or with the personal value orientations, and only few moderate correlations with the Rokeachean values. Expectedly enough, however, a strong correlation between the value of salvation and the religious activity pattern. This latter activity pattern predominantly expressive of metaphysical and ethical values and attitudes.

As expected, the pattern *Hunting & fishing* pattern is male oriented. It shows a weak negative correlation with a postmaterial value orientation, but none with the personal value orientations or with the Rokeachean values. Hunting and fishing are typically and traditionally male activities. People living in Växjö are particularly likely to engage in such activities, since the physical conditions for hunting and fishing in that area are better than in the Malmö area.

The *Exercise* activity pattern is a weakly female-oriented sports pattern. It lacks the element of competition present in a male oriented sports pattern. It is also related to such personal value orientations as personal and material development and the Rokechean values of excitement and happiness. Engaging in the physical activities constituting this pattern serves the function of improving one's physical health and capacity rather than winning against an opponent. That is probably the reason why females are more inclined to engage in these sports activities than in ones of the male-oriented sports pattern.

The *Media* pattern is a male-oriented activity pattern correlated with low education. It is also related to the personal value orientation of material security and the Rokeachean value of wealth. This is a mainstream pattern consisting of two activities engaged in by most young people, namely watching video and reading comics.

Finally, the *Travel* pattern is a postmaterial and middle-class based activity pattern related to the personal value orientations of personal and material development, and the Rokeachean values of excitement and a sense of accomplishment. The pattern consists of the two seemingly disparate activities of traveling abroad and doing extra work. However, there being a relation between people is understandable enough inasmuch as it is quite common in this age group to work extra so as to be able to travel for a year or so before starting work or beginning with higher education.

Figure 12. MCA-Analysis of the Relations Between Positional Variables, the Value of Wisdom and the Activity Pattern of Culture.

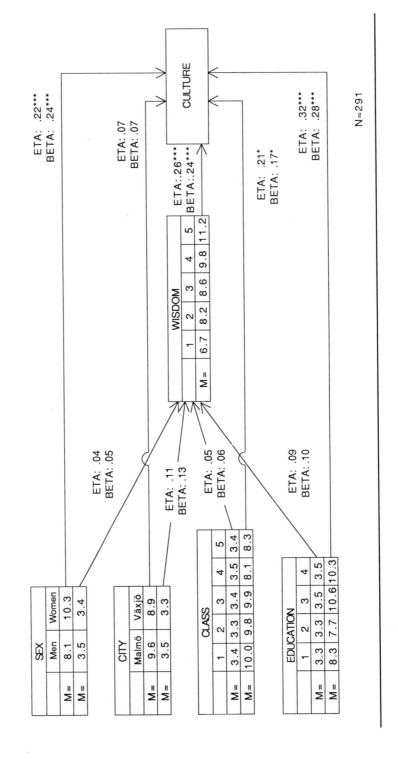

Figure 13. MCA-Analysis of the Relations Between Positional Variables, the Value of Wisdom and the Activity Pattern of Music.

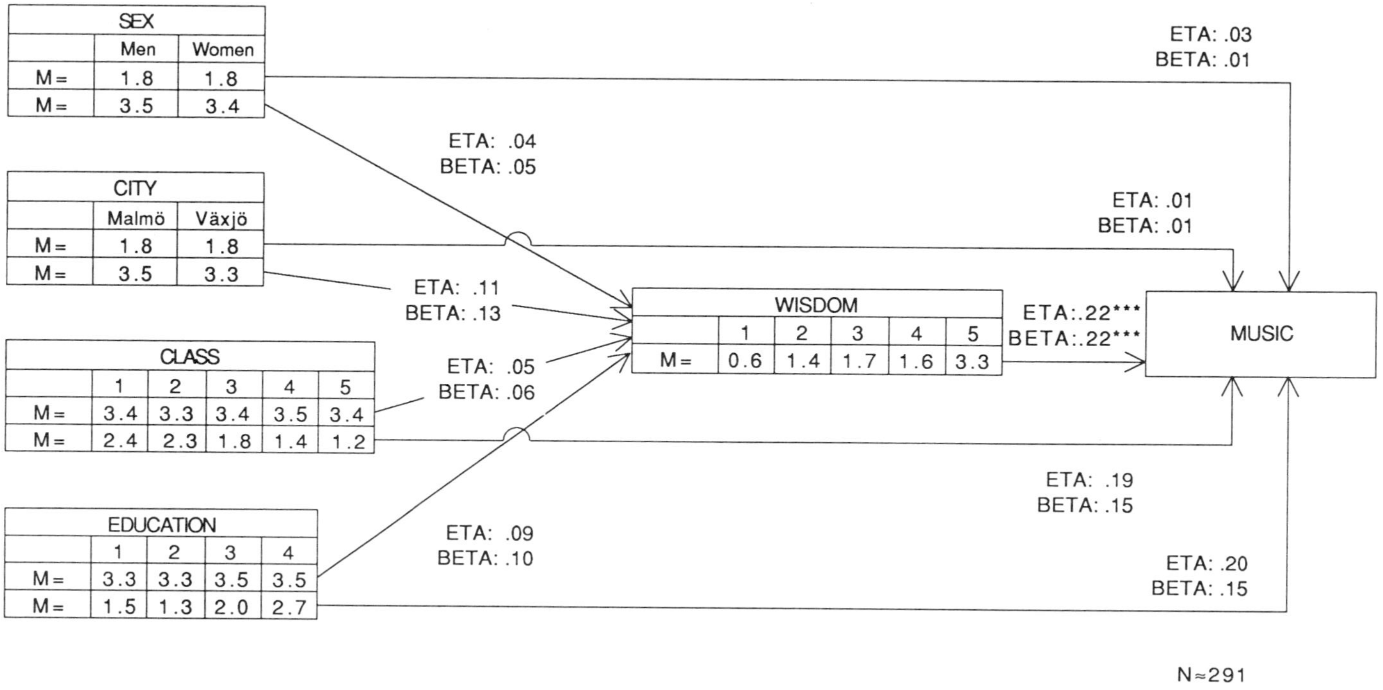

ETA: .03
BETA: .01

ETA: .01
BETA: .01

ETA: .22***
BETA: .22***

ETA: .19
BETA: .15

ETA: .20
BETA: .15

WISDOM					
	1	2	3	4	5
M =	0.6	1.4	1.7	1.6	3.3

ETA: .04
BETA: .05

ETA: .11
BETA: .13

ETA: .05
BETA: .06

ETA: .09
BETA: .10

SEX		
	Men	Women
M =	1.8	1.8
M =	3.5	3.4

CITY		
	Malmö	Växjö
M =	1.8	1.8
M =	3.5	3.3

CLASS				
	1	2	3	4	5
M =	3.4	3.3	3.4	3.5	3.4
M =	2.4	2.3	1.8	1.4	1.2

EDUCATION			
	1	2	3	4
M =	3.3	3.3	3.5	3.5
M =	1.5	1.3	2.0	2.7

N=291

In order to arrive at a more precise understanding of the relation between positional variables, values and various activity patterns we conducted, in the same way as reported earlier, two sets of MCA-analyses (Figures 12 and 13).

Figure 12 accounts for the *Culture* pattern. Although relations with the positional variables of gender, class and education provide an explanation of why certain of the people engage particularly in the activities included in the *Cultural* pattern, there is also an individual explanation. Whatever effect the positional variables may have, individuals who put strong importance on the value of wisdom also tend to engage in cultural activities more than do individuals who place lesser value on wisdom. This result once again illustrates the complex relations found between lifestyle and structural, positional and individual phenomena.

Figure 13 reports on the *Music* pattern. The absence of statistically significant relations between any of the positional variables and the activity pattern at issue, together with its rather strong correlation with the value of wisdom, indicates that the activities of this pattern are more closely related to individual than to structural and positional conditions.

In short, these results show once again that, despite the importance of structural and positional variables, there is also an individually determined factor involved in creating lifestyle. We will now discuss in a more comprehensive way the empirical results just presented.

Concluding Remarks

Individuals structure their leisure time in different ways depending, among other things, on their education, gender and values. In this chapter we have studied the relation between structural and positional variables and leisure time activities, on the one hand, and values as well as leisure time activities, on the other.

Just as in the cases of music and film taste there are some common activities in which young people engage irrespective of class or gender. Most young people like to go to a party, for instance. However, just as was the case with music and film taste, it is also quite obvious that there are considerable differences between men and women and, to a certain extent also, between persons of different educational background.

Drawing on the results involving the measurement of music and film tastes and leisure time activities, it seems possible to speak of separate female and male "worlds". There are such typically female activities as needlework, home decoration, cooking, light workouts, buying clothes, going to the hairstylist, and so on. There are also such typically male activities as hunting and fishing, team sports and reading comics. The activities constituting the female and the male "worlds", respectively, represent in some sense archetypical gender-related ways of structuring leisure time.

Although most of the activity patterns discussed here are to varying degrees related to gender, there are nevertheless some patterns which are not. Also, the activity pattern we call *Religion* is not at all related to the positional variables. The explanation of why certain persons engage in religious activities is probably to be found basically in their ethical and metaphysical values. In a similar vein one can argue that the activities included in the *Music* pattern can be largely explained on the basis of the aesthetic values embraced by the individuals engaged in those activities.

Apart from gender, the choice of different leisure time activities can be explained in terms of the security and developmental functions which values have. Just as with the mainstream tastes, the common youth cultural *Party* pattern cuts across class as well as gender. Involvement in such mainstream and common cultural tastes and activities can be at least partly explained by a general need to belong and to feel a sameness with a common youth culture.

Several respondents have just recently finished school or begun with a higher education, and in a few years' time most of them will be entering a more structured life, including having a family and a steady job. Therefore, many young people endeavor to use the last years of "freedom" to save money so as to be able to undertake a long journey before gradually entering into adulthood and its responsibilities. This experience is independent of gender, but — not surprisingly at all — is weakly related to social class and education (since those who left school and entered working life at an early age have already been through this phase). The involvement in activities constituting the *Travel* pattern can probably thus be largely explained on the basis of a common need and desire to gain experience and to develop before establishing a secure and structured life.

Apart from these activity patterns which are unrelated to gender, most of the other patterns are related either to security or to developmental values. It is interesting to note, for example, that the activity patterns of *Sport* and *Excercise* — both of which are oriented towards the cultivation of the body — are primarily related to developmental values. Concern with the body has increasingly become an important feature of youth culture. Mike Featherstone describes this development as a movement from words towards movement and gesture.

> The difficulty of evaluating an individual's competence on strictly rational criteria opens up the space for the performing self, schooled in public relations techniques, who is aware that the secret of success lies in the projection of a successful image. In the dense interpersonal environment of modern bureaucracy, individuals depend upon their ability to negotiate interactions on the basis of "personality". Impression management, style panache and careful bodily presentation therefore become important (Featherstone 1991a:191).

Perhaps the most striking results presented in this chapter, however, are these concerning the complexity inherent in an interest in clothes and fashion. As already discussed, interest in clothes and fashion are related to very different values depending on gender. For women, clothes are more often related to individual expression and the developmental functions of the values which they embrace, whereas men more often tend to look upon their clothes in terms of security and a means of expressing group belongingness or social status.

In next chapter we will comment briefly on some simple longitudinal findings concerning taste in music. After that we will sum up and comment upon the empirical results considered so far (chapter 18).

CHAPTER 17
LIFESTYLE — STABILITY AND CHANGE

The period of youth is characterized by profound changes of the individual's identity. We have distinguished three overlapping periods of youth, each characterized by the development of different components of identity. During the first two phases — the biologically and psychologically defined periods of youth — the individual's identity is relatively unstable and insecure. This almost chaotic state of personal identity makes the individual highly susceptible to external influences from the peer-group, from the mass media, from teachers and from parents.

Since during these periods young people have not yet developed a stable and secure individual identity, they often experience a need and desire for confirmation and recognition. As a result of this quest for security and confirmation they tend to join different groups in which they experience the security still lacking in their individual identity. Peer-groups thus play an important role during these years, providing the individual with a sense of belonging. The peer-group is often characterized by sharing of interests, tastes, and styles. During these years, the individual's identity is thus to be conceived as group identity rather than personal identity. One defines oneself in relation to the group to which one belongs, including the group's positive and negative relations to other groups with differing taste, interests and styles. The peer-group thus provides young persons with a secure environment in which they can try out different roles together with their peers and develop as well as find their own position within the peer-group (cf. Wulff 1988). To be identified as a distinct individual within the peer-group is of utmost importance for the individual's later ability to develop and refine an individual identity and lifestyle without having to rely on the peer-group and on confirmation and acceptance by it.

The third period of youth — the socially and culturally defined period — comes at the time when school life ends and entrance into the work situation or into higher studies has commenced. This means that an individual can no longer rely solely on peer-groups of the school years. The individual inevitably must confront new groups and new expectations, and consequently adapt to new and frequently more complex roles. Obviously, the individual does not cut his or her ties to the peer-group off, but anchoring one's identity in it is no longer possible. To a greater degree, the individual becomes dependent on his or her own personal identity.

During this period, therefore, the individual faces an increasing need and desire to develop an own identity and individuality of his own, so as to be able to relate to the different and often incoherent groups and role-expectations with which he or she is now confronted. To have one's identity confirmed and accepted by one's peers is no longer sufficient, since the peer-group's ability to satisfy one's need and desire for security and recognition has now become limited. The individual must rely more upon himself/herself and must consequently develop an own identity, able to supply the security formerly found in peer-group relations. When the individual's basic identification is no longer with peers, new demands are put upon his identity. To an increasing degree the individual must be able to interact with a variety of people and respect and accept their ideas, interests, tastes and styles. He or she must also be self-confident enough to maintain and develop his or her own personal social and cultural identity, an identity which must expand in scope so that it can replace the peer-group as the basic source of security and recognition. The individual must accept and adapt to the fact of no longer being primarily identified by the environment as "a member of this or that group", but instead as a single and individual person.

During the biologically and psychologically defined periods of youth personal identity gradually becomes more firm and stable. Since values compose a fundamental and solid component of the individual's identity, this means the individual has become more confident regarding his or her values. Once the individual has developed a satisfactory personal value structure, he or she also becomes more autonomous and self-confident, identity development coming increasingly to concern the social component of identity.

The individual is also in a better position now to firmly establish his or her attitudes (which, we have argued, are the individual's expression of his or her values). Since the individual's values have become relatively stable by now, the individual's attitudes tend to become more stable. The individual's taste in a number of areas, for example, music, film and clothes becomes more anchored in his or her own values and less in those of the peer-group.

In order to study how our respondents' tastes developed during the transitional period between the different periods of youth, we analyzed the relation between our respondents' attitudes towards music at the age of fifteen and the age of twenty-one.

The six music taste patterns presented in the left column of Figure 14 — *Avantgarde, Mainstream, Soft music, Rock, High culture* and *Heavy rock* — are the result of a factor analysis of our respondents' musical taste at the age of fifteen (table available from the authors). In this analysis 28 music genres were included. In Figure 14, relations between these six music taste patterns, on the one hand, and the twelve music taste patterns presented in chapter 15 (representing our respondents' musical tastes at the age of twenty-one), on the other, are shown. In the figure only the statistically significant correlations are presented.

The instruments of measurement used on the two different occasions are not identical, but they resemble each other enough to provide a general picture of the development of taste during these important years. Unfortunately, no value measurements were included in the questionnaire used when the individuals were fifteen years old, making it impossible to follow the development of their values and value orientations in a similar way. Results concerning the development of our respondents' attitudes towards music, however, reveal some rather interesting relationships.

The results in figure 14 indicate, on the on hand, that taste changes drastically during these years and, on the other, that it possesses a certain degree of stability. It appears that during these years individuals gradually become more flexible and self-reliant in their tastes. New tastes are often added to the old ones. This is quite obvious as regards tastes in music, where all the taste patterns distinguished at the age of fifteen are related to various of the taste patterns identified at the age of twenty-one. In a few cases the correlations are negative, but as a rule they are positive.

Although it is difficult to identify empirically the reasons for this diversification in musical taste, it can probably be at least partly explained by the fact that during these years individuals gradually stabilize their values, becoming more self-reliant and autonomous and thus less dependent on the peer-group in making judgements of musical taste.

Figure 14. Relations Between Music Taste Patterns at the Age of Fifteen and Twenty-one (Pearson´s Correlations).

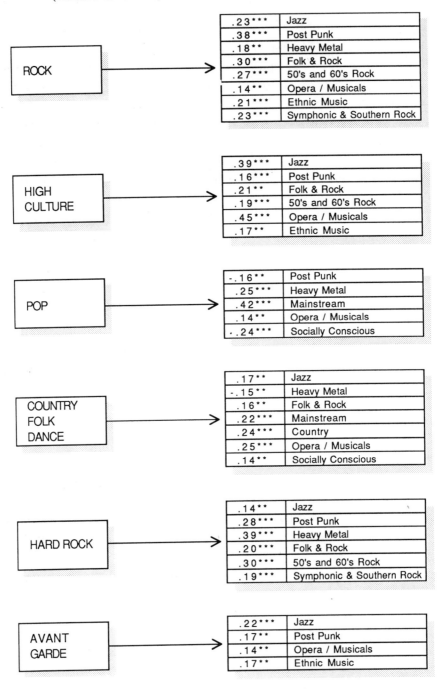

.23***	Jazz
.38***	Post Punk
.18**	Heavy Metal
.30***	Folk & Rock
.27***	50's and 60's Rock
.14**	Opera / Musicals
.21***	Ethnic Music
.23***	Symphonic & Southern Rock

ROCK

.39***	Jazz
.16***	Post Punk
.21**	Folk & Rock
.19***	50's and 60's Rock
.45***	Opera / Musicals
.17**	Ethnic Music

HIGH CULTURE

-.16**	Post Punk
.25***	Heavy Metal
.42***	Mainstream
.14**	Opera / Musicals
-.24***	Socially Conscious

POP

.17**	Jazz
-.15**	Heavy Metal
.16**	Folk & Rock
.22***	Mainstream
.24***	Country
.25***	Opera / Musicals
.14**	Socially Conscious

COUNTRY FOLK DANCE

.14**	Jazz
.28***	Post Punk
.39***	Heavy Metal
.20***	Folk & Rock
.30***	50's and 60's Rock
.19***	Symphonic & Southern Rock

HARD ROCK

.22***	Jazz
.17**	Post Punk
.14**	Opera / Musicals
.17**	Ethnic Music

AVANT GARDE

In this chapter we have touched upon an interesting and important issue in youth culture and lifestyle research, namely, that of the dynamic processes taking place in the development of young people's values, identity and lifestyles during these important years. Unfortunately, we do not have proper means for conducting more thorough and general empirical studies of this, but are restricted to exemplifying this development through measuring the changes in musical taste described above. These matters will be discussed more thoroughly in connection with the seven case studies. Although we cannot draw any general conclusions on the basis of the seven case studies, they provide us some concrete exemples of how the developments referred to are experienced and dealt with by young persons.

CHAPTER 18
PATTERNS OF LIFESTYLE, INDIVIDUALITY AND SYMBOLIC DEMOCRATIZATION

In this chapter we return to the three important questions adressed at the beginning of this part of the book. First, we discuss relations between values, attitudes and actions, on the one hand, and different manners of structuring of lifestyles, on the other. Secondly, we discuss the relations between the different levels of determination and also relate our conceptualization of these levels to Gidden's theory of the duality of structure. Thirdly, we discuss the function of popular culture in young people's lives and especially its function as a means for obtaining real and/or illusory power.

PATTERNS OF LIFESTYLE

In chapters 15 and 16 we analyzed and discussed our respondents' leisure time activities, their tastes in music and their taste in film separately. In this section we will relate these three different aspects of lifestyle to each other and discuss different *principles of structuring* of lifestyles. This is quite a natural step since lifestyles consist of several different components which are related to each other; the greater the number of components taken into consideration is, the better one can understand how lifestyles are structured in society.

In Figure 15 we present a schematic overview of the different relations between positional variables, on the one hand, and values and value orientations as well as taste and activity patterns, on the other. The figure should be regarded as a summary of the empirical results presented in chapters 15 and 16.

In the figure one can note that there are a large number of different relations and that these can be interpreted on the basis of several different theoretical perspectives. We shall discuss three such theoretical perspectives: a class and status oriented perspective, a gender perspective and a human values perspective.

Figure 15. Schematic Overview of Relations Between Taste and Activity Patterns and Values and Value Orientations.

	ROMANTIC	POETIC/PSYCHOLOGIC	SOCIALLY CONSCIOUS	SF/FANTASY	HORROR	PORNO & VIOLENCE	AGENT	COMEDY	WARGANGSTER	JAZZ	POST PUNK	HEAVY METAL	FOLK & ROCK	MAINSTREAM	COUNTRY	MODERN DANCE	OPERA/MUSICALS	ETHNICAL	SYMPHONY & SOUTHERN	SOCIALLY CONSCIOUS	50's AND 60's ROCK	CULTURE	PARTY	MUSIC	SPORTS	DOMESTIC	FASHION	RELIGIOUS	HUNTING/FISHING	EXCERCISE	MEDIA	TRAVEL
SEX	F			M	M	M	M	M	M	M	M						F		M	F		F			M	F	F		M	F	M	
CLASS	L					L									L				H			H			H	H						
EDUCATION			L	L	L		L						L		L				H			H			H						L	H
MATERIAL SECURITY	+	-	-	+	+	+	+	+		-			-	+					-			-			-		+			+		
PERSONAL SECURITY	+						+							+												+	+					
SOCIAL SECURITY	+													+												+	+		+			
PERSONAL DEVELOPMENT		+	+							+						+	+	+				+	+							+		+
MATERIAL DEVELOPMENT							+												+			+	+		+					+	+	
MATERIAL VALUE ORIENT.	+	-		+	+	+	+			-				+								-							+			
POST-MATERIAL VALUE ORIENT.	+	+	+								-		+				+		+			+		+	-		+				-	+
A CLEAN WORLD					F-								F				F															
TECHNOLOGICAL DEVELOPMENT				M	M	M	M	M	M	M									M-			M										
A COMFORTABLE LIFE	+						+																			+	+					
AN EXCITING LIFE	-	+																							+						+	+
A SENSE OF ACCOMPLISHMENT		+								+							+					+										+
PEACE	F												F				F		F						F	F						
A WORLD OF BEAUTY	F	F															F		F						F	F	F		F	F		
EQALITY	F	F		F-		F-											F								F-		F	F				F
FAMILY SECURITY	F												F		F-		F								F	F	F					
FREEDOM	F												F				F															
HAPPINESS	F												F												F	F			F			
INNER HARMONY	F																		F						F							
LOVE	F												F				F		F						F	F						
NATIONAL SECURITY	+			+	+	+	+							+					-			-					+					
PLEASURE	+			+	+	+								+													+					
SALVATION																												+			+	
SELF-RESPECT		+					+										+	+														
SOCIAL RECOGNITION				+	+	+	+							+								-									+	
WISDOM	-	+	+						-				+				+	+				+		+					+			
JUSTICE	F												F-		F										F	F						
POWER				M	M	M		M											M-			M-	M-								M	
HEALTH	+							+						+													+					
WEALTH				M	M	M	M	M	M							M			M-			M-	M						M-		M	

```
F = Female, M = Male        + = Positive  Correlation
L = Low, H = High           - = Negative  Correlation
```

The class and status perspective may be regarded as the dominant perspective within the sociological literature on popular culture and lifestyles (cf. Weber 1922/1968; Gans 1974; Bourdieu 1979/1984). According to this perspective, the most important structural principle here is the distribution of wealth and status in society. The most thoroughgoing theoretical and empirical work within this tradition is to be found in Bourdieu's *Distinction*. Our empirical results give some support to the assumption that class and education are important factors in the development and maintainance of lifestyles.

In Figure 15 we can note that several taste and activity patterns correlate with either class or education or both. Such activity and taste patterns as *Culture, Opera, Travel, Sports* and *Music* are clearly related to higher education and/or higher class, whereas such activity and taste patterns as *Country, Media, Comedies, Heavy Metal, Horror, Porno & Violence, Romantic* and *Science Fiction/Fantasy* are clearly related to low education and/or low class background. Thus, level of education and class background individuals seems to be related to the development of certain tastes and leisure time interests. Even though class and education constitute important and necessary explanations of why young people develop particular lifestyles, these do not suffice for providing an adequate explanation. Gender is at least as important a factor to consider.

On the basis of our empirical data we conclude that differences between men and women in their taste and leisure time activities, and thus in their lifestyles, are considerable. On a more general level it is also possible to discuss these differences in terms of two differing cultural spheres. The male sphere involves such taste and activity patterns as *Post punk, Heavy metal, Symphonic & southern rock, Science fiction/fantasy, Horror, Porno & violence, Agent, Comedy, War & gangster, Sports, Hunting & fishing* and *Media*. The female sphere consists of such taste & activity patters as *Opera/musicals, Socially conscious music, Romantic films, Culture, Domestic, Fashion* and *Excercise*.

Another interesting observation is that young men and young women tend to differ in the cultural distinctions they make and to express their identity in differing cultural areas. Whereas men seem to make greater distinctions within the areas of film and popular music, women tend to make greater distinctions within the area of fashion. The differences in tastes and other areas just referred to are, of course, related to gender roles. However, just as with class and education, gender is a necessary, but not a sufficient explanation of the differentiation of lifestyles within a society.

Apart from gender, class and education, there are also other structurally, positionally or individually determined phenomena which influence an individual's lifestyle. Among these are identity and the values the individual himself holds.

All the different taste and activity patterns distinguished in this study are in one way or another related to at least certain values and/or value orientations. The relations between values and value orientations, on the one hand, and taste and activity patterns, on the other, are rather complex. These relations are partly explained by the way values are structured among youth in Western society along the gender, class and status dimensions. As we have shown in chapters 15 and 16, however, the relations are found to be strong even when the positional variables are held constant. Thus, the values and value orientations of the individual tell a great deal about the way the person's own personal lifestyle develops within the structurally and positionally determined frames characterizing the person's society and culture.

The values embraced by the individual are inculcated into him or her by parents and peers at school or at work, as well as through other social institutions. during the process of individualization. Eventually all person's learn to function as individuals who incorporate into themselves to, the general material, aesthetic, ethic and metaphysic codes of society and culture and of particular groups and social networks in which they become involved during their lifetime. This adjustment to more or less commonly held values, norms, mores, etc., is necessary if the individual is to function as a social being. However, there are considerable variations, both between different groups in society and also between different individuals, regarding the relative importance put on these values, norms, mores, and the like.

One might say that even though most individuals share a common set of values, norms and mores with their fellow men, they nevertheless deviate from one other in their unique ways of relating to these values, mores and norms. Thus, the values and value orientations distinguished by Rokeach, Inglehart and others are all embraced more or less by all individuals, but the relative importance ascribed to each varies from person to person. These variations are important; obviously they exert a strong influence on the more specific attitudes and actions of the individual. These individual variations in turn are translated into the many highly differentiated lifestyles found in society.

The social and cultural structure of modern Swedish society is characterized by rather small variations in values between different classes and status groups among youth, but by rather strong variations between men and women (see Table 3, chapter 14). In our sample it is thus difficult to distinguish the values and value orientations of different classes or status groups. Those young people with higher education and of higher class background do tend, nevertheless, to emphasize the importance of development as opposed to security more than do individuals of lower education and of lower class background. Yet the major differences are to be found along the gender dimension, where we can identify a large number of values and value orientations tied to gender differences.

These gender differences are also expressed in variations in taste and activity patterns. Although there are class and status related taste and activity patterns, there are even greater gender-related ones. One can see in Figure 15 that there is a strong relation between the gender related values and value orientations, on the one hand, and the gender related taste and activity patterns, on the other. This seems to imply that values and value orientations, as well as taste and activity patterns, are strongly influenced by gender. The interesting thing, though, is that even when the gender variable is kept constant, the often rather strong influence of a particular value or value orientation on a taste or activity pattern remains intact (cf. Figures 7-11, 12 and 13 in chapters 15 and 16). Thus, the tendency to embrace certain values and value orientations and to develop certain taste and activity patterns is closely related to gender. At the same time, irrespective of gender, class and education, individuals embracing particular values are more or less likely to develop certain taste and activity patterns.

These empirical results can be considered to support the main thesis in this book, namely, that even though the lifestyles of individuals are partly determined by social and cultural structure and by class, status and gender, there is still room for considerable individual variation within this framework. In the final analysis, the lifestyle of an individual is individually determined.

The different taste and activity patterns empirically distinguished in our study are related to each other in several different ways which accord with the three strructural principles discussed above (A table showing relations between the different taste and activity patterns is available from the authors).

It would have been possible for us to construct a social and cultural lifestyle space similar to the one presented in Bourdieu's *Distinction* (Bourdieu 1979/1984). In constructing such a social space of lifestyle Bourdieu sorts the tastes of individuals along the dimensions of *composition of capital* and *volume of capital*. We could have sorted the taste and activity patterns of our respondents along the dimensions of gender, class and status in a similar way, but it would be of limited value for us to do so. The reason for this is that we consider the individual's values to be a central aspect of lifestyle, which means that we would have to introduce yet another dimension in constructing such a social space. Had it been possible for us to identify *one* such value dimension, the construction of such a social space of lifestyles might have been possible and have represented an achievement of considerable note. However, we found no way of arranging the Rokeachean values along a dimension of this sort, and it is probably impossible to do so.

One important issue in lifestyle research is whether one should try to capture and purify different ideal types of lifestyle, that is, abstract theoretical constructions. In much lifestyle research the categorization of tastes, actions, etc., into lifestyle patterns is carried out in a rather unreflected way on the basis of empirical measurements. Lifestyles have thus come to be viewed in terms of the operationalization of them. Our position in this respect is that it does not suffice to measure individuals' tastes, styles, actions, etc., to group these variables into different patterns, and to then call these lifestyles. In order to construct lifestyle types one has to develop a theory of lifestyles formulated in terms of certain concepts. If we wish to make meaningful empirical constructs concerning lifestyles, we must first understand the concepts we are using, and then develop instruments of measurements able to capture as much as possible of these concepts (cf. Hare 1981).

Central concepts in our theory of lifestyle are identity and value. We have primarily concentrated on cultural identity which can be seen as the locus of lifestyle. The most important aspect of cultural identity is values. We have distinguished between different types of values — material, aesthetic, ethical and metaphysical — in order to be able to examine dynamic aspects of cultural identity. The distinction between these different types of values and between the security and developmental functions of values may serve, we feel, as a point of departure in constructing an area of lifestyles suitable for analyzing the differentiation of lifestyles in contemporary Western society. Work in formulating such a social and cultural space of lifestyles and in developing adequate instruments of measurements has only just begun.

The theoretical and the empirical work reported in this book have been closely interwoven. The theoretical concepts formulated have influenced the instruments of measurement and vice versa. The distinction between different types of values put forward in the theoretical parts of the book are partly a result of a feeling of dissatisfaction with established methods of measuring values. The problem with these established methods of measuring values is that they were not designed to function within a theory of lifestyle such as the one presented in this book. It would have been easy for us to simply adapt to our approach the empirical results obtained and formulate concepts suitable for them. However, this would have been a form of cowardice almost since the empirical results themselves have been a source of insight into various weaknesses in our concepts and our methodology and have led to the development and refinement of both. Such developments have constituted a major difficulty in our work. Thus, our original theoretical notions were reformulated partly on the basis of the results of empirical efforts which originated from these ideas. The reformulated theoretical and conceptual notions, in their turn, called for new instruments of measurement and other operationalizations of the concepts central to our theory. Through such a dialectic interplay between theory and empirical results, both the concepts and the measurement methods have been continuously refined and developed. In the next part of the book we will discuss these problematic questions further and use our conceptualizations of different types of values in order to analyze seven young people's lifestyles.

STRUCTURAL, POSITIONAL AND INDIVIDUAL ASPECTS OF LIFESTYLE

An important theoretical and empirical problem discussed in this book is the construction of the subject and the relation between subject and object, that is the relation between agency and structure. In this section we will discuss the relation between our theoretical view on these questions and our empirical measurements of lifestyles.

Earlier in the book we have argued that lifestyles are determined on three different levels: the structural, positional and individual level of determination. In addition to examining these three different levels we have chosen to maintain the distinction between agency and structure. Such a view has been criticized by Anthony Giddens who has developed a theory of what he calls — *the duality of structure*.

Giddens has criticized the commonly employed analytic distinction between subject and object (Giddens 1984, 1991a). According to Giddens, structure may be seen as both the medium and the outcome of the conduct it recursively organizes. The structural properties of social systems do not exist outside of action but are chronically implicated in its production and reproduction. Structures are not to be regarded as constraints, but as both enabling and constraining features of social life.

> The duality of structure is always the main grounding of continuities in social reproduction across time-space. It in turn presupposes the reflexive monitoring of agents in, and as constituting, the *durée* of daily social activity. But human knowledgeability is always bounded. The flow of action continually produces consequences which are unintended by actors, and these unintended consequences also may form unacknowledged conditions of actions in a feedback fashion. Human history is created by intentional activities but is not an intended project; it persistently eludes efforts to bring it under conscious direction. However, such attempts are continually made by human beings, who operate under the threat and the promise of the circumstance that they are the only creatures who make their "history" in cognizance of that fact (Giddens 1984:27).

Giddens theoretical view of the collapse of the relation between agency and structure has been criticized from several different points of view (cf. Fielding 1988; Brewer 1988; Layder et al. 1991; Liedholm 1991). A common critique is that Giddens does not attach sufficient importance to constraint and thus does not acknowledge the pre-existence of social forms. Another type of critique deals with the problem of how Gidden's theory of structuration can be operationalized and applied in concrete situations (Fielding 1988; Brewer 1988; Layder et al. 1991). Although most authors acknowledge the important theoretical contribution Giddens, has made they hold that the distinction between subject and object may be an useful analytical tool if used with care.

The micro-macro distinction, some have asserted, is dead. It is the force of argument in this volume, even from a divergence of perspectives, that the assertion is misconceived. What is obsolete is the rigid separation, the dualism or opposition, between the micro and the macro. But even as this is recognized, we acknowledge the utility of a language which has these concepts, for easing out the signs of the external in the interaction and the symbolic meaning of action in the institutional environment. In that sense, the new province is all a middle ground (Fielding 1988:17).

In answering his critics Gidden's argues that his theory of structuration is not constructed primarily so as to analyze how *far* free action is possible in respect of social constraints, but rather in an attempt to provide social scientists with conceptual means of analyzing the delicate and subtle interlacings of reflectively organized action and institutional constraint (Giddens 1991b).

Gidden's theoretical work certainly deserves a more thorough discussion than we have provided, but we will nevertheless say something about the relation between his perspective and the theoretical perspective presented in this book.

In this book we have distinguished between the structural, positional and individual aspects of lifestyle. However, we are well aware of the fact that these aspects of lifestyle are far from independent of each other. In reality the structural, positional and individual aspects of lifestyle are closely related to each other, and often it is not even possible to be sure about what are structural, positional or individual influences. In this we agree with Giddens, but the theory of lifestyles we have presented also differs from the way Giddens conceptualizes the relation between agency and structure, since we emphasize the *relative* autonomy of the subject.

In our empirical analyses our aim has been to study individual influence on the development of different tastes and leisure time interests. We are well aware that in these analyses we have not considered all possible structural and/or positional influences but only a few important ones. We are also well aware of the fact that individuals' choices of lifestyle are deeply embedded in the structurally and positionally determined context of which they are part. Nevertheless, we want to stress the importance of individuals' reflective capacity and their possibility of transgressing the social and cultural milieux of which they are part (cf. also Giddens 1991a).

What is missing in most lifestyle research is a thorough discussion of how individuals conceptualize themselves and their place in reality. We have stressed the importance of the reflective capacity of individuals and their capability of to a certain extent, choosing lifestyles. In our discussion the various types of values occupy a central position. Individuals' ways of perceiving themselves and of presenting themselves in everyday life are intimately connected with each other. This relation may also be conceptualized in terms of Kamler's distinction between life-philosophy values and life-style values (in our terms, inner- and outer-directed values). Thus, what most lifestyle theoreticians have been concerned with have been attitudes and actions which are based on values that are held because of what other persons think. However, we stress that such values are highly dependent on those values which the individual embraces irrespective of others opinions. The fundamental question is which type of values are most important for the individual's development of his identity and lifestyle. Obviously it is much easier to discern empirically and to study, the outer-directed values, since by definition they lead up to visible actions and attitudes. This has to do with their function of relating the individual to other individuals or to groups of individuals. They serve the purpose here of distinction and adherence.

The life-philosophy values, on the other hand, are held, not primarily in order to relate to others or to distinguish oneself from them, but to understand oneself and to maintain and enhance one's conceptions of oneself and one's place in reality. Thus, without a satisfactory conception of oneself, the individual cannot relate satisfactory to others. This is why the inner-directed values are more fundamental to the individual's lifestyle than are outer-directed values. That is also why outer-directed values have been more important in lifestyle research than have inner-directed ones. Most lifestyle research has been concentrated on cultural and social distinctions, and not upon the individual preconditions for such distinctions. However, inner-directed and outer-directed values are intimately connected with each other, and values of the former kind may be held irrespective of other people's opinions, just as the latter may be embraced because of what others think.

In the MCA-analyses presented in this part of the book, we have shown that the values of the individual influence his or her attitudes towards different genres of popular culture and leisure time interests, even when the positional variables are kept constant. We take these results to be an indication of the existence of an individually determined component of lifestyle. However, due to the limitations of the instruments for measuring values, we cannot say what types of values such relations concern. However, we may argue theoretically that these values are held by the individual, at least partly on individually determined grounds. In order to obtain further empirical support for these assumptions, however, one must develop an adequate method for measuring the four types of values as distinct categories. Unfortunately, no such method is available. The development of such a method, therefore, would be highly desirable.

FALSE CONSCIOUSNESS OR SYMBOLIC DEMOCRATIZATION?

In the empirical parts of this book we have studied various central aspects of young people's identity and lifestyle. We have argued that popular culture constitutes a fundamental force in young people's lifestyle development. However, one might question whether it is the most important area or whether there are other ones which are even more important. As argued in the previous section, one's fundamental conceptions of oneself, of reality and of one's relation to it are probably more important to his lifestyle than are his relations to the restricted part of reality we call popular culture.

Thus, one's life philosophy and outlook on life and reality — that is, metaphysical and ethical values — occupy a much more fundamental position in one's identity than one's popular cultural tastes, style and attitudes — one's aesthetic and material values. Metaphysical and ethical conceptions are not as visible and easily observed as aesthetic and material conceptions. They are empirically less accessible. One might say that the four types of values we have distinguished stretch from mind to matter; obviously, mind is more abstract and less concrete than matter.

On the one hand, material and aesthetic conceptions and attitudes are influenced by metaphysical and ethical ones. On the other hand, material and aesthetic conceptions may also influence the metaphysical and ethical ones. Yet there is no doubt that the latter are more fundamental and lasting than the former. Thus, they represent the more stable and lasting component of identity.

If one wishes to understand individuals' use of popular culture and its importance to their identity and their creation of lifestyle it is thus necessary to grasp the complex relation between individuals' aesthetic, material, metaphysical and ethical values, evading the rather common mistake of concentrating entirely on consumption of and attitudes toward popular cultural goods.

The term *false consciousness* has been used frequently among Marxist as well as other social scientists to designate the process whereby, for instance, popular culture can be used as a tool for the ruling classes to inculcate their fundamental metaphysical and ethical conceptions into members of the working class, thereby making the latter accept and feel satisfied with their material and social conditions (cf. Eyerman 1981).

This view on popular culture and its function in society has been highly influential in social science and the humanities. Thus, popular culture has been seen as a pacifying component of everyday culture, restraining the opportunities of its users to further the material, intellectual and spiritual development. However, during the last few decades this view has been under more or less constant attack by a number of social and cultural theorists who established themselves during the 1950's and 60's, when modern popular (youth) culture originated. These theorists refused to dismiss popular culture as pacifying and non-creative, but stressed its importance for individual identity and lifestyle development (see, for instance, Turner 1990).

In this book we have refrained from using the concept of false consciousness, preferring the term and concept *symbolic democratization* (Ewen 1988). The reasons for this terminological decision are several. Contrary to the concept of false consciousness, the term "symbolic democratization" does not necessarily imply that people's use of popular culture is pacifying or creates a false consciousness (whatever that may mean). The process described as symbolic democratization is a central force in the making of contemporary lifestyle. Max Weber (1922/1968), Agnes Heller (1970/1984) and Richard Sennett (1976) all described how the use of different symbols was once tied to different positions in society. During the eighteenth century there were even laws in France and England prescribing who was allowed to wear certain clothes and garments. Today the use of different symbols and artefacts are not as tied to position as they once were; they may be used more freely, regardless of one's class or status position in society. The process of symbolic democratization may, of course, lead to an illusory transcendence of class; it may also function as a conscious disguise of class and status, emphasizing instead the image the individual wants to present. Thereby, the individual can escape the prejudices and notions towards the position he occupies and instead be regarded and recognized as an individual in his own right. Popular culture may thus function as an emancipating force in an individual's life, as well as an oppressing transmittor of false consciousness.

The empirical results we have presented in this book indicate that the use of popular culture to a certain degree depends on actual class or status. Individual freedom to transcend the limits of position are considerable, however. Through the use of popular culture the individual may break the limitations of class and status, even though he cannot remove the actual inequalities inherent in the real power and status relations of society. Thus, even if it cannot alter the status or recognition of the class to which he or she belongs, symbolic democratization may function as a way for an individual to obtain individual status and recognition.

To say this is also to state that if we restrict our analysis of lifestyle to structural and positional levels, we will probably find that power relations determined by class, gender and status are maintained and transmitted through popular culture. But if one takes one step further — as we have done — making individual determination a basic characteristic of lifestyle, we will also find that popular culture can be used, on the one hand, to enhance and increase the status and position of the individual, and on the other, to develop areas of identity not necessarily tied to status.

A discussion closely related to the one of false consciousness and symbolic democratization concerns the *double function* of popular culture and lifestyle. The most striking empirical result of our study is that among both taste and activity patterns there are some patterns related basically to the need and desire for security, and others related to the need and desire for development.

Most young people share the taste for mainstream music and film, and engage in a number of activities interesting to most young people. By adopting these tastes and engaging in these activities they become part of a general youth culture. Most individuals engage in a number of specific and rather distinct activities and also embrace tastes for a number of rather specific and distinct music and film genres. Such activities and tastes divide young people into different groups, but also allow them to cultivate and express their individuality. Quite naturally, the needs and desires for security, development and individuality are common to all young people.

The relative importance of the one or the other varies considerably from individual to individual, however, and also varies within one and the same person from one period of youth to another.

One can surely conceptualize and characterize youth culture as a rather coherent phenomenon involving conformity. It is also possible, however, on an empirical basis to distinguish a number of rather specific and distinct phenomena of youth culture which can be considered in terms of their incoherence and complexity, and the elements of creativity and development they involve. A common mistake in both youth culture and lifestyle research has been to stress only one of these views. The simple truth is that youth culture, like all culture, can and does serve both as a means of the individual's satisfaction of needs and desires to belong and feel security and as a means of personal and individual development and distinction. All youth culture is therefore conformist. All youth culture is likewise creative. It is also individual. Each individual tries to satisfy these two types of needs and desires in his or her own way. Therefore, if one really wants to understand how popular culture functions in relation to lifestyle, it is not sufficient to concentrate on rather abstract and quantitatively discerned general cultural patterns. One must also study the single and unique individual. That is what we intend to do in the next part of the book.

PART FIVE:

INDIVIDUAL LIFESTYLES — CAPTURING THE VARIATIONS

The achievement of every structure is at once a signal to seek out another one, in which the play — necessary structure, and necessary dissatisfaction with the structure as such — is repeated. As life it needs form; as life, it needs more than form (Simmel 1918/1971:370).

CHAPTER 19
INDIVIDUAL LIFESTYLES — SEVEN CASE STUDIES

INTRODUCTION

In this chapter we arrive finally at the core of lifestyle, the single individual. Hitherto we have mainly identified and discussed various general patterns of youth culture within the areas of music, film and leisure activities. Such patterns reveal much regarding the way Swedish young people structure their values, attitudes and actions into meaningful cultural patterns. Yet this alone is not sufficient. Whereas in principle we could assign each of the some 300 persons we have studied to one or more of the categories considered, however, this would lead to far too simple a description of the lifestyles they cultivate. One of our main theses is that, while its is certainly possible and meaningful, to identify such general patterns in order to arrive at a basic picture of the lifestyles of young people, we must carry out intensive studies of single individuals and their more specific lifestyles if we are to understand the role and importance of the lifestyle phenomenon for the individuals themselves.

Therefore, during a three year period, we conducted a number of intensive case studies in an attempt to comprehend the core of the individual lifestyle, which we argue is the individual's own and unique way of structuring a multitude of cultural artefacts and phenomena. The general patterns we have identified provide at least a rough impression of certain important aspects of lifestyle among Swedish nineteen to twenty-one year olds. This tends to underline the unity within the diversity of youth culture. The case studies, on the other hand, serve to illustrate the diversity within the unity portrayed by our theoretical and empirical lifestyle constructions.

Culture can be described both in terms of coherence, integration, and similarities, on the one hand, and of incoherence, inconsistence, disintegration and diversity, on the other (cf. Archer 1988). One of the main reasons for carrying out all those very time-consuming case studies is to present both the regularities and the peculiarities inherent in young person's use of culture. On the one hand, this shows how these individuals use culture to express their adherence to different social and cultural structures. On the other hand, it indicates their use of culture to express their own individuality and uniqueness. The detailed study of culture may thus serve to illuminate some conflicts resulting from the individual's cleveage between a private and a public self, between individuality and sociability, etc.

In the following, we present seven case studies. Each should be regarded as a separate example of individual lifestyle. We thus aim, not primarily at finding general patterns of lifestyle construction, or at categorizing these young persons in terms of differing lifestyles as such, but rather at studying the rich, individually determined variations which are vividly experienced as being variations in their styles of life.

Although we shall use these case studies basically as a means to exemplifying the considerable variety of individual lifestyles, and to support our theoretical thesis concerning lifestyle as a structurally, positionally *and* individually determined phenomenon, we nevertheless will also briefly discuss a number of general tendencies.

TOR

> "Well I stand on these hills and I watch her at night.
> A thousand square miles, a million orange lights
> wounded and scarred, she lies silent in pain
> raped and betrayed in the cold acid rain
> and I wish and I wish
> we could start all over again
> yes I wish and I wish
> we could win her back again"
> (New Model Army 1990).

Three Interviews With Tor

Tor grew up in a lower middle class family in Malmö. His high school period (1987-1990) was spent at two different schools oriented towards graphic design. After finishing his secondary school education he was called up for a year of military service, which he spent working in a photographic laboratory. Since then (autumn 1991) Tor has been unemployed.

The first time we met Tor he lived with his parents in a residential district in Malmö. He devoted the greater part of his time to two main interests. One of these was to construct and take part in so-called role games within the fantasy genre, and the other was to draw and paint. Tor's plans and dreams for the future were very concrete and well-defined, and his occupational plans and extra-curricular activities almost totally overlapped. He wanted to become a draughtsman or an illustrator, preferably within the genres of fantasy or science fiction.

> Hopefully I'll become a commercial artist, or a cover designer for books, book jackets or games and such things. I like to draw fantasy characters like dragons and monsters. You can do almost anything without risking how they'll look. But you have to make them lifelike. If you draw a dragon it must look as if it existed in reality. I'd like to develop this form of art in making book jackets or book covers, but I'll probably not get the chance to do this for a long time. However, this is what I'm aiming at.

Tor was indeed very purposeful in his ambitions. He was deeply committed to his interests in drawing and in fantasy-culture, and these interests formed the dominant elements in his cultural identity. During his leisure time Tor constructed his own fantasy games. He also painted, both mythical motifs and themes from different fairy tales and fantasy stories. In addition, Tor was a member of a fantasy club where he could attend lectures, meet like-minded people, and play role games. He also frequently played role games with his friends.

> It's roughly like being the main character in a book. One person leads the game and tells everyone what's happening. If the main character enters a room, for example, then the game leader informs everyone about what's in the room, who's there, what they look like and how they react. Then it's your turn to account for what you're going to do, and how you'll solve the different problems you're confronted with. The game often contains a lot of violence, but actually it's simulated violence, and I'm not a violent person. Those who play it are usually pretty calm people. There's a lot of mind- work. The rules are often very complicated, and the handbooks are really thick. It's all about simulating another person's life.

Tor's interests in fantasy and in drawing were expressed not only through his constructing and participating in different role games. His cinema, music and literary tastes were also strongly related to his interest in fantasy culture.

> Most of the films I care for are fantasy or science fiction, or other types of adventure films, like, for instance, *Indiana Jones*. *George Lukas* and *Steven Spielberg* are my favorite directors. I also like *Harrison Ford*. I seldom watch any really "deep" or "serious" films. In my opinion, people should go to the movies to be entertained and excited, not to become depressed. /.../ On the rock scene, my favorites right now are *The Mission, Magnum* and *Gandalf*. I bought Gandalf because of their name. It's one of Tolkien's characters, but I discovered that the music was really good, too. It's the feeling I get from listening to it. /.../

From what I say about books I guess you understand that it's mainly fantasy books I'm reading. I also read quite a bit of horror fiction, and some occult stuff.

The second time we met Tor, he was still living with his parents. He had the same leisure interests, characterized by the same deep commitment. He had not changed his future plans much either. He was approaching his goals gradually, taking various casual jobs and getting orders for different illustrations and paintings. He described his situation in the following way:

I'm going to become an illustrator. When I'm finished with military service I'll apply to an illustrator for an apprenticeship. Actually there is someone who's already offered me an apprenticeship, but I don't like his way of working. There's another one who's doing some fantasy stuff who'd like to work for. /.../ As an apprentice I don't care what I'll get while I'm doing my apprenticeship. I'll work as an apprentice for about a year and a half. Then I'll go to look for a job as an illustrator, or at an advertising agency. I'll probably have to do a lot of other stuff than fantasy, but if I get the opportunity to work with this other guy, that will be good, since he has a lot of contacts abroad. Hopefully, then, I'll have the chance to do jackets and covers for fantasy and science fiction books and to do ordinary illustrations for the daily press. I'm looking for a kind of mixture.

Tor had continued to develop not only his thinking regarding his future plans, but also his interest in fantasy culture. Together with his girlfriend he had visited a fantasy club in England, and together with some friends he had also founded a club for so-called lifelike role games.

When talking with a person like Tor, who maintains and cultivates his interests with such devotion, it is natural to ask how it all began.

During the eighth or ninth grade, there was a buddy of mine in school who told me about a hobby shop. I'd been there before and had noticed several shelves filled with boxes. I thought they contained models, but my friend said they were games. Several years later I heard about a game called *Dungeons and Dragons*. I read the rules, but I couldn't understand a thing. It was a failure as far as the rules were concerned when we started out, but we had lots of fun. Then we started to play more regularly, but the guys I played with couldn't live up to my expectations. For them it was a matter not of role games but of war games. It was fun, but I got no great kick. I became more and more interested in fantasy. I read a lot about it, and then, four years ago, I discovered the fantasy club. I got in contact with them. Everybody there was playing role games. I was accepted as a member and that's the way it's been ever since. /.../ There are mainly two guys who have influenced me. Both of them have played since they were children. They've played since the game was introduced into Sweden, and they've also been members of the Star War Association, which is only concerned with Star Wars. And then they have been occupied with SCA, a kind of Middle Ages game, where people fight in full armour. I've been hooked on it, too, but I've never made myself a suit of armour.

During these years, Tor was particularly involved in developing so called lifelike role games. In his description of such a role game, one can see his deep involvement.

It's during the Middle Ages. It's the Middle Ages all over the world. For example, you can be a Samurai. I've played the game a couple of times. People hit each other with rubber swords. We've also had other kinds of role games. We played one in my parents' house. It was a horror role game. We were having a barbecue when strange things started happening. The window-panes began to slam. Nobody knew what was going on. There was no electricity in the basement, and when people went into the bathroom they saw all sorts of mysterious things in the mirror. The game leader had put notes up beforehand with instructions about what you were supposed to do. When people appeared they had blood on their faces. Others fell into a trance. We didn't know what was going on. Everybody was provided with a manuscript of his special role. We played different characters. One was, a priest, for example. Finally, we were informed that there was a vampire causing all those things. We were told that there was something down in the basement, so we marched down the stairs carrying candles. One of us was a priest, and this helped us to pull ourselves together. We came down the stairs carrying a crucifix. It was so dark we could hardly see a thing. An ax went flying towards a wall. Our mission was doomed to fail, so we went back up again, but then we found that some people were missing. A lot of strange things had happened. There was a chess-board that was laid out on the table. We started to wonder, thinking the vampire must be someone we knew. When it was almost midnight the identity of the vampire was revealed. Then the priest disappeared. We still had the crucifix and we also found a silver dagger. We learned that, one way or another, we had to get hold of holy water. We put the crucifix into a tub of water which started to bubble. We hoped this would do the trick. We didn't dare go down into the basement. We took garlic powder and started towards the basement door. Then we discovered the vampire. He began following us, scratching in the air. We tried to pretend we were throwing garlic powder at him, but suddenly the lid went off, and the stairs got covered with garlic powder. We found all sorts of books containing rituals and things like that. We discovered a switch, and when we pressed it the wall opened. This brought to light everyone who earlier had disappeared. We threw holy water onto the vampire and succeeded in chasing him away. We woke those up who had been in trance. Finally, we succeeded in destroying the vampire. We had lots of fun.

Tor's style was thus strongly characterized by his intense interest in fantasy culture. One could even say that he was playing role games in his everyday life. He often dressed in different types of clothing symbolizing different roles.

I change between being the nice guy in blue jeans and a shirt and being a punk rocker. It depends on how I want to feel. Sometimes it's nice to feel like a ragamuffin. Then I wear that type of clothes. Usually my style of dressing changes from week to week. /.../ When I become older I'll probably wear a suit. Right now I just hate suits, but if I'm going to work in the advertising business it's standard. I'll have to wait and see. Maybe I'll become more extreme instead.

The third time we meet Tor he has just recently finished his military service. He is unemployed and looking for a job as an illustrator. Ever since we first met him, Tor has been firmly determined to become an illustrator or an art director. He wants to fulfill these plans even though it is difficult for him to find an appropriate job due to the current labor market situation. Tor is not prepared to compromise, but he is ready to start from scratch and successively advance to the position he desires. If needed, he is also prepared to get further education.

> I'm still determined to become an illustrator. You have to have a goal, and I know that I'll become an illustrator, one way or another. At first I might have to work at an office doing something simple, but as you learn the trade you can do more and more, and finally have enough knowledge and skill to do what you want. Maybe I'll have to get more education. There's an interesting school in Copenhagen, and there's a private school in Stockholm that I've been thinking about.

Tor's lifestyle is to a large extent characterized by his interest in drawing and painting, and it is quite natural for him to try to integrate this interest into his work plans. Although he undoubtedly has a strong need to express himself in his paintings and drawings he is well aware that it is almost impossible to make a living as an artist. He would like to be an artist, but he knows that this is no realistic plan for the future.

> I wouldn't mind being an artist, but to be one you have to be damned lucky. You need to become recognized and known. What you're doing is basically the same as when you're an illustrator. The difference is that as an artist you have no regular customers, no secure income. Art is something you create in your leisure time.

Tor is planning not only for his future career, but also for a chance to move to an apartment of his own together with his girlfriend, but he does not plan to do this until he has a steady job. When we ask Tor to describe how he has developed during the past four years, he tell us he has had the same interests and tastes all along, but that he has developed and become more mature and more sure of himself.

> I've become more self-assured. It's easier now to talk with people, partly because of military service, but also because of my interest in fantasy and in lifelike role games. I've become a member of a small group which I admired earlier. We've begun to play more of the real thing. It's more real theater now. I dare to act out and freak out more now. Before, the characters we played were more stereotyped. The lifelike role games, I think, have also made life easier for me in my contacts with other people in everyday life.

During the three years we have followed Tor he has had two major interests: painting and fantasy. He has developed these interests continually, and they have become increasingly integrated into his personality and lifestyle. Tor is an imaginative and artistically talented person, skillfully balancing between the realms of fantasy and reality. Among the seven young people we have followed, he is probably the one with the most stable identity. He is quite sure about, and also satisfied with, who he is and what he wants to do and become.

Tor's Life Plan

Except for his parents and school friends, the person Tor considered most important to him during the final period of his high school education was his drawing teacher. Tor wanted very much to develop his artistic talents, and he also felt that completing high school was important. During his four years of graphic arts courses while in high school, Tor came in contact with fantasy culture, and increasingly his drawings and paintings came to center on themes from the fantasy genre. During this period he also joined the fantasy and role game clubs of which he has been a member ever since. Towards the end of high school he met his present girlfriend. She, too, had an active and vivid interest in fantasy culture. Tor's interests kept growing ever stronger, and they culminated immediately after high school in his founding of a club for lifelike role games.

Tor is a young man of high ambitions, reflected in his conception of his future. The second time we met him (autumn, 1990) his plans were that, after finishing his military service, he would go to work as a low-paid apprentice to an illustrator who was oriented to the fantasy genre. Tor was convinced that, after completion of this apprenticeship (which he estimated would take approximately two years) he would be able to work as an illustrator on his own.

Tor's long-range plans for his private life were also fairly well elaborated. He felt that at about twenty-five he would get married and a few years later he expected to become a father.

When we asked Tor to sketch some alternative plan for the future, it turned out to be very similar to the first. The only difference was that, acording to this plan, after a few years of experience as an illustrator and as an assistent to an art director he would end up becoming an art director himself. He also had rather definite plans for his private life in connection with this.

The third time we met Tor he had not changed his plans for the future at all. He was certain, purposeful and self-confident in looking at his future. We hope he will succeed.

Some Comments on Tor's Lifestyle

Just as most young people's lifestyles, Tor's lifestyle is closely related to different types of popular culture. The central element of popular culture for him is his engagement in a variety of activities associated with fantasy — role games, fantasy literature, fantasy music, and fantasy films, etc. As mentioned before, popular culture serves a *double function* for young people's lifestyles. On the one hand, they use it to explore, develop and express what they consider to be their unique personal identity. On the other, they use popular culture to show their loyalty to various groups and persons and their sense of belonging.

This double function is quite obvious in Tor's case. He spends a great deal of his leisure time playing role-games with persons who are also influenced by fantasy culture. He is a member of an international fantasy organization. In addition, his interest in fantasy culture is intimately interwoven with his strong interest in painting and drawing. A fundamental feature of Tor's relation to the popular culture he is interested in, is that he creates it rather than merely uses it. He constructs role-games, writes adventure stories, paints fantasy motifs, and has founded an association for lifelike role-games. This is the creative aspect of Tor's use of popular culture.

However important fantasy activities may be for Tor, his most fundamental interests are painting and drawing. These interests color not only his leisure time, but also his career plans. It would seem that the overriding element in Tor's identity and in his personality is his need and desire to make use of his imagination and to create images and pictures anchored both in reality and in his own fantasy. His interest in the popular cultural sphere of fantasy can thus be regarded as a result of his more fundamental personal characteristics. The fact that he has adopted fantasy as his main popular cultural interest seems to be based on its being better able than any other form of popular culture to provide him with the chance to utilize his imagination and artistic creativity. Tor needs popular culture to develop his cultural competence, and through his engagement in role-games, fantasy clubs, and the like, he constantly strengthens and develops his social competences and thus his social identity. There is no doubt that Tor has succeeded in the difficult task of finding a balance between the personal and social parts of his identity. He has managed in his cultural identity to integrate, on the one hand, the solitary aspects of his desire for using his imagination and his creativity, and on the other, his need and desire to be part of a social community, to communicate and to find for himself a suitable position in society.

The constant interplay between the personal and social poles in Tor's identity is the driving force through which he constantly increases his cultural capital, at the same time developing his cultural identity. Since in Tor's case this interplay is relatively unproblematic and free of more serious conflicts, his identity has become very stable. Tor seems almost completely satisfied with his identity and with the lifestyle he has developed in relation to it.

When analyzing Tor's lifestyle as a function of his values, his aesthetic values appear to be the most salient. This is not to say that other values are unimportant to him, but merely that Tor first and foremost uses his aesthetic values, attitudes and actions to create and express his lifestyle. The latter, to be sure, is closely related to values, attitudes and actions of material, metaphysical and ethical character. Although these may in turn serve to express his fundamental material, metaphysical and ethical conceptions and convictions, it is to the aesthetic values he has best managed to give a concrete form in his attitudes and actions,

ANNA-KARIN

Each day can be an adventure
Between reality and dreams
Between secrets and lies
But my love is always there
Life is here
Life is now
Life is still here
(Niklas Strömstedt 1990, translated by the authors).

Three Interviews With Anna-Karin

Anna-Karin grew up in a working class family in a suburb of Malmö. Her secondary school education involved general studies. After its completion she began her college training to become a nursery-school teacher. Now, three years later, she is working as a nursery school teacher. Anna-Karin's ambition was to acquire a good education and a more interesting job than what she considers her parents to have.

> My dad is a butcher and mom works in an office. I don't want to work with the kind of things they do. I've tried it out during my summer holidays, but it didn't satisfy my needs. I want to work with people.

When first we met Anna-Karin (autumn, 1988), she lived with her parents in Malmö. During this period she had already decided to work with children in one way or another.

> Yes, I know roughly what I want to do. I want to take care of children. I don't know exactly how and where. Maybe I can specialize in some particular type of children. Anyhow it has to be something to do with children.

During her studies at college Anna-Karin had a wonderful time. She met people sharing the same kinds of interests as herself. She made a lot of new friends of different ages whom she met frequently, both in class and during her spare-time. She and her friends often met at home for a cup of coffee, talk, be together and watch TV. They often went to the movies. Now and then they went dancing.

> I'm often together with my schoolfriends. Sometimes we go to the movies, but we spend most of our time at home, chatting and watching TV, either at my home or at theirs. Some of the group live in Lund, and in Trelleborg, and sometimes we visit there. Since we belong to so many different age groups we seldom go dancing. For age reasons it's often difficult for some of my younger friends to get in. Unfortunately, there are not so many places that suit everyone.

The films Anna-Karin liked were largely quite popular ones. Horror films were the only film genre she expressed a clear dislike for.

> I like all kinds of films, but it's important that they're funny and exciting, and have some kind of story. The guys usually want to watch war and action films and stuff like that. We're more fond of, say, music films. Sometimes we go along with them, sometimes they go along with us. /.../ I'm not especially fond of horror films. I'm a bit afraid of the dark and sometimes I've got to go home alone afterwards. /.../ I like films with *Eddie Murphy*, he's funny. I also like romantic and tragic films. Once I saw a film called *Annie*. It was about a little

girl who was a foundling. It was "sob", "sob" all the time. I became both sad and glad after seeing it. It finally ended well."

Anna-Karin's music tastes were simple and straightforward. Mostly she listened to hit parade music on the radio.

> I listen to a lot of music on the radio, but I don't rush away to buy records. I listen to all kinds of music. *Roxette* is good, I also like the kind of music that was played in the film *Dirty Dancing*. I don't like heavy metal, but certain kinds of heavy rock can be rather good. *Europe* play some really good songs. I don't listen much to classical music or to jazz. If they play it on the radio I don't turn it off, but I don't listen very closely either.

Anna-Karin's literary tastes, too, were mainstream. Mostly she read best-sellers.

> The books I read are best-sellers. Right now I'm reading a book called *I Take Manhattan*. It's about the daughter of a man who owns a publishing firm. He tries to sell it. I like the book because it's both romantic and exciting, there are lots of plots. Still another book I liked a lot was about a woman in London. It was during the war, she met a guy who finally joined the army, and tried to survive to get back to London. The book follows this woman during all this time.

Two years later, when we met Anna-Karin again, she was still working at the nursery school, living with her parents. She was really satisfied with her work, and she wanted to continue her education in the same area so as to be able to work with handicapped children.

> I really get on well at my job. This is basically what I want to do — although in a somewhat different way. I want to work with parental guidance or handicapped children. I've read a lot about handicapped children, and even if it takes a long time, I'd like to be able to watch how a handicapped child who you're working with changes and develops.

Anna-Karin obviously had a clear and distinct idea of what she wanted to do in the future.

In her leisure time Anna-Karin did roughly the same sort of things she did two years before. She met with her friends, occasionally went to the movie, and very occasionally went dancing.

> Mostly we meet at home. We don't go out very often. The last time we did it, it was to Sodom (a discotheque) in Lund, and we've gone out dancing once or twice in Helsingborg. Mostly we arrange parties at someone's place.

However, Anna-Karin's most dominant leisure activity was in fact dancing. For a long period of time she had been a member of a team of folk-dancers, and at the moment she was active as a leader and instructor and also as a member of the committee. Her interest in folk-dancing was expressed not only through dancing, but she also read quite a number of books on subjects such as folk music, folk-dance and folk costumes.

> I dance folk-dance and I'm an instructor for the youth team. This takes quite a bit of time. We practice once a week, but we also have lots of courses and performances. Last weekend, for example, we were off performing down in Germany. We also have performances quite often in Malmö and in the vicinity. /.../ I'm really fond of Schottische, Hambo, and other types of big festival dances, since they have so many rotations and you're doing different things all the time. Everything have to match if it's going to work out all right. *Weave Rough Homespun* is a really nice dance symbolizing weaving. There are eight couples standing in a line, and there are lots of fusions which are supposed to be the weaving. You bend down again and again, and you're active all the time. Then we have the *Frykdals-dance*. It's quite a difficult dance that it takes a long time to learn, but when you know it, it's really great to dance. *English For Three Couples* is another dance that's difficult, that is, before you know how to do it, since everyone is doing things at the same time. /../ I've become ever more interested in folk-dance and everything surrounding it. I read a lot of differen books and I have lots of notebooks I use to research, which keeps me busy all the time. The costumes are really interesting. They have so many symbols, and ornaments symbolizing different things. These symbols are so abundant. Many are about marriage and such things. /../ We've had courses that deal with costumes, with dance, and with handicraft. All these things are part of our history. I have a costume with a white blouse and a big loose top, with a waist and waistcoat. It has lots of silver jewelry, and buckles on it, and a chain. All of this had meaning, showing how rich you were. The costumes we use nowadays were once used only by the rich.

At the time of the second interview, Anna-Karin's tastes were more or less the same. She listened mostly to music on the radio, and she watched popular movies.

> My taste is probably much the same: the same type of music, the same type of films, and the same kinds of books. I listen to lots of Swedish music, *Gyllene Tider*, for example, and to the hit parade. *Wilson Philips* are a singing group I like a lot. They are three girls who sing, not ballads, but rather quiet songs. I'm not exactly wild about opera and that kind of stuff, and not about heavy metal of the worst kind, but I guess I could say I like most kinds of music. /.../ You're not so dependent on music now as when you went to school, when you had to know the names of all the artists and be able to talk about them. I used to talk about music then. /.../ The latest film I saw was *Look Who's Talking*. I really liked it. Sometimes I like watching a comedy, sometimes a good thriller, it varies.

Anna-Karin said she had become more mature, self-assertive and sure about her own identity during the last few years. One way this was reflected was in her attitude towards clothes.

> When you become older it's easier to dare to be yourself. You don't have to be like all the others, and you don't fall for group pressure. In school you were easily influenced. For example, you should have the same sort of sweaters as the others. I've found my own style now. When you were in school you tested different styles. If everyone had brown clothes, I could easily put on something yellow or red. Afterwards, when you think about it, it was probably a lot for the sake of protest, to turn against the others. I'm more independent now. I usually dress in practical clothes, ordinary jeans and a shirt, but occasionally it turns out to be something different.

When we meet Anna-Karin for the last time (autumn, 1991), she is still working as a nursery school teacher. She has got a permanent job at a nursery school and is very satisfied with it. She has no thoughts of changing her occupation or starting some new program or studies. One of the biggest changes in Anna-Karin's life is that she has moved to her own apartment.

> I like my job even better now. I really feel it's OK. I've moved from home too, and that's nice. That's about everything that's happened. This year I've spent most of my time getting my new apartment ready. I moved in last Easter. It took quite a while before they had re-decorated it, and after that I had to move in my furniture. There hasn't been time to do very much else.

Anna-Karin's interests have been basically the same during the three years we have known her. Most of her leisure time is spent either sewing or dancing folk dance. She devotes more and more of her time to these activities, and she has scarcely had time for anything else. Anna-Karin even considers cutting down on the time she spends at the folk dance club. The rest of her time she spends either at home or with friends. She meets her friends more seldom, however, since most of them have moved elsewhere, and some even abroad. She also spends less time going to the movies or to discotheques.

> I have so little time, I've hardly been out at all this year. I have so much to do during the week that I don't get to see many people. I really enjoy being on my own.

In the evenings Anna-Karin devotes herself to one of her major interests, sewing. This is the interest she has developed the most since the last time we met her. On the whole, Anna-Karin seems to have a genuine need to create and to express herself aesthetically, not with the aim of gaining recognition by others, but rather of developing her own competence and her skills in different areas.

> Last year I got more interested in clothes. I find it rather amusing to look for sewing patterns and to see if they turn out the way I thought. I feel I create something. I haven't got enough fantasy to design clothes myself, except for simple things. Sometimes my friends ask me if I can make them a dress or whatever, then I make it and hope it will fit. Lately, I've begun to sew these Waldorf dolls. I've got a friend who gives courses in sewing them. The dolls become very personal. You've got a model, but no two dolls looks alike. /.../ The more you sew, the more experienced you become, so you can make more complicated things. It's stimulating with such *small challenges*. /.../ Being creative is important. Besides my sewing, dancing also contains creative elements. I try to use rhythm and motions in my work. Many children who have difficulties with reading and writing also have problems with their movements (Italics added).

When we ask Anna-Karin to describe her personal development during the three years that had gone by, she tells us she has become more self-reliant and independent. She feels her self-confidence has always been rather good but that it has nevertheless improved lately. She feels she dares to express herself and state her own opinions in different matters more freely.

Anna-Karin's Life Plan

With the exception of her parents, the persons Anna-Karin considered to be most important to her during her schooldays were a sewing teacher and a dance teacher. On the eve of her choice of a secondary school curriculum, Anna-Karin seriously considered becoming a sewing teacher. To be able to keep all her different possibilities open, she chose a social studies curriculum. Towards the end of her secondary school education she abandoned her plans to become a sewing teacher. Her plans to work with children then started to take more concrete shape. After finishing secondary school she elected for nursery teacher training. Taking part in this training gave her the feeling that she could start to "act naturally" and "be herself". Her friends and teachers encouraged a development of this sort. At the age of twenty she began to work as a nursery school teacher, and her colleagues here became very important to her. Anna-Karin felt she had been developing all the time at her work, learning new things continually, something she was very happy about.

The second time we met Anna-Karin, the picture she had formed of her future was not yet particularly differentiated. She knew that, one way or another, she was going to continue to work with children. She felt that at about the age of twenty-five she would move from home, and that at somewhere between twenty-five and thirty she would have a child. When we asked Anna-Karin to depict an alternative picture of her future she drew a big question-mark.

The last time we met Anna-Karin she was rather satisfied with life and how things had developed for her. This is not to imply, however, that she had no further ambitions. Though she had no plans to drastically change her life, she was very much interested in developing her own work, both in a formal sense and in terms of content. A dominant characteristic of Anna-Karin seemed to be her need to create continually and to express herself, to increase her skills and her competence, that is, to develop herself, her identity and her lifestyle.

Some Comments on Anna-Karin's Lifestyle

Anna-Karin shows a social consciousness in the sense of being highly concerned about the welfare of physically and mentally disabled children, of children with problematic home situations, and the like. She tries in many ways to help such children develop their capacities in her nursery school work. She also does a lot of reading about physically and mentally disabled children and about different methods used to help them. This concern for others suggests that ethical values constitute an important, and possibly a dominant, part of her value system. However, her interest in expressing herself aesthetically also characterizes her. This suggests strong aesthetic values as well. To summarize, Anna-Karin's lifestyle seems to be strongly influenced by both her aesthetic and her ethical values, attitudes and actions. She seems not much concerned about what other people think of her lifestyle. What is important to her is to be satisfied with and make use of her creativity.

In order to distinguish between our way of using it, and Bourdieu's definition of it, we have previously given a rather broad definition of the notion of cultural capital. In Anna-Karin's case it becomes obvious that an increase in cultural capital need not rest on strivings for a higher social position or status. Anna-Karin increases her cultural capital continually by developing and enhancing her skills and competence within the areas of folk dancing and sewing. This is important for her, not because it increases her social or cultural status, but basically because it increases her own satisfaction and helps her to develop her cultural identity and lifestyle.

SONJA

> Follow me
> Follow me to the land of your dreams
> You need not show respect for anyone
> You can do whatever you wish
> Who has told you that you have to
> live like everyone else
> Open your eyes and do what you wish
> (Mauro Scocco 1986, translated by the authors).

Three Interviews With Sonja

Sonja grew up in a lower middle-class family in Malmö. She chose a social studies curriculum for her secondary school education. Thereafter, she worked on and off as a nurse's aide.

When we met Sonja for the first time (autumn, 1988), she was still living with her mother. However, she had thought about moving to an apartment of her own. She got on well working as a nurse's aide, but had no intention whatever to spend her life doing that. Her thoughts regarding her future occupation were rather diffuse. Sonja wanted a job with much freedom and in which she would have the possibility of traveling a lot.

> Right now I work as a nurse's aide and it's okay. But it's actually not so great that I'd would like to work in the medical area all my life. It's something I'm doing right now before I've figured out exactly what to do later. I don't exactly have any specific plans on what I want to do in the future, but I do know I want an independent job in which I can travel a lot. I've thought about becoming a photographer, but I don't know. I'm not so good at taking photographs.

Sonja spent most of her spare time with her friends. She had five friends with whom she always did things together: going to a pub, going dancing, renting and watching video films, and seeing each other in general.

> I feel happy in Malmö. Actually I want to stay here because I've always lived here and I have all my friends here. /../ We're four or five friends who meet almost every day and telephone each other. I like that. We usually meet to have a nice chat, and we also go out quite often to a pub, and sometimes to a disco, but

not so much. In this city it's difficult to get into the discos. If we don't go out we usually rent video films. We watch video quite a bit.

Even if it covered several different genres, Sonja's film tastes were relatively distinct. When she and her friends decided to have a video night, which were rather often, it was almost always Sonja who rented the films.

> We are a couple of girls who have known each other ever since we were small. The others usually leave it to me to decide what we'll rent because they can never make up their minds. The kind of mood I'm in often decides what I rent, but usually it turns out to be an exciting film, a thriller, a penny dreadful, or a comedy that's kind of funny. I don't rent any really deep films, they're too heavy for me. They're usually so strange that one can't understand a thing. /.../ One film I liked took place in Africa. There were those tiny natives. I think it was called *The Gods Must Be Crazy*. It was funny, with small pygmies running around. Then I like horror films. Really bloody films like*The Texas Chainsaw Massacre* are not so funny, of course, but I really like to watch some kind of creepy stuff, more psychological. Sometimes it's just great to be scared. *The Hitcher* was a really good horror film. It was exciting every minute, without containing too much blood and such.

Sonja's music tastes were not particularly distinct, but just as many women in her age group, she liked the kind of music popular at the time, and she listened to a lot of it on the radio. However, she also listened quite a bit to old songs from the 1950s and 60s.

> I listen quite a lot to *Marie Fredrikson* and to most kinds of music that are popular now, but also to some old stuff. It's nice to listen to the old songs from the 1950s and 60s. /.../ I suppose that I don't have any particular artist who's my favorite, even if I listen quite a lot to Marie Fredrikson at the moment. When I buy records I mostly buy things I've heard on the radio, so you can really get stuffed.

Sonja's favorite author was *Leon Uris* and the reason was that she had worked for a year in a kibbutz.

Quite a lot had changed when we met Sonja the second time (autumn 1990). She had moved away from home and got herself a steady boy friend, but she still worked as a nurse's aide. Although she did not have any concrete plans for the future, two interests had increased and become really strong: her interest in films and photography and her interest in traveling.

> Since the last time we saw each other I've been to Mallorca for two weeks and I was also working in Iceland last autumn as a fisherwoman. I'd really like to travel more, preferably to Asia or to South America. I certainly don't have any plans at the moment to go there, but it would be nice to spend a year or so there. I could also imagine living abroad for a couple of years, or having a job where

you travel a lot. /.../ I thought about becoming a photographer, so I applied for a kind of media education, but there was only room for sixteen persons so they didn't let me start. I'll probably have to attend to a lot of evening classes instead, but right now it's hard to find the time. /.../ In one way or another, I think it would be great to work with pictures. You can always dream, of course, about having the opportunity to make a film and to stand behind the camera.

In her spare time Sonja did the same sort of things as she had done two years ago, and with the same friends. This meant that they watched a lot of films, both on video and at the movies. However, since she met her boyfriend she seldom went to discotheques. Instead, she did things together with him. This included going to the movies and watching video films.

When discussing her tastes, it seemed quite natural to take up her film tastes with her, since this was an interest she was developing at this time.

Yes, I watch lots of films and look at almost anything. Some of those I've seen recently are *Ghost*, *PrettyWoman* and *Sea of Love*. I can really recommend *Sea of Love*. Otherwise, I watch a lot of comedies like Peter Seller's *Pink-Panther* films, and sometimes a good horror film. I've also watched some of the really bad stuff, you know, like Jason with his hockey mask. They're more funny than they are frightening. They're so silly that it's almost impossible to get frightened. I don't like to watch rubbish films, which are completely meaningless, like *Casual Sex*, an American college film about two seventeen year old girls who were going to pick up some guys. /.../ I've thought about watching some more serious films. For example, they've been showing a series of Fassbinder films on TV just now that I thought I might watch, but never did.

Not only had Sonja's film tastes become more distinct but also her music tastes, something partly connected with her interest in traveling.

I can't remember what I said I liked last time, but I like most of what's popular. But not Hip-hop, of course, because it's so awfully tiresome. I listen quite a lot to Swedish music, like *Tomas Ledin*, *Roxette*, and others. After I had been in Mallorca I started to get a bit more interested in Spanish type music, in music that was a little more cultural, like *Gypsy Kings*. That kind of music is different, you can hear that it comes from Spain, and that kind of music hadn't existed in my world before. /.../ I buy many more records now than before and I'm also member of several different record clubs. When they have a sale of records somewhere I shop like a maniac.

Sonja was also rather interested in clothes and thought it was important to dress in her own way.

Clothes are really fun, everything from jeans to a ball gown. When I talk about colors, it's blue or red. I don't think it's interesting to buy clothes that everyone else is wearing. Usually I run all over the city to different shops to find clothes and combinations that are somewhat different, clothes that suit my own style.

Sonja's thoughts about the future were of two kinds: on the one hand somewhat abstract plans which nevertheless were achievable in a long-range perspective, on the other hand more concrete plans for the immediate future. At the same time that she developed in her own way her interests in films, photography and traveling, she knew that reality was something separate from her dreams. In line with this, she was working as a nurse's aide and also planned to work with her brother in his cleaning business for an extended period. However, these kinds of jobs were merely a temporary means in her quest for the things she really wanted to do later on.

The third time we meet Sonja she is still working in the same hospital as a nurse's aide. She is not very much satisfied with her work, but she does not care since she is going to become a mother in January. For that reason, she is going to quit working, for awhile anyway. Sonja has given up many of her earlier dreams of working abroad, of traveling, of becoming a photographer or a film director, and the like. She has not totally abandoned them, but she has realized that she will probably never be able to achieve them. Instead, she thinks a lot about her future role as a mother and prepares for this in different ways. She wants a safe and comfortable life for herself and her child. She also tells us that in a few years she is probably going to marry her boyfriend.

> Probably, I'll be moving into a row house. But I'm still working at the hospital. And in January I'm going to become a mother. I like that. I keep growing and growing. /.../ I still have the same dreams, but they've become weaker. First, I have to think about my child. In a few years I'll start working again. It'll probably be the same kind of job as I had before. It's nothing I'm looking forward to, I don't think it's so great. I know I'll probably never achieve the dreams I have. To do that you've got to be lucky, and usually I don't have that much luck. Well, I'm not pessimistic. I'm pretty realistic. It depends on your ambitions. You can always aim at the stars, but I'll probably only reach the grass-roots. But I don't care. The important thing is to have a stable income.

Sonja has about the same kind of leisure interests as earlier, but she feels she do not have as much time for them. She does not meet her friends as often as before, which she thinks is a pity. At the same time, she considers it quite natural, since both she and many of her friends have established stable relationships and this has changed their social lives as well. Instead, she spends more and more time with her mother and with her brother and his family. All in all, she is quite satisfied with the way she is living, though sometimes during the interviews we notice a restrained longing for a little bit of excitement.

Sonja's tastes are approximately the same as before. She still goes to the movies to enjoy a film, though more seldom. She also listens to the same kind of music, but does not buy as many records as before, since she cannot afford them.

To summarize, Sonja is gradually entering a safe and comfortable family life. She is looking forward to getting a child, a house, and, in a few years time, a husband. On the whole, Sonja is rather satisfied with the way her life has turned out, though she wants a job offering her some freedom and development. However, she is not sure what kind of work she actually wants.

> I've become more stable. I know what I'll be doing the next few years. You feel more confident when you know what you'll be doing. I want to live a pleasant life. Security is very important to me.

Sonja's Life Plan

Sonja's female friends had been important to her ever since she went to school. Several of her present friends had been with her since that time. It was together with two of these friends, Karin and Berit, that she went to Israel. When she returned home from Israel, she worked for awhile in a home for senior people. There she came in contact with older persons, and this influenced her way of looking at life and at herself, as she expressed it.

When Sonja was nineteen years old she traveled to Iceland together with her friend Karin, to work as a fisherwoman. Sonja felt that this trip had an impact on her maturity and openess similar to that of the earlier trip to Israel. When she returned from Island, she met her present boyfriend, Preben from Denmark. It really felt right with him, and they planned moving together.

When we asked Sonja to sketch a picture of her future, it contained such concrete plans as starting to work as a cleaning lady on the one hand, and some rather loose thoughts about becoming a photographer, on the other. Being able to travel was also part of her vision regarding the future. She imagined a life with a family of her own at the age of thirty. When we asked her to imagine an alternative vision concerning the future, she had some problems. Her thoughts were so many and so disparate that she found it very hard to formulate them in a concrete way.

The third time we met Sonja, her life plans had really changed. As already mentioned, she had abandoned several of her earlier plans, and was preparing for family life instead. Sonja's thoughts and desires were mainly focused on her future role as a mother. Therefore, she was not much worried or concerned about her future occupational role.

Some Comments on Sonja's Lifestyle

Sonja's lifestyle is primarily based on material values. Security type values as family security, material and economic security, convenience, etc., appear to be most important to her. Her values and lifestyle have undergone considerable changes during the three years we have known her.

During the two first interviews she wanted to experience different cultures and express herself aesthetically: to learn more about the world and about other cultures, make long journeys, live and work abroad. She also wanted to develop her aesthetic skills and competence in the area of film and photography. She even dreamed of becoming a film director. This suggests that at the time her aesthetic and metaphysical values were important to her lifestyle.

This then changed dramatically. The third time we met Sonja, her interest in other cultures and other ways of living had decreased. The same had happened with her desire to express herself aesthetically. Developmental values had become subordinate in her value system. The dominant values were now those aimed at social and material security and at comfort. This value change expressed itself in her altered lifestyle. Whereas she earlier was continually searching for new influences and new experiences, she had now found her place in reality.

Sonja's changes in values and in lifestyle were clearly related to the fact that she had become pregnant (which, of course, is one of the most crucial changes in a woman's life). Her desire to find and create meaning in life through traveling, experiencing different cultures and meeting people from other cultures, as well as her desire to create and express herself aesthetically, diminished when she found another way of creating meaning in her life. This new meaning was anchored in giving birth to and raising a child and living a good family life.

The change can also be seen in her social life. She meet her friends less often than before. Instead she spends most of her time with her boyfriend, her mother and her brother's family. It seems that Sonja has found a satisfactory meaning in her life. Therefore, her earlier desire to experience adventure and excitement has almost disappeared, having been replaced by a desire for security and comfort for her child and her family. Sonja's lifestyle has become almost entirely related to living a family life.

AGNETA

Mutual misunderstanding
After the fact
Sensitivity builds a prison
In the final act

We lose directions
No stone unturned
No tears to damn you
When jealousy burns
(Elton John 1989).

Three Interviews With Agneta

Agneta grew up in a lower middle class family in a municipality in the vicinity of Malmö. She graduated from high school with special training as an assistant nurse in the spring of 1988. Thereafter she started to work as an assistant nurse at an orthopeadic clinic.

When we first met her, she was 19 years old, still living with her parents. During this period her plans for the future were that she would continue her education at a School of Economics with the aim of becoming an economist.

> I plan to continue with my high school studies this autumn and to take the economics curriculum. I have to finish these studies first. Then I want to go on to graduate from a School of Economics, or become a travel agent, or do something like that. In some ways, the nursery job is quite nice, but I don't like the working-hours. Working evenings and weekends is really boring. After studying economics I'll have a better chance to get away and travel. The nursery school won't get me anywhere. /.../ I think it would be nice to be a tour leader, or a travel tourist agent, or to work with travels in some way.

Agneta's plans for the future were very uncertain, and vaguely formulated. Most of them had the character of fleeting dreams and immediate impulses. The picture of the future she gave us in the beginning of this interview had completely changed into another one by the end of it. However, a common theme in all of her dreams was the hope of being able to travel.

During her leisure time she had played soccer a lot, but because of a broken knee she was forced to give up her soccer career. This was quite a blow for her. Previously, Agnetas's leisure time had been almost totally dominated by soccer.

> Actually, I don't have any leisure time interests left since I quit playing soccer. I was active for eight years. My knee-cap was broken. It was a girl who kicked me in my knee. It was really hard to be forced to stop playing soccer. I grew up in a soccer family. My brother, father, sister — they all play soccer. Soccer meant so much to me. You had so many friends, the team spirit and all the fun to go with it. It feels really bad to have to be without it.

Agneta's film tastes could hardly be called distinct. She watched films that were popular at the moment. To some extent her film tastes were typically feminine. She watched films that girls of her age usually like, for example, romantic films and films about relationships (cf. Miegel & Dalquist 1991, and chapter 15 above). However, she also liked to watch some films that were more male oriented, for instance, satirical films like *Monty Python*, as well as action films.

> Yes, I really like comedies, *Monty Python*, as you know, is really funny. But I also like sad films. *Terms of Endearment* and films like that make me cry. *The Accused* was terrible, but it was a really good film about a girl who was raped. It was really unpleasant to watch her being raped while the three other guys were cheering. The latest film I've seen was *The Conducted Tour*; it wasn't so good. It was kind of long-winded; there wasn't so much that was happening. I like things to happen. I like real action, it's super. But I don't like horror films at all. If I watch one it's because the others want me to. It's not that I get frightened by them, but I think many horror films are piggish and actually pretty silly.

In music, Agneta's tastes were not particularly feminine, but more oriented towards rather rough rock music: Bruce Springsteen and Bryan Adams (cf. Miegel & Dalquist 1991).

> I like some of that rock stuff, like Bruce Springsteen and Bryan Adams. really rough, you know. Actually I listen to most kinds of music, but I really prefer rock. On the other hand, I don't like hard rock.

When, two years later, we met Agneta the second time, quite a lot had changed. She had bought an apartment of her own and moved away from her parents. She had also begun living with her boyfriend. She was still working at the nursing job, but her attitude towards her work had become still more negative. As a consequence, she had started looking for another job.

> I don't feel so good at my job. I'm looking for another one, any kind of job where they don't require anything more than a high school education. I've applied for a job at a travel agency. I'm so tired of the medical area, nothing but work, not rewarding at all. I've thought about applying for nurses' training but I'm not at all sure I want to continue working with medical care. It's hard not knowing what you want to do. I'll soon be twenty-two. Everybody seems to have their dreams, but I don't have any real dreams at all. You have to do something. Otherwise you'll soon be too old.

In spite of what Agneta told us, she did have some hopes of future occupation which would allow her to travel a lot. These hopes were evident in her account of her holiday travels and the different jobs she sometimes dreamed of.

> I was on the Canary Islands recently. I like it there. I love the atmosphere. Sometimes I dream of moving to Spain, maybe as a tourist guide. I think it's important that you do something before you get a family. Unfortunately, I'll probably never live in Spain. Not now anyway, I have so much here: my apartment, my cat and my job. You've got to take one day at the time. /.../ I'd like to become an air hostess. It must really be great to travel so much. I would probably rather become an air-hostess than a tourist guide. Yes, it would probably suit me well to be an air-hostess. I really ought to apply for the air-hostess course, but I'm too lazy. /.../ It bothers me that I never get going on things, and that I have a job I don't feel satisfied with.

In her leisure time Agneta spent quite a bit of time with her friends. They usually smoked and talked about their everyday problems and things they were happy about. They had recently attended a course on drying everlasting flowers.

> I've got three very special friends. We often see each other and we have such good contact. We usually sit around and smoke and talk about our boyfriends and different kinds of problems we have run into. We often simply sit and talk, and sometimes we go to a party together. /.../ During the week I don't give a damn how I dress, but on special occasions like that I usually dress up. I like to wear a black jacket and a white blouse. But I don't go out very much nowadays.

During the two years that had passed since the last time we saw her, Agneta had not changed in either her music or her film tastes. She seldom bought any records, but she liked to watch music videos on MTV. Bruce Springsteen was still her big favorite.

Everybody probably has one's special favorites, like*Bruce Springsteen* and *Elton John*. I don't have time to listen to music so much, but I usually hear some on MTV. I don't watch so many of the music videos, but I listen to the music. I don't like all that rap music on MTV. Music has to be pure. In fact, even Elton John plays some songs that are a little queer. /.../ My boyfriend doesn't like the same kind of music as I do at all. He likes Bob Marley, for instance.

Agneta said she thought she had become more mature since moving away from her parents. Although she still did not know what she wanted to do in her life, she had become more independent.

When you move from home you have to learn how to be responsible. It's not like living at home at all. I feel much more sure of myself now. Before, my mom and dad were always there backing me up and supporting me. Now I would rather struggle with my economy myself than letting them help me. My independence is very important to me.

The last time we meet Agneta she has changed her way of looking at life. After almost one year, she is not at all as pessimistic as before. Her self-confidence has increased. She feels it has to do with the fact that she has more money now. She feels that money is quite important to the way she feels.

Not having money ruins your self-confidence. I don't think I've felt as happy as I do now for a long time. Money is so important for your life. It affects everything from your self-confidence to your material welfare. Not having money really makes you feel down.

Agneta's life has changed in several ways. Together with her boyfriend, she is planning to move to another, cheaper apartment. Her reason for doing this is to improve her economy and have more money to spend on things she enjoys. It also give her the opportunity to save up enough money to realize one of her dreams, to attend a nine week course on Mallorca. Agneta has also become more satisfied with her situation at work, since she has learned the routines and got more responsibility. The idea of continuing to work at the hospital is no longer alien to her. She also nourishes some thoughts of getting further education to become a midwife. All these plans make a considerable change as compared with her previous pessimism about her future. She has finally achieved some of the dreams she spoke of in the earlier interviews.

The last time we met I'd just started to work. The job was new and I didn't know the routines. But I think I've matured during these two years. I know more about myself now, and how to enjoy life. I'm not at all as bored with my job as I was earlier. /.../ I don't know how long I'm going to work at the hospital. I've got other plans. Next year I'm going to follow a course on Mallorca for becoming a guide. I don't know if I'll ever get a job as one. I'm doing it just to have fun and do something different. I also have plans about becoming a midwife. I think it's what I want, but you never know. The important thing is to have a dream, to know what you want to do.

Agneta's lifestyle has become more oriented towards what she could experience and towards partaking of the pleasures in life. One might even say she has developed a hedonistic attitude towards living. "Why care about tomorrow, you live now", seems to be her new motto. She wants to feel free and to be able to realize some of her dreams while she is still young. When the time is right she will start thinking about marriage and children, but that time she has put off to a distant future. One reason for developing this attitude towards family life has been her reaction to what has happened to some of her friends who have had children.

I think it's important to enjoy yourself while you're young. Not that I'm afraid of getting old, but I'm afraid of how fast time flies. Why not have fun while you're young? I've become more certain about such things as children and marriage. Such things are distant to me. I'm too young. I have so many friends who have already got a family and children, who really are too young for that. I almost think it's become a fashion to have children. I'm definitely not ready for it yet. When I meet those friends everything has to do with babies, diapers, and such things. I enjoy meeting them, but it's not like it used to be. They've become so tied up, but I meet my childless friends quite often.

On the whole, Agneta has developed a more distinct, though not entirely stable, identity and lifestyle since we met her last time. Her desire to make the most of life while she is young could be interpreted as an indication that she is the one among the seven young people we have met who is going through the most dynamic changes. She does not know what will become of her, but she has developed a desire to experience as many different things as possible. Agneta does not think of herself as mature enough to settle down with a steady job and family. She first has to find out who she really is and what she really wants to do. Agneta has no fixed lifestyle, but one that is undergoing constant change, and she is rather satisfied with this state of affairs.

Agneta's tastes in film and music have been basically the same throughout the three years during which we have known her. She feels this taste is hers and no one else's. She likes what she likes, and she does not mind whether other people approve of her tastes or not. Neither does she experience any desire or need to change or to devolop her tastes. She is convinced that Bruce Springsteen and Bryan Adams will remain her favorite musicians.

In all the three interviews we had with Agneta, she talked a lot about how much she missed soccer. It is obvious that this interest, and the people she got to know through it, has been an important part of her childhood and youth. It has taken her a long time to accept the fact that she will never be able to play soccer again, and this has certainly influenced her way of looking at life. The last time we meet, however, she has become better reconciled to this fact. She now know better how to cope with it and thus with herself. Nevertheless, she persists in her conviction that she is never going to find another interest capable of completely replacing soccer.

Agneta's Life Plan

The persons particularly important for Agneta during her school years were her parents and siblings. All the members of her family were interested in soccer and devoted themselves to it. When her soccer life ended due to a serious knee injury, it was thus a very hard blow for her. Since then she had not managed to develop a leisure time interest that could replace the things soccer meant to her.

Thus far the most important event in Agneta's life was when she left her parents and bought an apartment of her own. She valued her own independence very much, and as soon as she moved away from her parents she felt that she could govern her own life to a much greater extent.

Ever since completion of her compulsory education Agneta's occupational plans have been rather unstructured. She has never worked in a goal oriented way to get a specific vocation for the future. Her choice of getting training as an assistant nurse was largely a temporary solution to her problems. This was an anchorage to reality, so to say, in relation to the more romantic and perhaps even unrealistic occupational dreams she had often entertained. At the same time, her medical care work involved some degree of security, which had a restraining effect upon her ambitions. She wanted to take steps to realize some of her dreams but could not make herself do so. Therefore, it was difficult for Agneta to imagine a picture of her own future, since the picture that she wanted to sketch did not fit with the picture that she really believed in. The picture she finally rendered was one of several ones she might have reported to us.

The last time we met Agneta she was still not sure what she wanted to do, but this did not bother her any more. On the contrary, she had been taking advantage of the poassibilities she had while she was still young. She was also determined to use this chance to explore different alternatives before deciding on too much. She had no plans at all concerning marriage and children. The important thing for Agneta was to take advantage of her opportunities for experiencing and enjoying as many different things as possible while she still had the chance.

Some Comments on Agneta's Lifestyle

Agneta's lifestyle is based to a great extent on her material values. However, it is not primarily material values connected with security, but rather developmental material values which she expresses in her lifestyle. What is important to her is to have enough money to be able to afford to travel, buy things she likes, and amuse herself in different ways. She also sees money as a necessary means to feel good and to be able to realize her dreams and develop herself. Also, aesthetic values are important to her. These values of hers are relatively stable, suggested by her rather distinct and seemingly unchanging tastes in music and films. Agneta's aesthetic values thus constitute an important part of her cultural identity and consequently of her lifestyle.

However, although her aesthetic values seem very stable, of all the seven people we met in our study, she nevertheless has the most unstable and changing identity and lifestyle. During the three years we have followed her, the perhaps most striking thing we noticed is that it was not until the last time we interviewed her that Agneta had entered the phase of identity and lifestyle development a phase the other six persons had been into since the first time we met them. Common to the other six was that during the three years we studied them they gradually developed more stable and distinct lifestyles and identities. Agneta, on the other hand, has only recently begun to realize and actively explore the different possibilities inherent in her identity. Therefore, she has had considerable difficulties in imagining what her life in the future will be like. What she eventually has come to realize is that she has to explore as many different alternatives as possible before making any concrete decisions or plans concerning her future. She has developed a number of rather loose ideas about a variety of possible alternatives she wants to try out before deciding. Therefore, she has also put all thoughts of getting a family and children far into an abstract future. As she says herself, she must first mature and find out who she really is and what she actually wants in life. She has only just begun to enjoy and find the excitement in this voyage of discovery.

These changes in Agneta's life can be ascribed at least partly to the difficulties she experienced when having to give up her major interest, that of playing soccer. During the earlier part of her youth, almost everything circled around soccer. Her friends all played on the same team, the other members of her family played soccer as well, and she often watched soccer games live on TV. Soccer thus constituted the fundamental ingredient in Agneta's identity and lifestyle. When she lost the possibility of engaging in this sport actively, she in a sense she lost her lifestyle and found herself forced to develop a new one. For many years, however, she was incapable of replacing soccer. This created problems for her in finding meaning in other areas of life. One might say that Agneta has gone through a minor identity crisis, which she finally successfully solved. She still misses soccer, but she has come to realize that even though she will never be able completely to replace it, there are other ways in which she can develop herself and her lifestyle.

ANNIKA

I give you my life
The only one I've got
And though I have reached something
There is so much left to do
Winter and Spring — Summer and Autumn
This heart is beating
Here in my breast
(Niklas Strömstedt 1990, translated by the authors).

Three Interviews With Annika

Annika grew up in a suburb of Malmö. Her family can be described as upper middle class. After completing her three years of the social studies curriculum at high school, Annika graduated in the spring of 1988. She has now (autumn, 1991) been studying for several years at the University.

When we met Annika for the very first time she was still living with her parents. Her life at the time was characterized by hard work with her studies and by the social contacts she had with her school friends. During that period she had no solid plans for the future. Instead, she had many differing ideas about what she might do after graduating from high school.

> It depends very much on my grades. One possibility is that I'll go to work first, at IKEA (a furnishings store). I'm working extra at IKEA now on weekends. After that I'd study for a term at a French university since I've been taking French now for several years. Another possibility is that I get accepted for the public relations program I want to study in. And then, of course, I could also take other courses.

One of the most characteristic things about Annika was that she had many different plans for her future. Several of these concerned her hopes and expectations regarding a profession. She had thought very much about what types of jobs that could promote her personal growth and at the same time be interesting. However, she had also thought quite a bit about traveling around in the world, and perhaps doing idealistic work abroad for some non-profit organization.

> I think I'll be getting a job as a copywriter in the advertising business. I have a feeling that that's the way it's going to be, and also that if I say so, it'll turn out that way. But it's true that there is a part of me that wants to go out in the world and work with something really important. I'm very much interested in animals, and the fact that so many animals live under the threat of extinction really bothers me.

In her leisure time Annika read a lot. Mostly it was her school books, but when she had time she also read books of other kinds. She often spent time together with her family. Friday evenings the whole family met and listened to the radio programme *Metropol*, ate popcorn, and talked about the past week. There was no doubt that Annika's family meant a great deal to her — and also had great impact on her.

> You get practically everything from your parents. A lot of your own thoughts are actually your parents' attitudes all over again. It's like that. You actually become a sort of miniature of them. Anyhow, that's the way I feel.

Annika's use of mass media was to a great extent oriented towards gathering information and knowledge about different things, but now and then she also escaped, in a sense, into her preoccupation with romantic love stories. She was very ambivalent towards the latter kind of reading. On the one hand, she liked to read romantic novels, on the other, she expressed her distaste for them.

> I also read those sickly-sweet novels, of course. They don't give you anything in return, but it can be an amusing pastime. It's dreaming and forgetting reality. It's a kind of escape, you know, not because I dislike reality the way it is, but still it's a nice feeling to read a romantic novel.

It was not only in relation to literature Annika had an ambivalent relationship of this type. She had the same kind of attitude towards the films she saw. She also felt that certain kinds of activities — like reading weekly gossip magazines, buying a lot of clothes, idolizing handsome films stars and reading romantic novels — were natural parts of a young girl's development.

> This Friday *Cocktail* was released, with Tom Cruise, an actor who's that kind of a handsome guy who all girls like. He plays the leading role. /.../ I buy a lot of clothes, I guess, even if it's become less now. I'm not as fixed on it as I was earlier. But anyhow it's probably a pretty common thing for most girls my age.

Annika did not have any distinct music tastes; she listened to many different types of music, but mostly to slow and somewhat romantic pop ballads. She did not at all like hard rock or noisy rock music, however.

The second time we met Annika, many things had changed, both regarding her future plans and her private life. She described these changes in the following way:

> Last summer, a year and a half ago, I left home. At first I stayed in a small one-room flat I rented from someone else. During that time I met Douglas. He is originally from Örebro, but he moved to Lund to study. /.../ I had been in line for quite a while in the housing queue before we got this apartment. We went and had a look at it, and since we liked it so much we accepted it. Said and done, all of a sudden we had moved in together there. I studied public relations then and had been working at IKEA for a year. At the moment I'm studying English full-time and public relations half-time. I'm quite busy this term trying to collect thirty points. /.../ I've decided that I want to work with marketing. This is something that's grown within me and I feel like it's possible to ignore all the other possibilities, because this is what I really want to do.

Annika's engagement in her studies and future plans were mirrored in her leisure time interests and tastes. Annika might even be said to have developed a rather distinguished lifestyle. During the two years that had passed since first we met her, her somewhat vague and unprecise thoughts about the future had been replaced by more concrete and precise thoughts and plans. This partly reflected the fact that her boyfriend had the same kind of interests as herself, and that they cultivated these interests together. They were both interested in the aesthetics of everyday life, above all in the areas of interior decoration and advertising.

> We had that in common from the beginning, that both of us were interested in interior decoration. We've developed this interest further in our relationship. It's grown.

Besides interior decorating, Annika was very much fascinated by advertising and marketing. Apart from the fact that she had thought about an occupational future within marketing or public relations, she thought about advertising and reflected on it a great deal in her leisure time.

> First, I think advertising is so much fun. When I go to the movies, I find the commercials the most amusing part. Maybe not the greatest part, but half the pleasure is gone if you miss the commercials. On buses and in other places I always look at the advertisements. I really think it's exciting. I'm fascinated by what it's possible to do with a small thing, what you can do with a bar of chocolate that makes all people want it. You can always imagine what you'd do yourself. You'd really buy it. And then there're the aesthetics. An advertisement that's similar to all the others isn't good. If it's going to attract me, it has to be odd. When you make something it has to be different. Doing advertising the way it's already been done before may function, but that's not the idea. I can also be angry at advertisements. Advertising can be a real lie when you mix an advertisement for a car with important world events, for example. It can also be unethical to advertise for certain things.

Annika emphasized the importance of being oneself, of being unique and of not attempting to be like someone else. She felt that she had learned to become herself. Earlier she had been easily influenced, doing things more or less the same way as her parents and friends.

> In high school you were strongly influenced by others. There were certain given norms about how you should look and what you should do. I don't feel like that any more. If a certain type of jeans was popular you had to buy that sort, and you could just as well skip buying jeans if you didn't buy that particular type of jeans. I thought it was difficult to skip buying them. My clothing style hasn't basically changed, but I'm less influenced now by what others say. However, I'm still influenced by advertising, but I'm not the slave I used to be. I have no desire to dress in a special way just to get people to look at me. I am what I am. Maybe I could change my clothing so as to fit in better, but I certainly wouldn't feel good about it.

When we first met her, Annika expressed an ambivalent attitude towards different kinds of popular culture products. She read what she described as sweet and sickly novels, and watched the big American movie hits. She had no distinguished music tastes, but listened to the songs that were played most frequently on the radio. During the two years that had passed since then her tastes had changed considerably. Annika had developed a more distinct taste, or rather what might be called a taste for high culture, without entirely rejecting her earlier preferences.

> Both Douglas and I have become interested in art. In this way we've come to visit different art exhibitions. Art has made me realize that something can be really strange but still be very good. However, if you want to reach most people with it, it also has to be realistic. /.../ At home I like to listen to *Vivaldi*, and it can be nice listening to good opera music and modern jazz. I like the same kinds of music as before. I like quite a lot of Swedish music: *Ratata, Niklas Strömstedt*, the ones that you hear quite a lot. /.../ I've always wanted to see good American movies, but it's rather boring if you've seen a lot of films lik that. I'm quite fond of somewhat odd films, but now and then I also like to see an American film. The former kind of films have a more lasting value. Still, *Tom Cruise* is the all American guy and I can't deny the fact that I like him. /.../ I read quite a lot. I don't like detective stories. I read *Jan Guillou*, but I didn't like him at all. What I'm most fond of is stories about everyday life. I like authors who can describe life as it is. Sometimes I read some sweet and sickly romantic novels, but I've stopped reading the worst ones.

At the end of this interview we asked Annika to give us a description of herself:

> Young, curious, has partly decided what she wants to do in life, but still pretty mouldable. Rather influenced by advertising, likes quality, has some cultural interests. A twentieth century girl. I suppose I aim at this thing of becoming something. Not merely for the money, but to get the money to buy that particular table. To be able to live somewhat outside everyday life, that's important.

The third time we meet Annika, she is twenty-one years old and has become even more convinced about what she wants to do in the future. She has taken a couple of courses at the University in the area of marketing and has recently started a year of studies at a school of adult education. Annika is prepared to continue her education for another two or three years, but then she wants to start working.

> I know what I want to do. I want to work with marketing. I've been interested in it for a long time. I just can't change my mind about it. I've started to learn how things work within the marketing area. It's got the creative aspect that

appeals to me. Thinking about getting a job is a problem. You know, I don't just want any job, it's got to suit me. It has to allow me to develop as a person.

Annika feels she has developed in her way of looking at life. The importance of money and material things has decreased. She feels shopping had lost its charm. Annika's values has changed. She is no longer as amused by consuming things as before. She had discovered that other things in life means a lot more to her. Her relationship with her parents, with Douglas and with her friends has become more important. She also values such things as nature, good environment, and fresh air more than before. Thus, physical comfort and an inner sense of well-being has become more important than economic wealth.

Unfortunately, in the type of society we live in, money is important, whether you like it or not. You can't just neglect the fact that you need money. But as you get older you realize more and more that the value of money and material things is only relative. You get to understand that money is not important in its own right. It's much more important to go out in the woods, for example, to pick flowers and mushrooms. I feel that shopping and city life have lost their charm. I'd like to live in the countryside. I don't want to spend the rest of my life in an apartment.

During the three years we have known Annika, she has gradually become more certain of herself. She has matured, her values have developed, and she has achieved a more satisfactory identity and lifestyle. Annika's tastes have varied during these three years. At the first meeting her tastes were rather mainstream, common to girls of her age. The second time we interviewed her she had become aware of the distinction between high culture and popular culture. She referred primarily to high culture in describing her tastes, but she also admitted that she still consumed what she described as cheap and vulgar cultural goods. The third time we met her, she did not make such clear distinctions between legitimate culture and vulgar culture. She had become more self-confident and more certain of her tastes. It was not as important to her what others thought of her tastes. The contradiction she had felt earlier between what she thought was good and what she thought was bad about her tastes had disappeared. She had become self-confident enough to have her own opinion of what she liked, and to accept those things which she had experienced as being contradictions earlier.

I'm rather satisfied with myself. I've got enough confidence to do what I feel is right. I feel I've grown as a person. My relation with Douglas is stable, which is important. I couldn't cope with a stormy relationship right now. I still think it's good to meet with my parents. Before, I thought I did it because I was immature and couldn't let go of them. But it's not like that. I've come to understand them better. It's the same thing with my friends. I've probably got fewer friends nowadays, but the friendships with them are more intense. We're not just friends, we're real friends. I think it's pointless to be too determined about just what you want to become, because if you fail, you'll probably be very disappointed. I've learned to accept the fact that not everything turns out the way you want. I can live with that.

Annika's Life Plan

The persons most important to her during her compulsory education were her parents, her siblings and a dear friend. During high school Annika chose social studies as her main subject. After a year of high school she decided to take a break and to go to the USA. Annika's "family" in the USA influenced her deeply. Family life there, as she expressed it, was very conservative. The members of the family were supposed to be active all the time. Cleaning and other household chores were particularly important. In that family her wish sometimes to be left alone was considered very odd. Annika almost entirely accepted the style of life and the attitudes of her American family, and she entered into the contract this involved. Annika told us that it was only quite recently that she had been able to free herself of the greater part of this influence.

When she returned to Sweden she started in a new class, got new teachers and new friends. Two among these friends were very important because they had, as she expressed it, a psychologically reassuring effect upon her. Her teachers helped her to understand that it was necessary to look for relationships between different things, to consider problems as a whole and to think critically, something that she had forgotten to do when she stayed in the USA.

After graduating from high school, Annika worked in a furnishings store. There she met a female director whom she really admired. She also established friendships with persons much older than herself. Annika felt that these persons helped her to become more mature and to look upon life from a completely new angle. During this period she also met her boyfriend Douglas and they became very closely engaged.

During the past two years Annika's future plans had developed from a confused heap of thoughts and ideas to plans that were somewhat, if not yet completely, firm. Annika could be characterized as having an open attitude towards different alternative plans for the future. The most desirable alternative appeared to her to be a career within the marketing and/or advertising business.

Annika's plans for her private life were not very easy to grasp, but they did involve both marriage and her having children by the age of thirty. She also dreamt of buying a house in the countryside, but this was quite a remote dream.

As already mentioned, Annika was open to other alternatives as well. Among other things she mentioned the possibility of living abroad or of increasing her knowledge in various areas. She also considered the possibility of changing her occupational plans completely and getting the training necessary to become, for example, a doctor. For Annika the future was to a great extent an unwritten chapter.

The last time we met Annika she had become more certain about how she wanted things to be in the future, both professionally and privately. She had started her education within the area of marketing and was quite certain that she would work within that field in the future. She had also deepened and stabilized her relation with her boyfriend, her parents and her friends. Even though she had no concrete plans for the immediate future, what had earlier been rather distant and alien thoughts of having children and of family life had become less threatening and seemed almost acceptable to her.

> A year ago I would certainly have had an abortion if I'd gotten pregnant. But now I'm older and I've changed my attitude toward having children. Not that I want a child now, but you never know what will happen. Since I've become much more mature, I think I'd be able to take care of a child now.

Some Comments on Annika's Lifestyle

During the past three years, Annika's lifestyle has undergone important changes. These changes are clearly related to a number of changes concerning what she regards as important in life. The changes in Annika's values can be described in terms of Kamler's (1984) distinction between life-style values and life-philosophy values. That is, in our terms, between outer-directed and inner-directed values. At the time of her first two interviews, Annika was very much concerned about demonstrating her status to others through her style. It was important to her to make clear the distinction between what she felt was legitimate culture and vulgar culture. Though she devoted herself to both, she was nevertheless eager to make clear to others that she knew that what she called "sweet and sickly love novels" were totally lacking in values of any deeper sort and that, although she read them from time to time, she actually despised the literary genre in question. At the same time, she stressed her interest in other literary genres which — together with her newly awakened interest in jazz and in classical music, in art and interior decoration — she considered more important. Annika was very much concerned about making clear distinctions and about seeking status through expressing high cultural style and tastes. She was also anxious to increase her material wealth, that is, to get a high status job, a good income and to be able to buy expensive things. All in all, Annika's lifestyle at this time was basically founded on her aesthetic and material values.

These values gradually changed during the three years we have known her, and at the time of the last interview she has become less sensitive about other people's opinions regarding her tastes and style. It is thus no longer as important to her to make as clear cultural distinctions as before. Instead, it has become more important to her that she grow on a personal level, realizing her own desires irrespective of other people's attitudes.

Annika's lifestyle has thus gradually shifted in accordance with changes in her way of looking at herself. From being rather concerned about status and about other people's opinions about her, she has become increasingly sure of herself and her identity. Consequently, she does not need other people's approval and recognition as strongly as before. Also, Annika has become more concerned about the environment, and about her relationships with her boyfriend and with her parents. To summarize, one could say that Annika's lifestyle is much more than before now based on her inner-directed metaphysical and ethical values, even though her desire to increase her cultural capital and status partly remains.

LASSE

I don't care about eternity
Give me a place here in reality.
Another life, another time.
But no peace now.

I live in playfulness
and in seriousness so deep, and so hot.
I dream of wonderlands

of other values
of up and down
that'll make right become wrong
Eva Dahlgren 1981, translated by the authors).

Three Interviews With Lasse

Lasse grew up in an upper middle class family in Malmö. After graduating from high school he started to work within the building trade. During this period he also took law courses at the University. During the autumn of 1990 he began his military service.

When we met Lasse in 1988, he was 19 years old and he had just moved away from his parents. He had found a nice apartment in downtown Malmö which he shared with a friend. Lasse was planning to continue his law studies at the University to become an attorney or a business lawyer. Actually, his dream was to become a doctor, but his grades were too low, and he was not prepared to put particularly much effort into reaching this goal.

> My dream job was actually that of becoming a doctor, but my grades weren't good enough. You need to have a five point zero average and I didn't have that much. You can take supplementary exams, but that takes at least four years. You have to either study two years to become a male nurse, or else become a physiotherapist, and then you have to work for another two years. So many things can happen in four years that you could end up changing your opinion on things completely. Four years is too high a price to pay.

However, Lasse regarded himself as something of a theoretician. Consequently, he felt that the right thing for him was to carry on with his academic studies, and that even though his plans for the future were hardly well thought-out, there would be no doubt of his obtaining a University education.

Lasse's two major leisure interests were karate and music. Most of his leisure time he spent playing in different rock bands. To keep himself fit he devoted many hours a week to karate training, but he was also interested in karate for the sake of the self-discipline and concentration it provided.

> I've always been fascinated by fighting sports. I felt I had to try it out and it suited me well. Above all, there was a lot of discipline, not military discipline, but self-discipline, which is a good feeling.

Lasse's interest in music was expressed in various ways. He played in several rock bands and he listened a great deal to music. He also listened to a wide variety of different music styles, but his tastes were nevertheless distinct. Lasse was interested in rock music, but also in jazz and classical music. In describing the strongest and most important experiences in his life he referred to incidents in one way or another connected to musical experiences he had had.

> I bought a CD-record. I don't have a CD-player of my own, but I've got a friend who has one. So I put this record on and played it all evening long, and all night long, too, and the whole morning the next day. It was a perfect experience. If you try and imagine an unbelievable bunch of voices that sang, such unbelievable chords. If I ever believed in God it was certainly then. /.../ Everything is so special with voices, it's so clear. It's not as clear as an instrument, but it's clear in another way.

Lasse's use of different media was characterized by his attraction to legitimate culture. This was especially true of his music tastes. However, there were also other tendencies in his patterns of taste. *Clint Eastwood* and *Charles Bronson*, for example, were two of his favorite actors. Lasse's tastes were characterized by a kind of pluralism, and the only types of films he objected to were those containing pornography and extreme violence.

> Extreme violence is something I really can't handle. It's so damned disgusting. Sure, you can sit and watch it, but in the end, I think, you feel pretty bad about it. And porno is actually pretty meaningless, but I did watch it when I was younger.

Many things had changed when we met Lasse for the second time (autumn, 1990). He had moved to an apartment of his own, and his girlfriend since three years spent a lot of time with him there. He had also been in Australia for half a year, where he had developed a new hobby, namely scuba diving, an interest he shared with his girlfriend. He had also resumed his thoughts of becoming a doctor.

> I've always wanted to become a doctor and it's what I'm going to be. It's the only thing that feels right. I've read quite a bit about medicine, so it would be nice to get started in medical school. There are new ways of applying now which may increase my chances of getting in. You work for five years and I'll be finished with that soon. /.../ I've got pretty definite plans, but it's still possible to change. You've got to always have some sort of escape route. I could imagine myself as a builder, but if everything works out as I want, I'll become a doctor.

During the past two years Lasse's plans for the future had become more firm and concrete. He worked purposefully toward realizing his dream of becoming a doctor.

His leisure interests were the same as earlier, but his attitudes towards popular culture had changed considerably. He was still practicing karate, and music was still important. However, he had stopped playing in rock bands since he felt he had more important things to do in his leisure time.

> I don't play in a band any more. It takes too much time. I mostly play for myself nowadays. I've discovered the good thing about playing on my own.

However, Lasse did actually miss the time when he had played in different rock bands, and the time when music was the most important thing in his life. His dreams of becoming a professional musician had been repressed, but somewhere deep inside himself they were still alive.

> My dreams of becoming a professional musician were shattered. I had some ideas about applying to a music school, but it didn't turn out that way because of my parents, and maybe that was good. But I think I would have been happy as a poor musician. Somewhere deep inside me I still have that dream, but it's far away now. I suppose it was those boyish dreams; they've changed a bit. You become aware of what it's really all about. For example, playing the piano professionally takes a lot of time, so you have to accept it as a hobby. I suppose there's a certain bitterness over the fact that it never came into being. /.../ I played together with a pretty well-known group before, and if I had quit school I could still have been playing with them. But I've got no regrets. I've gone through all that and realized that it doesn't feel so bad if you're forced to accept something. What I'm doing today is my own free choice and it feels right. But it took some careful consideration. If you've spent two and a half years in high school you don't quit like that. There are kind of norms from those around you, friends and parents. I could be furious about such norms when I was younger. I was a member of a country band once, and we really were top level. It was a full-time job and they have a record contract now. I've become calmer about it now, I'm not that angry anymore.

Lasse's cultural tastes had not changed appreciably, but they had become somewhat more distinct and "high" in a cultural sense. He often spoke, for example, of high quality and low quality films. He watched films of both kind, but was really conscious of the qualitative difference between the films of the two categories.

> I like both commercial films and other types of films. I spend more time now watching films than before. I watch a lot of documentaries, like portrayals of different countries, descriptions of nature, films with an educational purpose. /.../ I watch quite a few trash films. For instance I saw a *Dolph Lundgren* film, it was real rubbish, just as *My Stephmother Is An Alien* was. Those are real

junk films. I didn't feel so good about seeing Dolph Lundgren, but I felt OK about seeing the other films. Shit films are good, because for a couple of hours you can rest your brain. The bad thing is that everything is so stereotyped and show-offish, but sometimes there are some good parts i those films. /.../ Portrayals of family relations, problem films, and films about ordinary families, I think, tend to be pretty good.

A similar development could be seen in Lasse's relation to music. His distinctions between different categories of music and their qualities had become much more distinct.

Maybe it's easier to get heavily carried away by modern music, but listening to classical music, like *Mozart*, for example, makes you quite poetical. When it comes to modern music, I listen to a lot of trash and American West coast rock, and to *Docenterna*, *Ebba Grön* and that kind of stuff. You become a little bit nostalgic. When it comes to modern music I'm not changing my tastes. I'll probably be an old man when the rock bands I listen to stop playing. *Tubes, Journey, Scritti Politti* and *Van Halen* have been there all along, and they've been releasing records all the time.

Lasse had also changed his attitude towards clothes. He told us he was interested in clothes but that this interest was expressed differently than before.

I'm interested in clothes, but maybe people don't look at it that way. I put on the T-shirt that feels best. I'm getting more and more attracted to a functional style. Earlier you bought something because it looked fine, but now it's more because it's functional. When you were younger you dressed much more for getting an identity; the clothes gave you an identity. It's the same way now, but you don't try influencing people with your clothes in the same way as you used to. On the school grounds certain people wearing the same kind of clothes used to gather in a clump. You choose your clothes from from the viewpoint of the people you wanted to be with. Today it's not important at all. You don't dress the same way as your friends. /.../ I've got my hair cut short. I used to have awfully long hair, but I cut it because my grandpa wanted me to.

When we asked Lasse to describe how he had changed during the past two years, he replied as follows:

I've begun looking at things a lot more from my own point of view and I don't bother about how other people look at things. Before, I didn't work so much with the group, and I did't think so much about other people, but I just went ahead and trampled on others when I felt like it. I've changed. I've become more open to different ideas. Today I can look at myself the way I am without getting any bad vibrations.

The last time we meet Lasse, he has just finished military service and has started to work again in the building trade. However, his plans about becoming a doctor has grown stronger, and he is now sure he will apply to the medical school within a year. Lasse has also developed a more stable relationship with his girlfriend.

> The last time we met, I said that my family had become more important to me. You cut down more and more on your relations with your schoolmates and friends. I think I'm still in that phase. But I think I'm trying to change that a bit. I do try to contact my old buddies now and then.

Lasse's leisure time interests have changed considerably during the three years we have known him. In our first talk, Lasse virtually described himself in terms of his two dominant interests, playing music and practicing karate. He was certain he would never give these interests up. However, as it turned out, he did. He quit playing in rock bands, he replaced his electric piano with an acoustic one, and he totally abandoned karate.

These two interests can be considered as rather individually oriented, since Lasse basically practised them alone in order to develop and refine his skills, his competence and his self control. In their place, Lasse has now developed an interest in scuba diving, an interest he combined with an involvement in environmental questions and a newly acquired interest in archeology. These changes are probably related to more fundamental development in Lasse's identity. During the time we have known him he has gradually come to abandon his earlier individualism and to develop an interest in, and a concern for, his relations with other people.

> I've almost entirely abandoned karate. Music... well, I listen a lot but I play less. I've got rid of all my electric equipment and bought myself an acoustic piano, which was a good move. Now I play when I want to, not because I have to. The electronics were so pretentious. But karate I'll probably never pick up again. I'm doing a lot of scuba diving in the Sound. I help some environmental researchers take samples. It's fun but it's also scary. You know, in ten or twelve years there won't be any oxygen left, no vegetation, no animal life. It will be completely dead. Also, I help some marine archeologists diving for wrecked Viking ships. It's really interesting when you find a piece of wood or something and the archeologists make sense of it and tell you what it is. It's really fantastic. I read a lot about it. It's a great feeling being down in the deep, looking for Swedish history.

Music has always been one of Lasse's major interests. He has played a variety of different musical styles and has listened to most kinds of music. Contrary to many other young people, Lasse has not used his music tastes to distinguish himself from others or to express his group identity. Neither does he make sharp distinctions between the quality of different musical genres, but he can discover something he likes in most of them. Lasse's music tastes have been very diverse and heterogeneous. They have cut across everything from mainstream music, progressive and experimental pop and rock, heavy metal to jazz, classical music and opera. Nevertheless, during the three years we have known him, Lasse has gradually become more and more interested in high culture. Whereas his tastes in rock and pop music have remained approximately the same, he has gradually explored the field of classical music and found new pieces which have become favorites.

If he has cared to make any general qualititative distinctions in the field of music, the opposite goes for his film tastes. During the three years we have studied Lasse, his film tastes have clearly developed in the direction from mainstream to high culture. Though he enjoyed watching most film genres, he came to distinguish clearly between what is good and what is bad. He described certain films in such terms as "commercial", "standard plot" or "shit films". He also used different media for different film genres. He went to the movies only when he wanted to see what he called an artistic film or a film with a deeper meaning. The films he found amusing at the moment, he watched on video.

> I don't watch so many films nowadays. I have to know that a film is good, otherwise I don't go. But it does happen that I rent a piece of shit on video once in a while. So many shit films have been released recently, most of them for the broad American public. Earlier, there used to be much more technically interesting films with better plots. You know, deeper films. Several French films, for example. There were new plots all the time, but in American films it's always the same story.

What Lasse considers to be the most fundamental development having occurred in his sense of identity, is that he has become less self-centered and more concerned with groups and group relations. He talked about this in all three interviews, but in the last one he mentions one particular event that had influenced him very much in this respect. During his military service he took a course in group dynamics and leadership, which had a great impact on him.

> During my military service I went through something called UGL. It was about development of groups and leaders. It was a good course. At the beginning, I was very negative about military service, but that changed after a while. Knowledge about myself and the experience of leadership have changed me a lot. UGL is something everybody should go through. You're trained by people with a background in psychology. They're specially trained tutors. They give the group some material, and then it's up to the group to develop it. Some

groups can't handle the material, whereas other groups succeed well in handling the conflicts and problems that occur within the group. If someone makes a mistake during UGL training, intrigues and problems will inevitably occur. We had this guy, I can't say he went insane as a result of UGL training. He was probably insane before, but the week after having it he went totally nuts during a military exercise. They had to report him as being mentally instable, so he disappeared. He really wanted to do his military service, but after that exercise he was expelled. I'm sure UGL changes everybody who goes through it. I know it changed me. I've learned how important it is to listen actively to other people, that it's important to give the right signals. I've improved my ability to do that, and to keep things under control. I think it's very important to learn from other people, instead of just communicating things to others. Otherwise, you easily get burned out.

Lasse's Life Plan

Lasse describes his life as a roller-coaster with high hills and deep valleys. At one time, he was a model pupil with good grades, but then, towards the end of junior high, he lost his motivation. He became interested in matters which made it difficult for him to concentrate on his school work. These interests, as he expressed it, were women, music and wine. He then started to play in a rock band, which considerably improved his self-esteem. His grades became better, and he developed a solid interest in music. When he entered high school his motivation for school work once again decreased. He questioned the whole situation, why should he study, etc. He had some fights with his parents — a revolt of sorts, he said. However, he solved these problems, graduated from high school with good grades and showed very strong interest in music.

When he was nineteen, Lasse's life was beginning to stabilize. He had gone through a few broken relationships with girls, the relationship with his parents was improving, he had started to work, and he moved away from his parents. Also, he had established a lasting relationship with a woman he was really fond of. His interest in music had developed all the time and he had also spent half a year in Australia.

At the age of twenty-one, Lasse's plans for the future had become more firm and concrete and he was working in a purposeful way towards becoming a doctor. He imagined that by the time he will be thirty he will be working as a doctor. At the same time he also imagined that he is going to get himself a dog and then children. After that he was going to pursue a career as a doctor. Lasse also thought that his work would lead to his going through some kind of family crisis sometime.

Lasse said that although he imagined many different kinds of alternative plans for the future, it was very hard for him to sketch something more concrete while he was so occupied with his plans for becoming a doctor.

The third time we met Lasse, his plans for the future were very much the same as before. He was still planning to become a doctor and to get himself a family by the age of approximately thirty. What had changed, however, was his attitudes towards the importance of a career. He was still interested, to a certain degree, in a career within the medical field, but to attain this goal he was no longer prepared to sacrifice his family and his other relationships. He had become less individualistic and more altrustic.

Some Comments on Lasse's Lifestyle

Just as was the case with most of the seven persons, Lasse's lifestyle developed considerably during the four years. The first time we met him, he was rather materially oriented. He was also very much occupied with himself and with his own development. Since then he has become much more concerned about his relationships with others.

These changes in Lasse's identity are also connected with fundamental changes of his values, attitudes and· actions. From an originally material and outer-directed value orientation, Lasse's values have gradually become more postmaterial and inner-directed. That is, his ethical and metaphysical values have gained in importance to him, whereas material values have decreased. His aesthetic values were always an important part of his lifestyle.

All in all, Lasse's lifestyle has become increasingly based on his ethical values, which can also be seen in his attitudes and actions. He has almost entirely given up the individual leisure activities he used to be involved in, and has replaced them with activities of a group character. Lasse's interest in scuba diving is closely connected with his concern for the environment, which takes the form of an ethically based involvement in ecological problems of environmental pollution, and the like. He has also become more interested in psychology and more concerned about people's psychological health. This interest, as well as his plans of becoming a doctor, indicate his increasing ethical concerns. Furthermore, his tastes in film have changed in a direction mirroring his ethical attitudes and values. Lasse wants a film to contain a message and a meaning he can agree with. More and more, he expresses a distaste for films containing what he sees as meaningless violence, gender and race inequalities, and the like.

To summarize, Lasse's development of his leisure interests, his future occupational plans and his family relations, are closely connected with changes in his fundamental values, in his identity, and thus in his lifestyle.

TOBIAS

> You live as you teach
> and learn as long as you live.
> If you live long enough
> you will surely become old and wise
> (Kal P.Dal 1977, translated by the authors).

Three Interviews With Tobias

Tobias grew up in a lower middle class family in Malmö. He graduated from a high school program specializing in metal industry work. After that he commenced studies at a school for adult education in another county, in order to become a recreation leader.

When we first met him, Tobias was working temporarily at a warehouse. He lived in an apartment of his own close to downtown Malmö. Already then, he had plans for studying to become a recreation leader and a parish assistant.

> I'm doing this for one reason only and that's for money. I get really good wages here, but otherwise it's not so damned much fun. It's great to drive a truck, but you can't do that all your life. I've thought a lot about applying to an adult education program where you can study to become a recreation leader. The school I've been thinking about is a Christian one. It would be great to help other people later, but first I'll have to see if it's possible to get accepted. /.../ I've had several different jobs. Among other things I've worked as a bookbinder and a machine-operator. I studied to become a mechanic earlier, but I really got on badly with that. I had bad grades, but anyhow I graduated finally, though I wouldn't exactly want to continue working with such things.

Tobias was the only person in the group of seven young persons we interviewed who had been a member of a genuine subculture. He described this period as follows:

> I constantly questioned everything the teachers said, so they wanted to get rid of me. For that reason, I was thrown out, in ninth grade and had to start again in a new school. I've probably been some kind of a problem child. I really felt good when I was accepted by this gang. I became a kind of psychiatrist for these guys. I got involved with a heavy gang of punks or whatever they were. Long

shabby hair, rivets on their jackets, leather jackets with fifteen zippers, tight black trousers, ragged jeans, constant boozing, and lots of cursing. Not exactly the dream of a mother-in-law. I spent most of my time with them and I enjoyed it, but I was dressed the same as now. It was trashmetal, hardcore, well it's the same shit. They were problem children. Until I moved to Stockholm I spent lots of time with them, and I'm still in touch with them. We weren't criminal in any way, but if they were harassed or drank too much beer, they often beat someone up. Several of them have been nailed for assault and battery. One of the guys works as a bouncer in a porno-club in the USA, but he's trying to get something going with his music. He played in a rock band in Malmö before. They played karate punk, real hardcore, speed metal, and heavy trash music. Three of the guys have been nailed for assault and battery. I've never been of the violent type myself.

Tobias's tastes were, of course, influenced by this gang and he listened to different types of hard rock, among others so called hardcore, trash metal and speed metal.

At the same time as Tobias was spending considerable time together with this gang, he was also meeting different persons who were deeply Christian, and he was a member of the youth organization within the church. During this period he developed a faith of his own in his strong belief in Jesus and in God.

It all started after confirmation. I then begun taking part in youth activities in church. It was not exactly a religious thing. Instead, you treated the place just like any kind of youth recreation center. /.../ And then the woman who was a parish assistant quit and was replaced with a younger guy who was easier to get to know. He was really good. And then, well I just discovered that this was the way it was. It came sneaking upon me, so to say. It took probably two or three years. And then when you started believing in things you were eager to know more about them.

At the same time as all this happened, Tobias also started developing plans to become a parish assistant and a recreation leader, something his parents were not particularly enthusiastic about.

At first, when I told my parents that I wanted to become a parish assistant they thought I should choose some job where I could earn more money. I didn't give a damn about that. I'm more inclined to follow my conscience than to want to earn money. I suppose they wanted me to have a good job with lots of money. I certainly did earn a lot of money while I was working as a truck driver. I had fifty-seven kronor an hour and my wages were going to be increased even more.

The second time we met Tobias, in the autumn of 1990, he was well on his way to realizing a good deal of his plans. After working for a year in

Stockholm as a church volunteer, he was accepted for studies at the school for adult education which he had mentioned about two years before.

> I felt I wanted to become a parish assistant. I wanted to work with people on the basis of my faith. I felt it would really be terrific. I applied to this school but was rejected. Later I heard that you could work and get practical experience, so I moved to Stockholm and stayed there for a year with a really lousy economy. Then I was accepted at the school, and I've been here for a year now this summer. I can't see anything negative about it. Theology, education, psychology, almost everything is nice and I benefit privately from it too. /.../ You can't cope with being a parish assistant for more than ten years, though, then you're burned out, have no more ideas, and have to do something else. I'll have to change my profession then. I've got some thoughts about becoming a clergyman, but then I'd have to study quite a lot. These are only small, very small, thoughts. You don't simply become a clergyman, it's a vocation, a pretty heavy one, and in fact more than a profession, it's a way of living. When you're hungry you know it; when you feel called, you know what to do. It's simply a feeling you get. /.../ Here you work ordinary school days, and then you're free until the next day. You do your homework, talk with your friends, go out for sports and are always up to your ears.

Since the first time we met Tobias, his tastes had changed rather radically. He did listen to the same kind of music as before and did watch the same types of films, but he had certainly added something important to his tastes.

> Roughly speaking I listen to the same kinds of music as before. It's mostly old blues inspired music, AC/DC, and Thin Lizzy. I mix hardcore with Swedish punk. Hardcore is a kind of raw rock, a kind of masturbation with sounds, real tough heavy metal. I haven't changed my musical tastes so much, but I listen more now to Freda and Ratata, and more to classical music. Freda is supposedly a Christian group, but there are music styles and if they're Christian or not, is nothing I care about. A Christian rock band consists of people who play rock music and then they fill it up with some commandments. As long as it's good music it doesn't matter if they're Christian or anti-Christian. It's the instrumental part I'm after. There's a group called Rififi, they're referred to as a Christian group, but they could just as well be just any group.

Even if Tobias's film tastes had become more distinct, he still watched much the same kinds of films as before.

> I watch less TV now than before, and I'm also more choosy. The plot and the actors are important. I love turkey movies, I didn't like them the last time we met, but I'm tired of American ideal films. I watched a lot of college films before, but I don't like them anymore. Pretty Woman was the latest film I saw. It was pretty funny, a modern copy of My Fair Lady. /.../ I don't know what I go for when I choose films. You often just go along with your friends and watch something. Although I don't think I watch any different kind of films now, I certainly have different ideals than I had earlier. I'm not as easy on films as I used to be. American films are constructed according to a certain pattern. It has to be a little bit cheap and sweet and so forth. I don't like that anymore.

Since Tobias started at the adult education school, his leisure time interests had changed considerably. He spent much time with his friends, and was often busy with the kinds of activities offered at school. He took part in different kinds of sports activities, spent a great deal of time photographing and processing photos, he made his own video films, participated in services, and read books. Later he became interested in guitar playing and in old cars. He owned an Austin A-35 from 1957, which he liked to work with now and then. He was eager to play down his being a Christian, and he felt that his daily lifestyle was not particularly influenced by his Christian faith.

> There are so many prefabricated beliefs about Christians, and I don't fit into any of them. I curse like hell and I really like to go out and have a couple of beers. I wouldn't exactly call myself a milksop.

It is difficult to describe Tobias completely. His lifestyle is very complex, and it sometimes contains incoherent and inconsistent elements. One could say that Tobias is something of a seeker after truth, although the second time we met him he had become more structured and had also achieved some kind of order in his life.

> I suppose I've become more mature in my old days. I've gained control over myself and over my life. I have more self-esteem now, and I know more about where I am, and I can control myself better. I suppose my biggest crisis was in the sexual area, bad self-esteem and difficulties with the opposite sex. It calls for self-esteem and now I've got some. I've realized that as soon as you get to know me better I'm a person who's easy to talk with. Sometimes it can be difficult, because you either hate me or love me. People have told me I'm a funny guy, because either you dislike my style a lot or you really like it. I'm not easily impressed by people who want to be important, so I usually make fun of them. I like to pull their leg, but I've got more control over that now.

The third time we meet Tobias, he has spent almost two years at a Christian adult education. During this period he has become more certain of his religious convictions. His faith in God has grown stronger. This development also has had implications for his plans for the future. He has serious plans of continuing his theological studies after finishing at the adult education. He wants to become a lay worker. Even though Tobias says that his faith in God is stronger than ever, he does not deny that his faith fails him now and then. As most Christians he sometimes has periods of doubt. However, these periods, which tend to be short, does not seem to cause him any serious or lasting problems regarding his faith. Rather, they make it necessary for him to work actively with his beliefs. This, he feels, helps him become even stronger in his faith.

If he does not experience his personal religious beliefs as particularly problematic, he does have some problems in integrating what remained of his pre-religious self-image with his present self-image. This conflict is particularly evident in his account of his social life. Tobias has always been rather fond of hanging out at pubs and drinking a few beers, and he has not changed this habit very much since becoming an active Christian. Drinking beer has taken on a new meaning for him, however. A new symbolic meaning has now been added to what he previously regarded as just a way of having a good time with his buddies. Through drinking beer, smoking and swearing, Tobias also wants to counteract the prejudices he felt many young people has against Christians.

> If I go to a pub, and I do that a lot, I often end up talking with somebody about what I'm doing. When I tell them I'm at a Christian school, their mouths often drop. They seem rather puzzled and surprised at my using bad language, drinking a few beers, laughing and even occasionally going for a pee.

During the interview Tobias often returns to what he obviously experiences as his twofold role of being both the convinced Christian and the fun-seeking beer drinker. Tobias is clearly afraid of being considered a bore. Since he thinks that most non-Christian young people regard Christians as boring moralists, and since he himself considered many Christians to be like that, it is particularly important to him that he tries to counteract this prejudiced conception of Christians. For Tobias, his faith in God was of extreme importance, but he is nevertheless much concerned about other people's attitudes towards him. He wants to be a good Christian without being a moralizing social bore. At the same time as Tobias's faith in God has grown stronger, his concern about other people's attitudes and prejudices towards him has decreased. He had become more certain regarding his identity even though he still experienced certain difficulties in combining his pre-Christian and present identities. These difficulties gradually became easier for him to cope with, however.

During the three years we have known him, Tobias's music tastes has undergone a development. He listens to basically the same sort of music as he did three years before, but some of the genres constituting his tastes have increased in importance. His interest in Christian rock music, for example, has increased, while his taste for heavy metal and trash metal has decreased.

He still characterizes himself as a "rock'n'roller", however. One interesting aspect of Tobias's music tastes is his fascination with a Swedish pop music genre characterized by deliberate simplicity and naiveté both musically and lyrically, as represented by groups like Torson, Perssons Pack and Traste Lindéns kvintett. Such bands often originate in small Swedish towns, and their lyrics frequently concern everyday situations in small towns. They can be about tractor exhibitions, third division soccer games, fishing for eels, hunting elk, etc. The deliberately backward naturalism of these groups' lyrics is often accompanied by a great deal of irony and humour, turning big city prejudices towards people in small towns to the advantage of the latter. In a way, the jokings of these groups regarding big city prejudices towards rural and small town life correspond with Tobias's way of coping with the prejudices against him as a Christian.

Similar trends may be discerned in Tobias's film tastes. On the one hand, his attitudes towards popular Hollywood films has become more negative, and on the other, his interest in films of existential or religious content has increased. He mentioned Martin Scorcese's *The Last Temptation of Christ* and Monty Python's *Life of Brian* as two of his favorites at the moment.

All in all, Tobias had developed a more stable identity, and in particular a more solid Christian identity, during the three years we had known him, something of which he was also aware.

> A lot has happened during these three years. I've matured and become more stable. I've got new and better values in life. I've changed some of them. I've discovered more about myself.

Tobias's Life Plan

Tobias's parents and the family security they provided were an important part of his life. Towards the end of his studies in school he had been down in the dumps, as he expressed it. He had had difficulties with members of the opposite sex and had experienced his own body as awkward and ugly. However, when he met Karin, who was his girlfriend for nearly two years, this negative self-image changed in a positive direction. All the time, he had experienced his different jobs as very disappointing and of little value, and it was not until he had worked for a year in Stockholm as a volunteer, and had decided to become a parish assistant, that he achieved a more positive conception of himself. During the same period he also met his present girlfriend, Helen. She is also strongly Christian. They met at a camp in France arranged by the Church of Sweden.

Tobias's future has already been staked out. After completing his education he plans to work as a parish assistant. He also plans to marry his girlfriend and have his first child. This is what he wants to do, and he sees no alternatives to this. He always was deeply convinced that this is the way things were going to turn out.

The third time we met Tobias his future plans were approximately the same, though since last we met him they have become more solid. Tobias wants to work in a Christian environment, preferably with children or young people as a recreation leader. In accordance with his growing faith in God, Tobias has also developed extensive plans for becoming a lay worker. This is connected with an increasing interest in spiritual guidance. Tobias told us he had become a "psychologist" of sorts for his schoolmates. He had got a reputation for being a good person to talk with when having love problems, problems of faith, or other kinds of personal problems. Apart from these plans, Tobias also wanted to spend a year or two abroad, working in one of the foreign branches of the Church of Sweden.

Concerning his private life, Tobias had become a bit more uncertain since the last time we had met. Since his girlfriend lives in a town approximately 500 kilometers from Tobias's school, they meet rather seldom. This unlucky situation has created certain relational problems for them. Since he often discusses these difficulties with her, however, he is convinced that the problems can be solved, and he is still planning to marry her.

Some Comments on Tobias's Lifestyle

It is rather obvious that Tobias's lifestyle rests basically on his inner-directed values, and perhaps most of all on the metaphysical ones. His religious beliefs and thoughts cut through all areas of his life. His present studies, his future plans, his leisure time activities, and his tastes in music and film are all colored by his metaphysical convictions. This does not mean, however, that Tobias's entirely lacks outer-directed values. As we have seen, he is concerned about what other people think of him. Consequently he deliberately uses different symbols and artefacts to express and visualize his taste and style. He does this primarily in order not to be identified as, as he says, a boring Christian. Thus considered, Tobias's style can be seen as a symbolic expression of his need to express what he considers as his unique and individual way of relating both to Christianity and to profane culture. It is reasonable to assume, however, that the majority of Tobias's ethical, aesthetic and material values, attitudes and actions are strongly related to his metaphysical values. The metaphysical values are the overriding ones in Tobias's personal value system, and, consequently, also in his lifestyle.

In terms of mobility, the changes in Tobias's occupational plans, taste and style, can be described as horizontal, that is, as involving cultural mobility. The direction of Tobias's changes in taste is not from popular culture towards high culture, but rather from one area of popular culture to another. Whereas his tastes for profane popular culture are relatively stable, his interest in Christian popular culture has become stronger. He listens increasingly to Christian rock and pop music, such as to the Swedish Christian group *Freda*. Neither the music nor the lyrics of these groups differ much from profane pop and rock, but their members have declared themselves to be Christians. It is interesting to note that the Christian performers Tobias likes do not go primarily for a Christian audience but for consumers of popular music generally. These artists thus resemble Tobias in that they openly express their Christian faith and at the same time attempt to counteract prejudices against Christians through playing music usually regarded as profane. The same goes for the films he likes. Both *The Last Temptation of Christ* and *Life of Brian* were rejected by many Christians as blasphemous and blameworthy, whereas Tobias's rejected such attitudes towards the films. Indeed, he considered both films to represent the Christian gospel in a positive and entertaining way that was suitable both for Christians and non-Christians.

Tobias's tastes in the areas of film and music thus correspond well with his individual lifestyle, and with his way of relating to Christianity.

CHAPTER 20
LIFE HISTORIES AND LIFESTYLES

A major thesis in this book is that lifestyle is at least partly an individual phenomenon. To really grasp the phenomenon of lifestyle, therefore, it is necessary to study how single individuals create, develop and maintain their lifestyle. Furthermore, we have criticized the tendency within lifestyle research of defining lifestyles in relation to such limited aspects of it as musical taste, film taste and leisure time activities, for example.

In our view, lifestyles are complex systems consisting of a multitude of relations between individuals' values, attitudes and actions. Since values constitute the basis for the individual's attitudes and actions, it is in the values of the individual that we find the basis for his or her lifestyle as well. Furthermore, since the identity of an individual to a large extent consists of his or her fundamental conceptions regarding ethical, metaphysical, aesthetic and material issues, values also constitute a basic component of identity.

Our theoretical views on lifestyle have important implications for our empirical study of it. It is very difficult to satisfactorily measure people's values, even though various methods can give at least a rough picture of how the values are structured among people in a given society. It has proved almost impossible, however, to identify the lifestyles prevailing in a society by means of value measurements alone. Thus, it is much easier to operationalize and measure attitudes and actions than it is lifestyles. Consequently, most empirical lifestyle studies have been conducted at the level of attitudes and actions, this in the case of young people often involving attitudes towards popular cultural areas such as music and film, as well as leisure time activities.

In this book we have done the same thing, and thus arrived at a number of taste and activity patterns which could be called lifestyles. Aware of the importance of values, however, we have refrained as a rule from calling these patterns lifestyles and used instead the terms taste and activity patterns. Such patterns are very useful, since they can provide a general picture of how a certain lifestyle area are structured within a population. However, they cannot provide a complete picture. This becomes very evident in the analysis of our case studies. In these, the importance of individuals' values becomes obvious. None of the seven young people whom we studied so intensely considered their musical taste, film taste or taste in clothes to be the most central component of their lifestyles. Rather, they emphasized their more fundamental conceptions of life and its meaning.

The rather abstract patterns of culture identified in the quantitative part of this book may serve as a kind of map against which the dynamic character of individuals' lifestyles stands out. Using Goffmans's terms one might also refer to abstract cultural patterns as a figure providing the field an individual needs to "cut a figure in a figure that romps, sulks, glides, or is indifferent". When relating the lifestyles of the seven individuals to general patterns of culture, it becomes obvious that each individual relates to these patterns to some extent while deviating and gaining a distance from them at the same time.

In studying individual lifestyles one is studying subtle variations in lifestyle which are impossible to capture by means of the instruments of measurement used to identify general patterns of culture. Looking at the portrayals of the seven individuals, we can conclude, on the one hand, that each of them can be described in terms of such general patterns and, on the other hand, that they deviate from them in various important respects.

Tor constitutes a good example of this state of affairs. He may certainly be partly described in terms of the film taste pattern of *SF/Fantasy*, the music taste patterns of *Heavy metal* and *Symphonic and southern rock*. However, whereas these patterns are related to low education and such values and value orientations as material security, technological development and wealth, Tor does not regard these values as very important. Instead, he emphasizes values of aesthetic development, personal development, self-respect, wisdom and so on. Furthermore, it is definitely not proper to describe him as being of low education. Tor also listens to other types of music than the ones constituting the patterns mentioned above, and the same goes for the films he watches. Watching films and listening to music are also not the only activities Tor engage in. He has several other interests which are at least as important to his lifestyle. Although this may seem obvious and self-evident, it is nevertheless important, since herein lies the key to the distinction between lifestyles and individual lifestyles. Whereas the former term designates general, theoretically and empirically constructed patterns of culture common to several individuals, the latter term designates the individual's relations to such patterns, and also how he or she deviates from them. Whereas the former concept is used to distinguish characteristics common to a large number of people for characterizing them into a limited number of lifestyles, the latter is used to distinguish the single individual as a unique person with his or her own individual way of relating to the multitude of social and cultural phenomena inherent in lifestyle. As already mentioned, general patterns of lifestyles allow us to find unity within diversity, whereas individual lifestyles allows us to find diversity within unity.

A central theme in theories of modernization and individualization is the individual's inclination to reflect upon one's identity and one's presentation of oneself in everyday life (cf. Giddens 1991; Wouters 1992).

> Although feelings of ambivalence, insecurity and disorientation will to some extent accompany each new round in the process of self-distantiation, articulating and emphasizing one's distinctive features still seems to have become a sport and an art, and increasing numbers of people seem to have become more and more aware both that they have to put their minds and hearts into it, and how it is to be done (Wouters 1992:243).

This reflective attitude is also expressed by the seven individuals studied here. Tor, for instance, dresses in different clothes depending on how he feels and how he wants to present himself to his environment. "I change between being the nice guy in blue jeans and a shirt and being a punk rocker. It depends on how I want to feel", says Tor.

Tobias is very much aware of the fact that he can be categorized as Christian, and he also expresses his dissatisfaction with this categorization since he objects to several of the notions inherent in this category. "There are so many prefabricated beliefs about Christians, and I don't fit into any of them", says Tobias.

Anna-Karin described how she became more mature and sure of her own identity during the last few years, and how she also dared, therefore, to present herself as an individual rather than as a member of a particular peer-group. "When you become older it's easier to dare to be yourself. You don't have to be like all the others, and you don't fall for group pressure", says Anna-Karin.

We will now try to further demonstrate how each one of the seven individuals' lifestyles differ. As we shall see we are dealing with seven very different lifestyles, in spite of the fact that when we originally chose these individuals, they belonged to either or the other of two empirically distinguishable taste and activity patterns.

Tor's lifestyle is clearly based on developmental values. For him the important thing in life is to be able to develop his imagination, to create and express himself aesthetically. His two major leisure time interests — painting and fantasy culture — both give him the opportunity to develop in the way he wants. Therefore, it is quite natural that Tor has also incorporated these interests in his future work plans. In fact, his creative and imaginative needs and desires are so important that he is prepared to sacrifice a great deal of material welfare and security if he only can get the chance to continue to develop his creativity and imagination.

Of our seven individuals, Tor is definitely the one who possesses the most stable lifestyle and identity. He is well aware of his talents in drawing and painting and of his imaginative abilities. He has used this awareness in developing his identity and lifestyle. Tor knows who he is, what he wants and where he is going, and he is satisfied with his lifestyle as well as with his identity.

Agneta has only recently begun to realize and actively explore the different possibilites inherent in her identity. What she eventually has come to realize is that she has to explore as many different alternatives as possible before making any concrete decision or plans concerning her future. What is important to her is to have enough money to be able to afford to travel, buy things she likes, and amuse herself in a number of different ways. Agneta's lifestyle is thus based on her fundamental material values. During the four years we have known Agneta, her lifestyle and values have thus drastically changed from material values connected with security to developmental values. However, in her lifestyle she expresses developmental material values rather than material values that are connected with security.

These changes in Agneta's lifestyle can be ascribed at least partly to the difficulties she experienced when she had to give up her major interest, that of playing soccer. One might say that Agneta has gone through a minor identity crisis, which she has finally successfully solved. Agneta has put all thoughts of getting a family and children far into a distant and rather abstract future. She is more concerned with trying to find out who she really is and what she actually wants in life.

It is rather easy to follow Annika's identity and lifestyle development. The first time we met her, she was extremely concerned with her future career and social status. She wanted a well paid high status job, and she was determined to work hard in order to achieve this goal. Her values were clearly material, and she was aiming at material development rather than security. During the three years we followed Annika, she developed considerably, which she was also aware of herself. Even though her wishes and desires for wealth and high status remained, they gradually became subordinated to other life values. As Annika matured, she found that material wealth was not the most important component of a good life. She gradually developed, and included in her identity and lifestyle, other values. The last time we met her she was more interested in self-development and life satisfaction than in social recognition. This development was especially visible in her attitudes towards her future work. When we met Annika the last time, she emphasized job satisfaction, creativity and personal development rather than high salary and high status as being the most important features of a future occupation. Annika still emphasized development. However, she emphasized not simply material development, but ever more her personal and cultural development.

Towards the end of his high school studies, Tobias went through a kind of identity crisis. He had had difficulties with members of the opposite sex and he felt his own body was awkward and ugly. When he met Karin, however, this negative self-image changed in a positive direction. After finishing school he experienced his different jobs as being very disappointing and of little value, and it was not until he had worked for a year in Stockholm as a volunteer, and had decided to become a parish assistant, that he achieved a more positive image of himself.

This development went hand in hand with Tobias's growing image of himself as a Christian. It is rather obvious that Tobias's lifestyle rests basically on his inner-directed values and, perhaps, most of all on the metaphysical ones. His religious beliefs and thoughts cut across all areas of his life. However, this does not mean that Tobias completely lacks outer-directed values. Tobias's style can be interpreted as a symbolic expression of his need to express what he considers his unique way of relating to both Christianity and profane culture. His values and lifestyle are thus colored by the fact that he has a strong faith in God.

Anna-Karin's lifestyle can be described as altrustic. She is not at all interested in social recognition for its own sake. She gets her life-satisfaction from helping and taking care of other people, and especially people with some kind of problems. Her main interest is in children and their development. Her work at a nursery school is characterized by a high degree of involvement. In her work she actively engages in developing and improving the possibilities of children to develop their cognitive, emotional and creative abilities and skills, through trying new ways of teaching and fostering.

For Anna-Karin personal creativity and development are main features of her lifestyle and identity. She is not at all interested, however, in using her creative competence as a means of acquiring social recognition or social status. Rather, she uses her creativity in order to develop herself, and she finds great satisfaction in acquiring new skills. As she puts it, the important thing is not to be the best, but to gradually become better and better by facing the *small challenges* in life. Through her folk-dance and sewing she satisfies her creative needs and desires. The altruistic character of her identity becomes obvious one notes that she uses the skills she develops not to impress others but to transmit her skills and to help other persons to develop their creativity.

During the four years we have known her, Sonja's lifestyle has changed considerably. On the first two occasions we met her, she was very much concerned about her own personal and social development. She wanted to travel and she also entertained plans of becoming a photographer. At that time her aesthetic and metaphysical values were important to her lifestyle. Sonja's lifestyle then was primarily based on developmental values. Material and social security were not as important to her as personal and social development. This then changed dramatically.

The third time we met Sonja, her interest in traveling and photography had decrease in favor of plans for a secure and comfortable family life. Developmental values had become subordinate in her value system. The dominant values had become those aimed at social and material security and at comfort. Her value change was expressed in her altered lifestyle. Sonja's changes in values and lifestyle were clearly related to the fact that she had become pregnant. She had found another way of creating meaning in her life. This new meaning was that of giving birth to and raising her child and to live a good family life. Sonja's values and lifestyle and her conception of her future had thus become intimately connected with living a family life. Consequently, her life plan had become closely related to needs and desires regarding her future child and her boyfriend.

Sonja still had some dreams, but she was more than willing to suppress these dreams and to postpone her own personal and social development.

Sonja had become much more interested in developing herself *in relation* to her child and her family.

Lasse's lifestyle has changed dramatically during the years we have known him. During the first interview, he was a rather self-centered and laissez-faire minded young man primarily occupied with his interest in music. He was a member of a number of different rock bands and dreamed of becoming a professional musician. He did not care much for other people and often argued with his parents and friends. He was well aware of this feature of his identity and dissatisfied with it. By the second time we met him he had managed, as he stated it himself, to think and care more about other people and therefore also become able to look upon himself without "getting bad vibrations".

The last time we met Lasse, he had further developed his concern for other people's welfare and happiness. He had simply become more altrustic. His lifestyle and identity development were perhaps mirrored best in the development of his occupational plans. He had totally abandoned his previous plans of becoming a celebrated musician; he was determined instead to become a medical doctor. His interest in music remained strong, however. He was no longer playing in any rock bands, but only for himself when he felt like it. Just like Annika, Lasse had gradually become less interested in social status and recognition and had found more important qualities and values in life. Personal and cultural development, life satisfaction, self-realization, and also concern for the well-being of others had become more important aspects of a good life for Lasse.

It is quite obvius that for these seven persons, lifestyle is not equivalent with their musical taste, their film taste or their taste in clothes. Lifestyle is something much more important to them than is popular culture. The basis for their respective lifestyle is to be found in their quest for a good life, and what they consider to be a good life differs considerably due to difference in their fundamental conceptions, that is, their basic values. Another way of putting it is to say that they all are aiming at "doing the right thing", and that what all of them are looking for is the right thing to do.

During the socially and culturally defined period of youth, young people's lifestyles and identity change, often dramatically so. These changes are frequently based on dramatic life-events, such as personal identity crisis, pregnancy, diseases, injuries, etc. It is symptomatic that those individuals whose lifestyle have changed the most during the years we have followed them have also experienced such events. Whereas Tor's and Anna-Karin's lifestyles have been relatively stable, Agneta's knee injury, Lasse's unsatisfaction with himself, Tobias' religious awakening, Sonja's pregnancy and Annika's identity crisis after returning from the USA, have had a considerable impact on their identity and lifestyle development (cf. Erikson 1968b).

Another interesting observation to make is that the life plans of the seven young people we have studied have changed considerably between the different interviews. Their views of their past and future lives also change continually as they mature and develop new values and goals in life. One might say that there is a constant revaluation of past events, as well as a constant re-orientation regarding their outlook on the future. Hanna Arendt expresses this in a somewhat philosophical way:

> In this gap between past and future, we find our place in time when we think, that is, when we are sufficiently removed from past and future to be relied on to find out their meaning, to assume the position of "umpire", of arbiter and judge over the manifold, never-ending affairs of human existence in the world, never arriving at a final solution to their riddles but ready with ever-new answers to the questions of what it may be all about (Arendt 1978: 210).

The changes in the seven young people's life plans and lifestyles can be described in terms of mobility. The cultural and social development described above is probably characteristic of young people at this age. They are gradually entering into adult life and facing new responsibilities and new possibilities. The changes concern their cultural as well as their social identity and status (cf. figure 5, chapter 8). Changes in cultural and social identity, of course, are often intimately connected with one other, but sometimes one identity changes without affecting the other. Most young people are both socially and culturally mobile during this period of youth. That is not to say, of course, that everyone alters his social or cultural status, but merely that all of us develop our cultural and social identity. Sometimes these alterations coincide with changes in status as well. Thus, horizontal cultural and social mobility is common to most young people, whereas vertical cultural and social mobility is less frequent.

Looking at our case studies it becomes clear that, during the three years we have followed them, all seven individuals have more or less developed their cultural and social identities. They have developed new tastes, new leisure time interests and new styles, established new relationships, developed their plans for the future, altered their values and attitudes, started new jobs or programs of education, etc. Some of them have also acquired a new social and cultural status. Anna-Karin, for example, has moved from a traditional working class background to a lower middle class profession, and Lasse and Annika are well on their way to acquiring a higher social and cultural status through their education.

Common to all seven individuals is that they have developed their values during the period we studied them. A general tendency regarding these value changes is that purely material values have gradually become less important than ethical and metaphysical ones. That is the case for Lasse, Annika and Tobias, for example.

Clearly, no single taste or activity pattern empirically distinguished coincides with any of these individuals' lifestyles. Although each of them uses elements from different areas of popular culture in building their lifestyle, it would be unfair to categorize them on the basis of their taste in music, film and clothes. Their activity patterns, on the other hand, seem to be a better lifestyle indicator, since these cover a much broader and more differentiated area. However, of the 56 activities used in the questionnaire, none involved scuba diving, folk-dancing, and lifelike role games, activities which were of extreme importance for the lifestyles of Lasse, Anna-Karin or Tor. This indicates certain of the problems inherent in lifestyle measurements.

To summarize: most individuals have one or a few dominant interests on the basis of which they can develop, define and express their values and their identity, forming their own individual lifestyles. Apart from these dominant interests, most people also practice a number of other activities of less importance for their lifestyle. To understand the unique lifestyle of an individual one must thus concentrate on his or her dominant interests. Popular music, film and clothes can each constitute such dominant interests, but none of these are dominant among all young people. Therefore, it is only in a very limited sense that one may equate taste patterns with lifestyle, even though most young people listen to and have attitudes towards the two important popular cultural areas of music and film.

Now, as we are approaching the end of the book, one can ask what we have achieved, and how our theoretical and empirical efforts can be used in lifestyle research.

A great deal of lifestyle research has aimed at distinguishing a number of lifestyles in society, at identifying various social and cultural patterns and at putting different labels on them. Much lifestyle research has thus been conducted at an aggregated level of analysis. It might have been possible for us to also identify a number of social and cultural patterns and label them as lifestyles. In fact, we have identified such patterns (taste and activity patterns) using our measurements of leisure time activities and taste in music, film and clothes. However, we have not combined these different areas in order to distinguish a number of lifestyles. This has not been our purpose in this study. Instead, our main intention has been to discuss the lifestyle phenomenon on an aggregated as well as an individual level of analysis, in order to show the relative advantages of each of these levels, and the importance of considering both levels when constructing lifestyles.

Our work may perhaps best be described in terms of a continuous oscillation between *categorizations* and *particularizations*. On the one hand, we have categorized empirically a multitude of leisure time activities or genres of film and music in terms of a limited number of aggregates, and on the other hand, we have shown how seven particular individuals both can be described in terms of these categories and deviate considerably from them. One advantage of such an oscillation between different levels of analysis is that one can identify, and thereby take into consideration, various limitations and problems related to lifestyle studies on both the aggregated and the individual level of analysis.

Our constant struggle with those two different levels of analysis — categorization and particularization — has led to the development of a number of concepts of some importance in a theoretical discussion of lifestyles. These include, different types of mobility (horizontal and vertical, social and cultural), of capital (economic, social and cultural), of values (material, aesthetic, ethical and metaphysical), and of functions values can have (security versus development). In order to construct a social and cultural space of lifestyles which may be used in order to understand the lifestyle phenomenon in recent modern context, one has first to operationalize these different concepts. As already indicated, we do not have any fully adequate instruments for measuring these phenomena. An important task is therefore to operationalize the concepts and develop functioning instruments of measurement. That may possibly be our next move.

CHAPTER 21
CONCLUDING DISCUSSION

During the last decades the concept of lifestyle has experienced a renaissance within the social sciences. An almost uncountable number of articles and books have been written in the area, and the concept has become an important analytical tool in contemporary social and cultural studies.

The concept of lifestyle has a long history within sociology. In fact it has been applied by sociologists ever since the days of the founding fathers of sociology. The lifestyle concept has thus proved to be really enduring, probably because of its constant development and the reformulation of its scope. In the late nineteenth century, lifestyle was conceptualized basically in relation to different classes or status groups in society. The function of conspicuous consumption of luxury goods as a means of expressing status distinctions soon became the dominant area of application for lifestyle theories.

When consumption of mass produced goods sold at a market had come to involve increasing numbers of persons, Weber, Simmel and Veblen all carried out a considerable amount of scholarly work explaining and analysing the rise of early consumer culture and its functions for the individual and society. These authors all noticed its importance as a symbolic way of expressing power and wealth. They observed that the lower classes, through consumption of cheap, mass produced imitations of the status symbols of the higher classes, at least symbolically transcend their status, irrespective of the actual power relations inherent in society. This symbolic transcendence of status was doomed to be rather temporary, however. As soon as the lower classes had incorporated a specific status symbol into their culture, it lost its symbolic value for the higher classes and was consequently replaced by something new.

During the latter half of twentieth century we have witnessed a constantly expanding mass market, not only in consumer goods but also in the areas of mass media, popular culture in general and youth culture in particular. It was during the forties and fifties that young people — teenagers — were first recognized by market forces as an interesting group of consumers. With this, youth culture begun to flourish and expand.

During the post-war period the access to material wealth has increased throughout the Western world. Most people have enjoyed the possibility of not buying their daily bread, but also consuming for pleasure. The mere ability to consume is thus no longer a sufficient sign of social status. In contemporary Western society consumption of goods has for most people become a matter of routine. It has, therefore, also become saturated with a large number of new symbolic meanings and functions. Consumer goods have frequently been used as a means of distinctions between male culture and female culture, youth culture and adult culture, and between different types of youth cultures.

Parallel with these social and cultural changes, use of the lifestyle concept has also changed. Although it is still applied in connection with power and status relations, its scope has become much broader. The most significant development of the concept is in its close relation to the concept of identity and increasing emphasis on the individual. In short, the development of the lifestyle concept has moved from an almost total interest in class and status towards an increased interest in ethnicity and gender, on the one hand, and in the relation between consumer culture and identity creation, on the other.

This book has been written during a period when the lifestyle concept has again become fashionable within social sciences. The book's main purpose has been to develop a general theory of lifestyle — not to identify, investigate or answer any particular sociological or empirical question. The empirical parts of the book, therefore, do not cover all the theoretical arguments we have put forward. Rather, they must serve as particular examples or illustrations of matter dealt with in the general theoretical discussions. We hope, however, that our theory of lifestyle will be applied to future empirical research on more or less specific lifestyle issues.

We have tried to develop a theory which includes structurally, positionally and individually determined aspects of lifestyle. Basically, however, we have been concerned with individual aspects of the phenomenon. The two main concepts we have used to provide an understanding, within a structural and positional frameworks, of how the individual develops his or her lifestyle, have been those values and identity.

To summarize, we have argued that lifestyle is a structurally, positionally *and* individually determined phenomenon. We have also argued that the identity of the individual strongly influences the way the individual develops and forms his or her own lifestyle and that the central component of the identity of an individual is that of the values he or she embraces. We have also tried to shed light empirically upon the dynamics inherent to the construction of lifestyles. We shall now turn to a brief summary of the main theoretical and empirical results presented in the book.

During the twentieth century the process of individualization has accelerated, resulting in changing values among persons in the West. Increased material welfare has led to a common experience of material and physical security for a major part of the population. Therefore, the values of Western man have come to an increasing extent to concern also non-material aspects of life as well. Psychological growth, self-realization, personal development and the like have gradually become central concerns for modern man.

Our assumption that lifestyles are not determined by social structure only, or by the individual's position within it, but to a considerable extent *also* by the individual's unique characteristics, personality and identity, obtains substantial empirical support in our analyses of the relations between positional variables, values and tastes or activities. We have shown that even whenthe positional variables are held constant, the values they embrace have a considerable impact on our respondents' attitudes towards film and music and their choices of leisure time activities. The assumption that lifestyles are influenced not only by class, gender, education but also by individuals' own free choice, therefore, seems to be reasonable.

During the course of life, individuals alter their positions in the social structure, sometimes drastically so. Thus, they are mobile in various respects. Such mobility can be defined in terms of access to cultural, social or economic competence. Even though it is difficult to study mobility empirically since it is a developmental process, we do have certain empirical indications that such processes actually take place during youth. Especially the seven case studies show the close relation between social and cultural mobility and the development and changes of identity, values and lifestyle. Also the comparison of our respondents' musical tastes at the ages of fifteen and twenty-one clearly indicates young people to be culturally quite mobile during late adolescence.

In order to understand how lifestyles are constructed and how they develop, one must realize that behind all the visible expressions and signs of individual lifestyle there are a relatively small number of basic values. If one does not understand the relations between individuals' fundamental values and their more or less conscious use of their taste in different areas, in their leisure time interests and so on, it is also impossible to understand lifestyle. We have shown empirically that most — but not all — of the general taste and activity patterns we have identified are related to specific values and value orientations. The fact that these relations remain even when the impact of other types of variables is controlled for offers strong support for the thesis that behind attitudes towards specific objects and events — as well as particular actions — lie a number of general and abstract values.

We have also shown empirically that there are different types of values, serving different purposes in the identity of the individual. The values of an individual may serve both security functions and/or developmental functions. Values may be outer-directed or inner-directed, material or postmaterial. The differing functions of values appear in the general quantitative analyses as well as in the more specific qualitative analyses.

During what we have called socially and culturally defined youth individuals grow more autonomous, more aware of their cultural identity and their lifestyle, and less dependent upon their peer-groups and parents. Youth culture contains both innovative and conformist elements, and the more the individual becomes aware of himself/herself as an automous cultural being, the better he or she can use culture to cope with his or her contradictory needs and desires. The individual learns how to express and develop his or her individuality, on the one hand, and to define himself/herself and to act as as a member of different cultural and social groups, on the other.

Although it is empirically and methodologically possible to distinguish quantitatively between a number of taste or activity patterns termed lifestyles, such patterns are by definition quite general and do not say much about the characteristics of the individual lifestyle. Rather, they supply a preliminary categorization of tastes and activities and thus help us to discern some general characteristics of lifestyles. In order to capture individual variations in these general patterns as well, one must obviously study how the single individual constructs his or her lifestyle. One might argue that the general patterns distinguished quantitatively illustrate the conformist components of lifestyle, whereas studying single individuals makes it possible to also capture the creative components.

Another way of putting it is that throughout the empirical parts of the book we have moved to and fro between abstract patterns of lifestyle and individual lifestyles. We have been aware all the time of the fact that it is impossible to identify all lifestyles in a society, or even all aspects of one individual lifestyle. All we can do is to shed some light on some basic features of the lifestyles of modern youth. We hope that our contribution to lifestyle theory will be of some use in future research related to the lifestyle and value discourse.

REFERENCES

Abercrombie, N., Hill, S and Turner, B.S. (1986) *Sovereign Individuals of Capitalism*. London: Allen & Unwin.

Abrams, M. (1959) *The Teenage Consumer*. London: Press Exchange.

Adorno, T. W. (1957/1964) Television and the Patterns of Mass Culture. In Rosenberg, B. & White, D. M. (Eds.) *Mass Culture. The Popular Arts in America. New York: The Free Press*.

Alexander, J. C. (1988) *Action and its Environment.Toward a New Synthesis*. New York: Columbia University Press.

Alexander, J. C. (1989) Durkhemian Sociology and Cultural Studies Today. In Alexander, J. C. (Ed.) *Durkhemian Sociology: Cultural Studies* Cambridge: Cambridge University Press.

Alwin, D. F. & Krosnick, J. A. (1985) The Measurement of Values in Surveys: A Comparison of Ratings and Rankings.*Public Opinion Quarterly 49*.

Ang, I. (1985) *Watching Dallas. Soap Operas and the Melodramatic Imagination*. London: Methuen.

Angus, I. & Jhally, S. (1989) *Cultural Politics in Contemporary America*. New York: Routledge.

Archer, M. (1988) *Culture and Agency. The Place of Culture in Social Theory*. Cambridge: Cambridge University Press.

Arendt, H. (1978) *The Life of Mind. Volume Two: Willing*. London: Secker & Warburg.

Ariès, P. (1962) *Centuries of Childhood. A Social History of Family Life*. New York: Vintage Books.

Back, K. W. (1985) Modernism and Fashion: A Social Psychological Interpretation. In Solomon, M. R. (Ed.) *The Psychology of Fashion*. Toronto: Lexington Books.

Ball-Rokeach, S. J., Rokeach, M., Gruber, J. W. (1984) *The Great American Values Test. Influencing Behavior and Belief Through Television*. New York: The Free Press.

Baudrillard, J. (1987) *The Esctacy of Communication*. New York: Semiotext(s).

Baudrillard, J. (1988) *Selected Writings*. Poster, M (Ed.) Stanford: Stanford University Press.

Beck, U. (1986) *Risikogesellschaft. Auf dem Weg in eine andere Moderne.* Frankfurt a.M: Suhrkamp.

Bell, D. (1976) *The Cultural Contradictions of Capitalism.* London: Heinemann.

Bellah, R. N., Madsen, R., Sullivan W. M., Swidler, A and Tipton, S. M. (1985) *Habits of the Heart. Individualism and Committment in American Life.* Berkeley: University of California Press.

Bendix, R. (1968) Weber, Max. In Sills, D. L. (Ed.) *International Encyclopedia of Social Sciences.* Macmillan Company and The Free Press.

Benjamin, W. (1968) *Illuminations.* London: Fontana.

Berardo, F.M., Greca, A. J. and Berard, D. H. (1985) Individual Lifestyles and Survivorship: The Role of Habits, Attitudes and Nutrition. *Death Studies*, 9:5-22.

Berger, P. & Luckman, T. (1966/1987) *The Social Construction of Reality. A Treatise in the Sociology of Knowledge.* Harmondsworth: Penguin Books.

Berger, P. (1967) *The Sacred Canopy. Elements of a Sociological Theory of Religion.* New York: Anchor Books.

Berger, P., Berger, B and Kellner, H. (1973) *The Homeless Mind. Modernization and Consciousness.* New York: Vintage Books.

Berman, M. (1983) *All That is Solid Melts Into Air. The Experience of Modernity.* London: Verso Editors.

Blos, P. (1962) *On Adolescence.* New York: Free Press.

Blos, P. (1967) The Second Individuation Process of Adolescence. *Psychoanalytic Study of the Child* 22:162-86.

Blos, P. (1979) *The Adolescent Passage: Developmental Issues.* International Universities Press.

Blumer, H. (1969) Fashion: From Class Differentiation to Collective Selection. *The Sociological Quarterly*, 3:275-91.

Blumler, J. & Katz, E. (Eds.) (1974) *The Uses of Mass Communications.* Beverly Hills: Sage.

Bourdieu, P. (1977) *Outline of a Theory of Practice.* Cambridge: Cambridge University Press.

Bourdieu, P. (1979/1984) *Distinction. A Social Critique of the Judgement of Taste.* Cambridge: Harvard University Press.

Bourdieu, P. (1988) *Homo Academicus.* New York: Polity Press.

Bourdieu, P., Boltanski, L., Castel, R., Chamboredon, J-C. and Schnapper, D. (1965/1990) *Photography. A Middle-Brow Art.* Cambridge: Polity Press.

Bourdieu, P. & Passeron J-C. (1977/1990) *Reproduction in Education, Society and Culture.* London: SAGE.

Brake, M. (1980) *The Sociology of Youth Cultures and Youth Subcultures: Sex and Drugs and Rock'n'roll.* London: Routledge & Kegan Paul.

Braunstein, P. (1985/1988) Toward Intimacy: The Fourteenth and Fifteenth Centuries. In Aries, P and Duby; G (Eds.) *A History of Private Life. Revelations of the Medieval World.* Cambridge: Harvard University Press.

Breakwell, G. (1986) *Coping With Threatened Identities.* New York: Methuen.

Brewer, J. D. (1988) Micro-Sociology and the "Duality of Structure". Former Fascists "Doing" Life History. In Fiedling, N. G. (Ed.) *Actions and Structure. Research Methods and Social Theory.* London: SAGE.

Broady, D. (1990) *Sociologi och epistemologi: Om Pierre Bourdieus författarskap och den historiska epistemologin.* Stockholm: HLS förlag.

Burke, P. J. & Franzoi, S. L. (1988) Studying Situations and Identities using Experiental Sampling Method. *American Sociological Review*, 4:559-568.

Burnett, R. (1990a) From a Whisper to a Scream. Music Video and Cultural Form. In Roe, K. & Carlsson, U. (Eds.) *Popular Music Research.* An Anthology from NORDICOM-Sweden.

Burnett, R. (1990b) *Concentration and Diversity in the International Phonogram Industry.* Göteborg: Kompendiet.

Campbell, C. (1987) *The Romantic Ethic and the Spirit of Modern Consumerism.* Oxford: Basil Blackwell.

Carey, J. (1988) *Communication As Culture. Essays on Media and Society.* London: Unwin Hyman.

Carter, E. (1984) Alice in the Wonderland: West German Case Studies in Gender and Consumer Culture. In McRobbie, A. & Nava, M. (Eds.) *Gender and Generation.* London: MacMillan.

Chambers, I. (1986) *Popular Culture: The Metropolitan Experience.* New York: Methuen.

Chodorow, N. (1974) Family Structure and Feminine Personality.In Rosaldo, M. Z. & Lamphere, L. (Eds.) *Woman, Culture, and Society.* Stanford: Stanford University Press.

310

Chodorow, N. (1978) *The Reproduction of Mothering. Psychoanalysis and the Sociology of Gender*. Berkeley: University of California Press.

Christenson, P. G. & Peterson, J. B. (1988) Genre and Gender in the structure of Music Preferences. *Communication Research*, 3:282-301.

Clark, T. N. & Lipset, S. M. (1991) Are Social Classes Dying? *International Sociology, 4:397-410*.

Clarke, J., Hall, S., Jefferson, T and Roberts, B. (1976) Sub-cultures, Cultures and Class. In Hall, S. & Jefferson, T. (Eds.) *Resistance Through Rituals. Youth Subcultures in Post-War Britain*. London: Hutchinson.

Clarke, G. (1981) Defending Ski-Jumpers. A Critique of Theories of Youth Subcultures. In Frith, S. & Goodwin, A. (Eds.) (1990) *On Record. Rock, Pop and the Written Word*. London: Routledge.

Cohen, A. (1955) *Delinquent Boys: The Culture of the Gang*. Chicago: Free Press.

Cohen, S. (1972/1987) *Folk Devils and Moral Panics. The Creation of the Mods and Rockers*. London: Basil Blackwell.

Coleman, J. S. (1961) *The Adolescent Society*. Glencoe: Free Press.

Coleman, J. S. (1988) Social Capital and the Creation of Human Capital. *American Journal of Sociology. Suppl. S95-120*.

Coleman, J. S. (1990) *Foundations of Social Theory*. Cambridge: The Harvard University Press.

Collins, J. (1989) *Uncommon Culture. Popular-Culture and Post-modernism*. New York: Routledge.

Connolly, W. E. (1989) *Political Theory & Modernity*. London: Basil Blackwell.

Cook, D. A. (1981/1990) *A History of Narrative Film*. New York: W.W Norton & Company.

Curran, J. (1990) The New Revisionism in Mass Communication Research: A Reappraisal. *European Journal of Communication, 2-3:135-64*.

Dahlgren, A. (1979) *Två världar. Om ungdom och könsroller. Ett kunskapssociologiskt perspektiv*. Stockholm: Raben & Sjögren.

Dahlgren, R. (1985) *Unga arbetare: en sociologisk studie i en mellansvensk industrimiljö*. Lund: Akademiska avhandlingar vid Sociologiska institutionen, Lunds Universitet.

Dalquist, U. (1991) *Insamlingsrapport 1988 och 1990*.

Damon, W. (1988) Socialization and Individuation. In Handel, G. (Ed.) *Childhood Socialization*. New York: Aldine De Gruyter.

De Casper, H. S. & Tittle, C. K. (1988) Rankings and Ratings of Values: Counseling Uses Suggested by Factoring Two Types of Scales for Female and Male Eleventh Grade Students. *Educational and Psychological Measurement 48.*

d'Epinay, L. C. (1991) Individualism and Solidarity Today. *Theory, Culture & Society, 2:57-74.*

Denisoff, R. S. (1988) *Inside MTV.* New Brunswick: Transaction.

Denisoff, R. S. & Levine, M. (1972) Youth and Popular Culture: A Test of Taste Culture Hypothesis. *Youth & Society,* 4: 237-55.

Donohew, L., Palmgreen, P. and Rayburn, J. D. (1987) Social and Psychological Origins of Media Use: A Lifestyle Analysis. *Journal of Broadcasting & Electronic Media,* 3: 255-278.

Drotner, K. (1991) Intensities of Feeling: Modernity, Melodrama and Adolescence. *Theory, Culture & Society, 1: 57-78.*

Durkheim, E. (1893/1988) *The Division of Labour in Society.* Hampshire: McMillan.

Dyer, R. (1986a) *Stars.* London: British Film Institute.

Dyer, R. (1986b) *Heavenly Bodies. Film Stars and Society.* New York: St. Martin's Press.

Eichorn, D. (1968) Adolescence. In Sills, D. L. (Ed.) *International Encyclopedia of Social Sciences.* New York: The Macmillan Company and the Free Press.

Eisenstadt, S. N. (1956) *From Generation to Generation. Age Groups and Social Structure.* Glencoe: The Free Press.

Elias, N. (1939/1982) *The Civilizing Process. State Formation and Civilization.* Oxford: Basil Blackwell.

Elias, N. (1939/1978) *The Civilizing Process: The Development of Manners.* New York: Urizen Books.

Erikson, E. H. (1959) *Identity and the Lifecycle.* Psychological Issues, Monograph I:1. New York: IUP.

Erikson, E. H. (1968a) *Identity, Psychosocial.* In Sills, D. L. (Ed.) *International Encyclopedia of the Social Sciences.* New York: The Macmillan Company and The Free Press.

Erikson, E. H. (1968b) *Identity, Youth and Crisis.* New York: W.W Norton & Company.

Erikson, R. (1971) *Uppväxtförhållanden och social rörlighet.* Stockholm: Allmänna förlaget.

Ewen, S. (1988) *All Consuming Images. The Politics of Style in Contemporary Culture.* New York: Basic Books.

Ewen, S. & Ewen, E. (1982) *Channels of Desire. Mass Images and the Shaping of American Consciousness.* New York: McGraw-Hill Book Company.

Ewen, S. (1990) Marketing Dreams. The Political Elements of Style. In Tomlinson, A. (Ed.) *Consumption, Identity, and Style.* London: Routledge.

Eyerman, R. (1981) *False Consciousness and Ideology in Marxist Theory.* Stockholm: Almqvist & Wiksell.

Featherstone, M. (1987) Lifestyle and Consumer Culture. *Theory, Culture & Society,* 1:55-70.

Featherstone, M. (1990a) Perspectives on Consumer Culture. *The Journal of the British Sociological Association,* 1: 5-22.

Featherstone, M. (1990b) *The paradox of Culture and the Globalization of Diversity.* Utrecht: ISOR.

Featherstone, M. (1991a) The Body in Consumer Culture. In Featherstone, M., Hepworth, M and Turner, B. (Eds.) *The Body. Social Process and Cultural Theory.* London: SAGE.

Featherstone, M. (1991b) *Consumer Culture & Postmodernism.* London: SAGE.

Featherstone, M. (1992) Postmodernism and Aestheticization. In Lash, S. & Friedman, J. (Eds.) *Modernity and Identity.* Oxford: Blackwell.

Fenster, M. (1991) The Problem of Taste Within the Problematic of Culture. *Communication Theory 1-2:87-105.*

Fielding, N. G. (1988) Between Micro and Macro. In Fielding, N. G (Ed.) *Actions and Structure. Research Methods and Social Theory.* London: SAGE.

Fiske, J. (1987) *Television Culture.* London: Routledge.

Fiske, J. (1989) *Understanding Popular Culture.* Boston: Unwin Hyman.

Fornäs, J. (1990) Popular Music and Youth Culture in Late Modernity. In Roe, K & Carlsson, U (Eds.) *Popular Music Research.* An Anthology From NORDICOM-Sweden. Göteborg.

Fornäs, J., Lindberg, U., Sernhede, O. (Eds.) (1987) *Ungdomskultur. Identitet-Motstånd.* Lund: Symposion.

Fornäs, J., Lindberg, U och Sernhede, O. (1989) *Under rocken. Musikens roll i tre unga band.* Lund: Symposion.

Fox, W. S. & Wince, M. H. (1975) Musical Taste Cultures and Taste Publics. *Youth & Society*, 2: 198-224.

Frisby, D. (1985) Georg Simmel: First Sociologist of Modernity. *Theory, Culture & Society*, 3:46-67.

Frith, S. (1978) *The Sociology of Rock*. London: Constable.

Frith, S. (1983) *Sound Effects. Youth, Leisure, and the Politics of Rock'n'Roll*. London: Constable.

Frith, S. (1985) *The Sociology of Youth*. Lancashire: Causeway.

Frith, S. (1988) *Music For Pleasure. Essays in the Sociology of Pop*. Oxford: Basil Blackwell.

Fromm, E. (1962) *Beyond the Chains of Illusion*: *My Encounter With Marx and Freud*. New York: Pocket Books Inc,.

Gans, H. J. (1972) The Politics of Culture in America. A Sociological Analysis. In McQuail, D (Ed.) *Sociology of Mass Communications*. Harmondsworth: Penguin Books.

Gans, H. J. (1974) *Popular Culture and High Culture. An Analysis and Evaluation of Taste*. New York: Basic Books, Inc,.

Garnham, N. & Williams, R. (1986) Pierre Bourdieu and the Sociology of Culture: An Introduction. In Collins, R., Curran, J., Garnham, N., Scannell, P., Schlesinger, P and Sparks, C. (Eds.) *Media, Culture and Society. A Critical Reader*. London: SAGE.

George, N. (1988) *The Death of Rhythm & Blues*. London: Omnibus Press.

Gibbins, J. (1989) *Contemporary Political Culture. Politics in a Postmodern Age*. London: SAGE.

Giddens, A. (1984) *The Constitution of Society*. Oxford: Polity Press.

Giddens, A. (1991a) *Modernity and Self-Identity. Self and Society in a Late Modern Age*. Oxford: Polity Press.

Giddens, A. (1991b) Structuration Theory: Past, Present and Future. In Bryant, C. G. A. & Jarry, D. (Eds.) *Gidden's Theory of Structuration: A Critical Appreciation*. London: Routledge.

Gillis, J. R. (1981) *Youth and History. Tradition and Change in European Age Relations, 1770-Present*. London: Academic Press.

Glover, J. (1985) *I — The Philosophy and Psychology of Persona Identity*. Harmondsworth: Penguin Books.

Goffman, E. (1969) *Where the Action is: Three Essays*. London: Penguin Books.

Goffman, E. (1982) *The Presentation of Self in Everyday Life.* Harmondsworth: Penguin Books.

Goldhammer, H. (1968) *Social Mobility.* In Sills, D. L. (Ed.) *International Encyclopedia of the Social Sciences.* New York: The Macmillan Company and The Free Press.

Grossberg, L. (1989) MTV: Swinging on the (postmodern) Star. In Angus, I. & Jhally, S. (Eds.) *Cultural Politics in Contemporary America.* New York: Routledge.

Habermas, J. (1975) *Legitimation Crisis.* Boston: Beacon Press.

Habermas, J. (1981/1984) *The Theory of Communicative Action. Volume One: Reason and the Rationalization of Society.* Boston: Beacon Press.

Habermas, J. (1981/1987) *The Theory of Communicative Action. Volume Two: Life-world and System: A Critique of Functionalist Reason.* Boston: Beacon Press.

Hall, S., Hobson, D., Lowe, A and Willis, P (1980) *Culture, Media, Language. Working Papers in Cultural Studies 1972-1979.* London: Hutchinson.

Hall, S. & Jefferson, T. (Eds.) (1976) *Resistance Through Rituals.Youth Subcultures In Post-War Britain.* London: Hutchinson.

Handy, R. (1969) *Value Theory and the Behavioral Sciences.* Illinois: Charles C Thomas Publisher.

Hare, R. M. (1981) *Moral Thinking.* Oxford: Oxford University Press.

Harker, R., Mahar, C. and Wilkes, C. (1990) *An Introduction to the Work of Pierre Bourdieu. The Practice of Theory.* London: MacMillan Press Ltd.

Hebdige, D. (1979) *Subculture. The Meaning of Style.* London: Methuen.

Hebdige, D. (1988) *Hiding in the Light. On Images and Things.* London: Routledge.

Hedinsson, E. (1981) *TV, Family and Society. The Social Origin and Effects of Adolescents' TV Use.* Stockholm: Almqvist & Wiksell International.

Heller, A. (1970/1984) *Everyday Life.* London: Routledge & Kegan Paul.

Höjrup, T. (1983) *Det glemte folk. Livsformer och centraldirigering.* Köpenhamn: Institut for Europaeisk folkelivsforskning.

Holman, R. H. (1984) A Values and Lifestyles perspective on Human Behavior. In Pitts, R. & Woodside, A. G. (Eds.) *Personal Values and Consumer Psychology.* Lexington: Lexington Books.

Holman, R. H. & Wiener, S. E. (1985) Fashionability in Clothing: A Values and Lifestyle Perspective. In Solomon, M. R. (Ed.) *The Psychology of Fashion*. Toronto: Lexington Books.

Inglehart, R. (1977) *The Silent Revolution: Changing Values and Political Styles Among Western Publics*. Princeton: Princeton University Press.

Inglehart, R. (1990) *Culture Shift in Advanced Industrial Society*. Princeton: Princeton University Press.

Israel, J. (1979) *Alienation: From Marx to Modern Sociology*. New Jersey: Humanity Press.

Jameson, F. (1989) Postmodernism and Consumer Society. In Kaplan, E. A. (Ed.) *Postmodernism and its Discontents: Theories, Practices*. London: Verso.

Jarlbro, G., Lööv, T., Miegel, F. (1989) Livsstilar och massmedieanvändning. En deskriptiv rapport. *Forskningsrapporter i kommunikationssociologi,14*. Lund: Sociologiska Institutionen.

Jay, M. (1973) *The Dialectical Imagination. A History of the Frankfurt School and the Institute of Social Research 1923-1950*. London: Heinemann.

Jensen, K. B. & Rosengren, K. E. (1990) Five Traditions in Search of the Audience: Towards a Typology of Research on the Reception, Uses and Effects of Mass Media Content. *European Journal of Communication, 2-3: 207-238*.

Kahle, L R., Beatty, S E., Homer, P. (1986) Alternative Measurement Approaches to Consumer Values: The List of Values (LOV) and Values and Lifestyles (VALS). *Journal of Consumer Research 13*.

Kamler, H. (1984) Life Philosophy and Lifestyle. *Social Indicators Research 14(1):69-81*.

Kaplan, E. A. (1987) *Rocking Around the Clock: Music Television, Postmodernism and Consumer Culture*. London: Methuen.

Kaplan, E. A. (Ed.) (1988) *Women in Film Noir*. London: BFI.

Kellner, D. (1989) *Jean Baudrillard. From Marxism to Postmodernism and Beyond*. Cambridge: Polity Press.

Keniston, K. (1975) Prologue: Youth as a Stage of Life. In Havighurst, R. J. & Dreyer, P. H. (Eds.) *Youth*. Chicago: The University of Chicago Press.

Kim, J-O. and Mueller, C. W. (1978) *Factor Analysis. Statistical Method and Practical Issues*. London: SAGE.

316

Kothari, R. (1980) Life-style. A Political Analysis. *Alternative*, 6:591-98.

Kroeger, J. (1989) *Identity in Adolescence. The Balance Between Self and Other*. New York: Routledge.

Layder, D., Ashton, D., Sung, J. (1991) The Empirical Correlates of Action and Structure: The Transition from School to Work. *The Journal of the British Sociological Association, 3:447-64*.

Leming, J. S. (1987) Rock Music and the Socialization of Moral Values in Early Adolescence. *Youth & Society,* 4:363-83.

Lewis, G. H. (1978) The Sociology of Popular Culture. *Current Sociology, 3: 1-64*.

Lewis, G. H. (1981) Taste Cultures and Their Composition: Towards a New Theoretical Perspective. In Katz, E. & Szeeskö, T. (Eds.) *Mass Media and Social Change*. Beverly Hills: SAGE.

Lewis, G. H. (1989) Taste Cultures. In *Encyclopedia of Communications*. New York: Oxford University Press.

Lichtheim, G. (1968) Alienation. In Sills, D L (Ed.) *International Encyclopedia of Social Sciences*. Macmillan Company and The Free Press.

Liedholm, M. (1991) BO. Inflytande och deltagande som fenomen och social process. Lund: Sociologiska Institutionen. Lunds Universitet.

Lull, J. (1987) Listener's Communicative Uses of Popular Music. In Lull, J (Ed.) *Popular Music & Communication*. London: SAGE.

Lukes, S. (1973a) *Individualism*. Oxford: Basil Blackwell.

Lukes, S. (1973b) *Emile Durkheim. His Life and his Work. A Historical and Critical Study*. London. Penguin Books.

Lüdtke, H. (1989) *Expressive Ungleicheit: Zur Soziologie der Lebenstile*. Opladen: Leske & Budrich.

Lööv, T. (1990) Music Video and Lifestyle. Modern or Postmodern Aesthetics? *Lund Research Papers in the Sociology of Communication, 24*.

Lööv, T. & Miegel, F. (1989) The Notion of Lifestyle: Some Theoretical Contributions. *The Nordicom Review 1:21-31*.

Lööv, T. & Miegel, F. (1991) Sju livsstilar. Om några malmöungdomars drömmar och längtan. *Forskningsrapporter i kommunikationssociologi, 29*. Lund: Sociologiska Institutionen.

Magnusson, D. (1988) *Individual Development From A Interactiona Perspective: A Longitudinal Study*. Hillsdale, New Jersey: Lawrence Erlbaum Associates.

Mahler, M. S. (1963) Thoughts About Development and Individuation. *The Psychoanalytic Study of the Child*, 18: 307-24.

Mahler, M. S., Pine, F., Bergman, A. (1975) The Psychological *Birth of the Human Infant*. New York: Basic Books.

Marcus, G. (1990) *Lipstick Traces. A Secret History of the Twentieth Century*. London: Secker & Warburg.

Marsh, P., Rosser, E., Harre, R. (1978) *The Rules of Disorder*. London: Routledge & Kegan Paul.

Marx, K. (1852/1969) *The 18th Brumaire of Louis Bonaparte*. New York: International Publishers.

Marx, K. (1844/1975) *Early Writings*. Harmondsworth: Penguin Books.

Maslow, A. (1968) *Toward a Psychology of Being*. New York: Van Nostrand Company.

Mayntz, R. (1968) Simmel, Georg. In Sills, D. L. (Ed.) *International Encyclopedia of Social Sciences*. Macmillan Company and The Free Press.

McClelland, D. (1967) *The Achieving Society*. New York: The Free Press.

McRobbie, A. and Garber, J. (1976) Girls and Sub-Cultures. In Hall, S. and Jefferson, T. (Eds.) *Resistance Through Rituals: Youth Subcultures in Post-War Britain*. London: Hutchinsson.

McRobbie, A. (1984) Dance and Social Fantasy. In McRobbie, A. and Nava, M. (Eds.) *Gender and Generation*. London: MacMillan.

McRobbie, A. (1991) *Feminism and Youth Culture. From Jackie to Just Seventeen*. London: MacMillan.

Mead, G. H. (1934/1962) *Mind, Self and Society: From the Standpoint of a Social Behaviorist*. Chicago: The University Press of Chicago.

Merton, R. K. (1963) *Social Theory and Social Structure*. Glencoe: The Free Press.

Middleton, R. (1990) *Studying Popular Music*. Milton Keynes: Open University Press.

Miegel, F. (1990) Om värden och livsstilar. En teoretisk, metodologisk och empirisk översikt. *Forskningsrapporter i kommunikationssociologi, 25*. Lund: Sociologiska Institutionen.

Miegel, F. and Dalquist, U. (1991) Värden, livsstilar och massmedier. En analytisk deskription. *Forskningsrapporter i kommunikationssociologi, 31.* Lund: Sociologiska Institutionen.

Mill, J. S. (1859/1984) *On Liberty.* Harmondsworth: Penguin Books.

Miller, J. B. (1976) *Towards a New Psychology of Women.* Boston: Beacon Press.

Miller, J. B. (1984) The Development of Women's Sense of Self.*Work in Progress 84:01. Wellesley: Stone Center Working Papers Series.*

Mishra, V. M. (1982) The Psychographics or Lifestyles Characteristoics Nature and Pattern of Uses Mass Communication Media by Adults. *Indian Journal of Social Research,* 1:90-97.

Mitchell, A. (1983) *The Nine American Lifestyles. Who We Are & Where We Are Going.* New York: Warner Books.

Modleski, T. (1986) *Studies in Entertainment. Critical Approaches to Mass Culture.* Bloomington: Indiana University Press.

Munson, M. (1984) Personal Values:Considerations on Their Measurement and Application of Five Areas of Research Inquiry. In Pitts, R. E. and Woodside, A. G. (Eds.) *Personal Values and Consumer Psychology.* Toronto: Lexington Books.

Nedelmann, B. (1991) Individualization, Exaggeration and Paralysation: Simmel's Three Problems of Culture. *Theory, Culture & Society, 3:169-93.*

Nietzsche, F. (1886/1990) *Beyond Good and Evil.* Harmondsworth: Penguin Books.

Norusis, M. J. (1988) *SPSS/PC + Advanced Statistics.* Chicago: SPSS Inc.

Nylöf, G. (1990) Trends in Popular Music Preferences in Sweden 1960-1988. In Roe, K. and Carlsson, U. (Eds.) *Popular Music Research.* An Anthology From Nordicom-Sweden.

O'Connel, A. M. (1980) Correlates of Life-Styles: Personality, Role-Concept, Attitudes, Influences and Choices. *Human Relations, 8:589-601.*

Parsons, T. (1942/1964) Age and Sex in the Social Structure of the United States. In *Essays in Sociological Theory.* New York: The Free Press.

Parsons, T. (1964) *Social Structure and Personality.* London: The Free Press of Glencoe.

Parsons, T. (1966) *Societies. Evolutionary and Comparative Perspective.* London: Prentice Hall, Inc.

Parsons, T. (1968a) *The Structure of Social Action. Vol 2: Weber.* New York: The Free Press.

Parsons, T. (1968b) Durkheim, Emile. In Sills, D. L. (Ed.) *International Encyclopedia of Social Sciences.* New York: Macmillan Company and The Free Press.

Patrick, J. (1973) *A Glasgow Gang Observed.* London: Methuen.

Pearson, G. (1983) *Hooligan. A History of Respectable Fears.* London: The MacMillan Press.

Petersen, A. C. and Taylor, B. (1980) The Biological Approach to Adolescence: Biological Change and Psychological Adaptation. In Adelson, J *Handbook of Adolescent Psychology.* New York: John Wiley & Sons.

Peterson, E. E. (1987) Media Consumption and Girls Who Want To Have Fun. *Critical Studies in Mass Communication,* 4:37-50.

Pettersson, T. (1988) *Bakom dubbla lås. En studie av små och långsamma värderingsförändringar.* Stockholm: Institutet för framtidsstudier.

Pitts, R.E. and Woodside, A.G. (1984) *Personal Values and Consumer Culture.* Toronto: Lexington Books.

Postman, N. (1982) *The Disappearance of Childhood.* New York: Delacorte Press.

Postman, N. (1985) *Amusing Ourselves to Death.* New York: Elizabeth Sifton, Viking.

Radway, J. (1984) *Reading the Romance: Woman, Patriarchs, and Popular Literature.* Chapel Hill: The University of North Carolina Press.

Rahbek, L.C. (1987) *Hver vor veje. Livsformer, familietyper og kvindeliv.* Odense: Etnologiskt Forum.

Reimer, B. (1985) *Values and the Choice of Measurement Technique. The Rating and Ranking of Postmaterialism.* Working Paper 8. Göteborg: The departement of Mass Communication.

Reimer, B. (1988) No Values — New Values? Youth and Postmaterialism. *Scandinavian Political Studies 11.*

Reimer, B. (1989) Postmodern Structures of Feeling. Values and Lifestyles in the Postmodern Age. In Gibbins, J R (Ed.) *Contemporary Political Culture Politics in a Postmodern Age.*

Riesman, D. (1954) *Individualism Reconsidered and Other Essays.* New York The Free Press.

Riesman, D., Glazer, N and Denny, R (1950) *The Lonely Crowd.* New Haven: Yale University Press.

Riesman, D. (1950/1957) Listening to Popular Music. In Rosenberg, B. and White, D. M. (Eds.) *Mass Culture. The Popular Arts in America.* New York: The Free Press.

Roe, K. (1983) *Mass Media and Adolescent Schooling: Conflict or Co-Existence?* Stockholm: Almqvist & Wiksell International.

Roe, K. (1990) Adolescent's Music Use. A Structural-Cultural Approach. In Roe, K. and Carlsson, U. (Eds.) *Popular Music Research.* An Anthology From Nordicom-Sweden.

Rokeach, M. (1973) *The Nature of Human Values.* New York: The Free Press.

Roos, J. P. (1983) On Way of Life Typologies. In Uusitalo, L.(Ed.) *Consumer behavior and Environmental Quality.* Aldershot: Gower.

Rosenberg, B. and White, D. M. (Eds.) (1957/1964) *Mass Culture. The Popular Arts in America.* New York: The Free Press.

Rosenberg, B. (1957/1964) Mass Culture in America. In Rosenberg, B. and White, D. M. (Eds.) *Mass Culture. The Popular Arts in America.* New York: The Free Press.

Rosenberg, B. and White, D. M. (Eds.) (1971) *Mass Culture Revisited.* New York: Van Nostrand.

Rosengren, K E., Wenner, L A and Palmgreen, P. (Eds.) (1985) *Media Gratifications Research. Current Perspectives.* Beverly Hills: SAGE.

Rosengren K. E. and Windahl, S. (1989) *Media Matter.TV Use in Childhood and Adolescence.* New Jersey: Alex Publishing Corporation.

Rosengren, K. E. (1991a) Media Use in Childhood and Adolescence: Invariant Change? Some results from a Swedish Research Program. In *Communication Yearbook,* 14.

Rosengren, K. E. (1991b) Combinations, Comparisons and Confrontations: Towards a Comprehensive Theory of Audience Research. *Lund Research Papers in Media and Communication Studies, 1.*

Roszak, T. (1969) *The Making of the Counter Culture. Reflections on the Technocratic Society and its Youthful Opposition.* New York: Anchor Books.

Rundell, J. F. (1987) *Origins of Modernity: The Origins of Modern Social Theory from Kant to Hegel to Marx.* Oxford: Polity Press.

Sebald, H. (1977) *Adolescence. A Social Psychological Analysis.* New Jersey: Prentice Hall, Inc.

Schudson, M. (1986) *Advertising, The Uneasy Persuasion: Its Dubious Impact on American Society.* New York: Basic Books.

Schutz, A. and Luckman, T. (1974) *The Structures of the Life-World.* London: Heineman.

Schwartz, S H., Moore, R. L. and Krekel, T. H. (1979) Life Style and the Daily Paper: A Psychographic Profile of Midwestern Readers. *Newspaper Research Journal*, 1:9-18.

Schwendter, R. (1990) Theoretiker der Subkultur. In Bruckert, H. and Wefelmeyer, F. (Eds.) *Kultur Bestimmungen Im 20.Jahrhundert.* Frankfurt am Main: Suhrkamp.

Shepherd, J. (1986) Music Consumption and Self-Identities: Some Theoretical and Methodological Reflections. *Media, Culture & Society, 8:305-30.*

Shepherd, J. (1991) *Music as Social Text.* Oxford: Polity Press.

Sennett, R. (1976) *The Fall of Public Man.* Cambridge: Cambridge University Press.

Simmel, G. (1903/1971) The Metropolis and Mental Life. In Levine, D N (Ed.) *On Individuality and Social Forms.* Chicago: The University of Chicago Press.

Simmel, G. (1904/1971) Fashion. In Levine, D. N. (Ed.) On *Individuality and Social Forms.* Chicago: The University of Chicago Press.

Simmel, G. (1908/1971) Group Expansion and the Development of Individuality. In Levine, D. N. (Ed.) *On Individuality and Social Forms.* Chicago: The University of Chicago Press.

Simmel, G. (1908/1971) Social Forms and Inner Needs. In Levine, D. N. (Ed.) *On Individuality and Social Forms.* Chicago: The University of Chicago Press.

Simmel, G. (1918/1971) The Transcendent Character of Life.In Levine, D.N. (Ed.) *On Individuality and Social Forms.* Chicago: The University of Chicago Press.

Singer, P. (1983) *Practical Ethics.* Cambridge: Cambridge University Press.

Sklar, R. (1975) *Movie-Made America. A Cultural History of American Movies.* New York: Random House.

Snow, R. P. (1987) Youth Rock'n'Roll and Electronic Media. *Youth and Society*, 4:326-343.

322

Statens Ungdomsråd (1972) *Ungdom i Köping, Mölndal och Östersund.* Stockholm: statens ungdomsråd.

Steenbergen, B. and Feller, G. (1979) Emerging Life-Style Movements: Alternative to Overdevelopment. *Alternative,* V:275-305.

Stoecker, R. (1991) Evaluating and Rethinking the Case Study.*The Sociological Review,1:88-112.*

Taylor, C. (1975) *Hegel.* Cambridge: Cambridge University Press.

Thunberg, A M., Nowak, K., Rosengren, K. E. and Sigurd, B. (1982) *Communication and Equality. A Swedish Perspective.* Stockholm: Almqvist & Wiksell.

Toffler, A. (1970) *The Future Shock.* New York: Random House.

Turner, B. S. (1988) *Status.* Milton Keynes: Open University Press.

Turner, G. (1990) *British Cultural Studies. An Introduction.* Boston: Unwin Hyman.

Turner, R. H. (1968) Role. In Sills, D. L. (Ed.) *International Encyclopedia of Social Sciences.* New York: Macmillan Company and the Free Press.

Turner, R. H. (1978) The Role and The Person. *American Journal of Sociology, 1:1-23.*

Turner, R. H. (1990) Role Change. *Annual Review of Sociology,* 16: 87-110.

Veblen, T. (1899/1979) *The Theory of the Leisure Class. An Economic study of Institutions.* Harmondsworth: Penguin Books.

Veltri, J. J. & Schiffman, L. G. (1984) Fifteen years of Consumer Lifestyle and Values Research at AT & T. In Pitts, R.E. & Woodside, A. G. (Eds.) *Personal Values and Consumer Psychology.* Lexington: Lexington Books.

Wallis, R. and Malm, K. (1984) Patterns of Change. In Frith, S. & Goodwin, A (Eds.) *On Record. Rock, Pop and the Written Word.* London: Routledge.

Wallis, R. and Malm, K. (1990) The Implications of Structural Changes in the Music Industry for Media Politics and Music Activity. In Roe, K. and Carlsson, U. (Eds.) *Popular Music Research.* An Anthology from NORDICOM-Sweden.

Weber, M. (1904/1930) *The Protestant Ethic and the Spirit of Capitalism.* London: Unwin University Books.

Weber, M. (1922/1968) Class, Status, Party. In Gerth H. H. & Mills, C. W. (Eds.) *From Max Weber. Essays in Sociology.* London: Routledge & Kegan Paul Ltd.

Weber, M. (1924/1968) *Economy and Society* (II) *An Outline of Interpretive Sociology*. New York: The Bedminister Press.

White, D. W. (1971) Mass Culture Revisited. In Rosenberg, B. and White, D. W. (Eds.) *Mass Culture Revisited*. New York: Van Nostrand.

Wicke, P. (1990) *Rock Music. Culture, Aesthetics and Sociology*. Cambridge: Cambridge University Press.

Williams, R. (1961/1978) *The Long Revolution*. Harmondsworth: Penguin Books.

Willis, P. (1977) *Learning to Labour. How Working Class Kids Get Working Class Jobs*. Aldershot: Gower.

Willis, P. (1990) *Common Culture. Symbolic Work at Play in the Everyday Cultures of the Young*. Milton Keynes: Open University Press.

Willmott, P. (1966) *Adolescent Boys of East London*. London: Routledge & Kegan Paul.

Wilson, B. (1970) *The Youth Culture and the Universities*. London: Faber & Faber.

Wilson, B. (1988) Values and Society. In Almond, B. and Wilson, B. (Eds.) *Values. A Symposium*. Atlantic Highlands: Humanities Press International.

Winnicott, D. W. (1963/1987) *The Maturational Process and the Facilitating Environment*. London: Hogarth Press.

Winnicott, D. W. (1971) *Playing and Reality*. London: Tavistock Publications.

Wouters, C (1992) On Status Competition and Emotion Management: The Study of Emotions As A New Field. *Theory, Culture & Society, 1:229-52*.

Wulff, H. (1988) *Twenty Girls. Growing up, Ethnicity and Excitement in a South London Microculture*. Stockholm: Social Studies in Social Anthropology.

Zablocki B. D. & Kanter, R. (1976) The Differentiation of Life-Styles. *Annual Review of Sociology 2:269-298*.

Zetterberg, H. L. (1977) Arbete, livsstil och motivation. Stockholm: SAF.

Zetterberg, H. (1983) *Det osynliga kontraktet*. Stockholm: SIFO.

Ziehe, T. (1975/1984) *Pubertät und Narzissmus. Sind Jugendliche Entpolitisiert?* Frankfurt a.M: Europäische Verlagsanstalt.

Ziehe, T. (1989) *Kulturanalyser: Ungdom, Utbildning, Modernitet* Stockholm: Symposion.

324

Zigler, E. and Seitz, V. (1978) Changing Trends in Socialization Theory and Research. *American Behavioral Scientist*, 5:731-756.